two-drop
PEYOTE
PATTERNS

D1644447

HOLLY KURZMAN

Kalmbach
Media

DEDICATION

To Chris, who always encouraged and supported my bead addiction. You were the only husband who encouraged his wife to buy more beads. I miss you every day and hope you are proud of my little book.

Kalmbach Media
21027 Crossroads Circle
Waukesha, Wisconsin 53186
www.JewelryAndBeadingStore.com

For technical and artistic reasons relating to photographic reproduction, colors reproduced in these images may not be exact representations of the original work.

Step-by-step photos and patterns by the author. All other photography © 2020 Kalmbach Media except where otherwise noted.

The jewelry designs in *Two-Drop Peyote Patterns* are the copyrighted property of the author, and they may not be taught or sold without permission. Please use them for your education and personal enjoyment only.

Published in 2020
24 23 22 21 20   1 2 3 4 5

Manufactured in China

ISBN: 978-1-62700-756-6
EISBN: 978-1-62700-757-3

Editor: Erica Barse
Book Design: Lisa Bergman
Assistant Editor: Katie Salatto
Proofreader: Dana Meredith
Photographer: William Zuback

Library of Congress Control Number: 2019949372

Contents

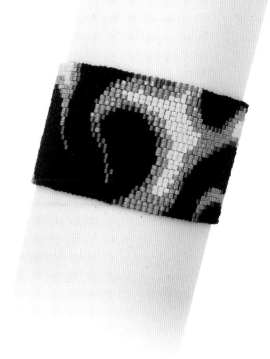

PROJECTS

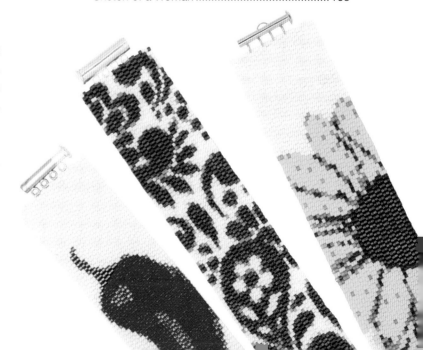

Introduction

One day over lunch in 1999, a colleague and I went for a walk and stopped in the bead shop across the street because she wanted to buy buttons for a dress she was making. While she was browsing the button selection, I wandered around the store, looking at all of the beautiful beads. Then I noticed the finished pieces hanging on the walls; they were samples of what could be made in the various classes offered. One bracelet immediately caught my eye, and I decided to sign up for the class. That class was so much fun that I signed up for another class, which turned out to be the beginning of my peyote stitch obsession.

One of the great advantages of beadwork is that one can start with basic tools and supplies. There is no need to invest in a lot of expensive equipment. I am continually amazed at what can be created with just a needle, thread, and a few piles of beads. This holds true for every project in my book — you will need 11° cylinder beads, a needle, thread, and a clasp. That's it!

Beaded jewelry also requires patience. Yes, even though two-drop peyote is quicker than the "regular" stitch, it will still take you hours to finish a bracelet. However, when you are finished, you will have something unique, handmade, and precious. I find that the time I spend at my bead mat brings me a sense of calm; the focus on my beads de-stresses me, so it's time well spent.

I hope you enjoy creating jewelry from my patterns.

Happy beading!

Holly

Supplies

For a lot of beaders, even-count peyote stitch is the first off-loom technique we try. It's easy to learn, versatile, and a seemingly endless range of projects can be created using the stitch. For many years, it was my go-to stitch for those reasons... and then I discovered two-drop peyote stitch, which was a game-changer for me.

The most often mentioned benefit of two-drop is that it works up more quickly than "regular" peyote. That's true, though that's not what really drew me to it. When I started designing peyote stitch patterns, I found that I preferred the results when I used two-drop peyote because I was able to create more complex and detailed designs. In particular, curves look smoother and less choppy, which adds to the overall aesthetic of the finished piece.

CYLINDER BEADS

All projects in this book are made with 11° Miyuki Delica cylinder beads; changing the beads you use will alter your results. Delica beads are high-quality, affordable, widely available, and uniform in shape and color (though you will occasionally come across a bead that needs to be culled). Delicas nestle together well, so as long as you maintain consistent tension, your finished piece will be straight and even. Cylinder beads are a bit more expensive than round seed beads, but the quality is worth it. If you're going to put in hours on a bracelet, you want the finished piece to look great, and that means using quality materials.

note I prefer using opaque rather than transparent beads, not only because of their depth of color, but because the thread will be less visible than with transparent beads. Many projects in this book combine beads with different finishes (see below) because the variety adds visual interest.

Common finishes

Opaque beads are solid-colored beads that don't allow light to pass through them. You also shouldn't be able see your thread through the beads. Unless otherwise stated, opaque beads are shiny.

Transparent beads will allow some light to shine through. There are two reasons I rarely use transparent beads in my designs: Your thread is more likely to be visible through the beads, and the colors aren't as saturated and rich as the opaque beads.

Matte beads are acid-etched to remove their shine; they can be slightly more fragile than non-matte beads, and you might need to cull more defective or broken beads from your stash. Some beads have a **semi-matte** finish, which means the beads are slightly less shiny than regular beads, but not as etched as full matte beads.

AB (aurora borealis) is a rainbow finish that's added on top of the main color; this finish is available for opaque, transparent, and matte colors. It can appear to change color, depending on the lighting and the angle from which you're viewing the beads. The AB effect is usually more noticeable on darker beads.

Ceylon is a luster finish most commonly seen on lighter color beads and is reminiscent of a pearl's sheen.

Dyed beads are not 100% color-fast, so colors could fade or wear off over time (though I have never had this problem with any of my finished pieces).

Color-lined and luminous beads have color added inside the hole; these colors do tend to wear off or fade over time, especially the bright colors.

Silver-lined beads are similar to color-lined, but the interior is a silver color. These beads have a vivid appearance, almost as if there was a light shining inside.

Duracoat finish is a clear coating that makes the colors more durable than regular dyed or galvanized beads.

Galvanized beads are plated; Duracoat galvanized finishes are more durable than regular galvanized beads because of the coating added over the plating. Those with acidic skin might find that the Duracoat galvanized finish reacts less to the skin so the beads retain their brilliance.

Picasso finish looks almost like you splattered paint on a batch of beads. Each bead will have a slightly different color, which gives your finished piece a textured appearance.

Silk satin beads are very fragile and prone to sharp edges that cut the thread, so I don't recommend using them for projects in this book. Compared to the way they look in the tube or packet, the colors can wash out when incorporated into your stitching.

note These beads are glass, so they can break if you bang your bracelet against something hard.

You can substitute another brand of cylinder beads (Toho, for instance), but the available colors will be different from the specified Miyuki colors. Please don't mix brands in the same project—each brand's beads have slightly different dimensions, which will be evident in your finished piece.

note Your local bead shop or online bead supplier might use slightly different names for some of the bead colors, but the Miyuki color numbers should remain the same. Also, some suppliers maintain the 4-digit protocol (DB-0010) while others delete the initial zero(s) (DB-10).

Color notes

• There are some projects in this book that really allow you to be creative and choose your favorite colors, while for others (especially the Renaissance pieces), you will get the best results if you stick to the colors listed in the pattern.

• For most of my designs that use white beads, I prefer opaque bisque white (DB1490) rather than opaque white (DB200) because it is less stark—but feel free to use whichever you like best.

Bead counts

There are approximately 190–200 11º cylinder beads per gram. When calculating the number of grams per color needed for each project, it's better to be on the safe side. Although cylinders are high-quality, there will no doubt be an occasional broken or irregular bead that needs to be culled. The bead finish can also affect the bead count per gram, so calculating the number of grams is not an exact science. Therefore, when the project's bead count shows that you could *probably* get by with 2g, I recommend having 3g on hand; better safe than sorry. 195 rows of beading will yield 6½ in. (16.5cm) of beadwork, not including the clasp.

THREAD

For most of the pieces in this book I used either Fireline 6-lb. test in smoke or crystal, or Wildfire .006" in green. If you want a slightly stiffer finished piece, try using a thicker thread. Both Fireline and Wildfire are fishing line, so they were designed to be strong. Many of us have favorite threads, so use whatever you prefer, especially if you want to choose a thread color that matches your beadwork. That said, color is important—so try to avoid using smoke Fireline or dark thread if your project has a white or light background, for example, because your thread may be visible.

note The color of the smoke Fireline sometimes rubs off on my fingers as I bead. If this bothers you, run your thread through a dryer sheet several times. It removes most of the excess color and also serves as a thread conditioner to help minimize tangles and knots.

NEEDLES

My favorite needle is a size 10 or 11 Tulip. I find them easy to thread, and they hold their shape better than any other needles I've tried. I am hard on my needles, so it's worth spending a little bit extra on needles that last longer. They come in a handy small storage tube with a cork.

Threading a needle

To thread your needle, flatten the end of the thread by pinching it between the tips of a pair of flatnose pliers, and then hold the thread between your thumb and forefinger so only a small tip is visible. Bring the eye of your needle down to the thread. In other words, "needle the thread" rather than thread the needle. (I have tried using a needle threader, but I broke both the needle and the threader while doing it, so I don't recommend it.)

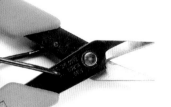

CUTTERS

Fireline and Wildfire will quickly dull the blades of scissors, so it's important to have scissors or snippers that will stay sharp enough to cut the thread. Oddly enough, my inexpensive children's scissors hold up better than more expensive ones—go figure. You can also try using tools specifically designed to cut fishing line. When it's time to end the thread, I usually burn it with a thread burner (Thread Zap or equivalent) because it allows me to get in very close to the beadwork while also cauterizing the end of the thread so it will stay put. Only burn the end, not any of the threads in your piece.

CLASPS

I use 3- or 4-loop magnetic tube clasps to finish my bracelets. There are several reasons I like them: The length of the clasp fits well with the width of the bracelet; they are secure and stay fastened; they only add ½ in. (1.3cm) to the length of the beadwork; the spacing of the clasp's loops line up well with the spaces between pairs of beads; and they are available in several metallic colors (silver, bronze, gold, rose gold, etc.). Of course, you can choose your favorite closure (or even make your own), but be sure to adjust the length of your beadwork accordingly.

tip End your beading after an odd-numbered row so the clasp will be equally positioned on each end.

Attaching a clasp

1. To attach a 4-loop tube clasp to a bracelet that's 28 beads across, first position the first loop so it nestles inside the second "ditch," or open space between beads, from the end. Note: For bracelets that are wider or narrower, you'll need to adapt the positioning of the clasp. Follow the thread path so your thread is exiting a pair of "up" beads (beads that protrude at the ends), and then sew through the clasp's loop, through the next pair of "up" beads, and so on.

2. Change direction by working your way back to the "up" beads just before the clasp loop. Repeat on the other end of the bracelet, making sure the clasp is oriented correctly. Keep the two pieces of the clasp attached when you are ready to sew on the second side; it helps avoid having to remove an incorrectly attached clasp.

3. Reinforce by retracing your thread path and stitching back in the opposite direction a couple of times. Clasps take the brunt of wear and tear on your finished piece, so it's important to reinforce your thread paths at least twice (a minimum of three total passes of the thread).

tip Don't shower or swim while wearing finished stitched bracelets. Water, chlorine, shampoo, etc. can affect the bead finishes and the metal of your clasp, and can even weaken the thread over time.

tip Bead scoops are handy to help get your beads off the work surface and back into their containers.

ADDITIONAL TOOLS

A **tape measure** or **ruler** is important, especially one that has both inches and centimeters.

You might find it handy to have a set of inexpensive **alphabet beads** to help keep track of your colors, especially for patterns that use more than three or four colors. Simply place the "A" alphabet bead on your mat next to your color A 11º cylinder beads, etc.

I have two **bead boards,** and I love them! The fabric surface of the mat helps keep your beads in piles, and the padded raised edge not only keeps your beads from rolling off the mat, but also serves as a pincushion. My smaller board is from Bead Wrangler (www.etsy.com/shop/BeadWranglerBoards), and it even has my name embroidered on it.

If you don't want to buy a board, you can put a bead mat or piece of felt on a rimmed baking sheet or tray.

Good **lighting** is important, especially when working with darker colors. I've tried beading without good lighting, and it really strains my eyes. I don't use a **magnifier** (yet!), but you might find it helpful if you struggle to see the beads as you work.

A small **scale** (the kind made for weighing cooking ingredients; you should be able to set it to measure in grams) helps when weighing your bead packages to see how many grams you have on hand.

ORGANIZATION TIPS

When preparing to buy my beads, I make a list in a notebook: project name, bead color numbers, and any additional supplies needed for that project. Before placing my order, I go through my bead stash to see whether I already have a sufficient quantity of any of the beads on hand; those I mark "H" (have). When my order arrives, it's easy for me to gather the materials for each project.

Cylinder beads arrive from my supplier (because of where I live, nearly all my bead purchases are made online) in small zip-top bags, labeled with the color number and name. At the start of each project, I mark each label with "A", "B", etc. to correspond with the project.

I have acquired quite a large stock of cylinder beads over the years and found it necessary to organize them in a way that makes sense to me. I bought some small plastic boxes in two sizes and then labeled them according to colors. I keep my beads in the small zip-top bags sent by my supplier; each has a label with the color number and name, which is very useful. When I have a lot of beads in a particular color group, I also arrange the baggies in numerical order within the boxes. The small boxes fit into two shoebox-size bins.

Two-Drop Peyote Stitch

BASIC TECHNIQUE (EVEN-COUNT)

1. Pick up an even number of beads as directed in the project. These beads become rows 1 and 2.

2. To begin row 3, pick up two beads, and sew through the third and fourth bead from the end. (As you stitch, every other pair of beads drops down half a space to form row 1.) Pick up two beads, and sew through the seventh and eighth beads from the end. Continue across the row. End by sewing through the first pair of beads picked up. To count peyote rows, count the total number of bead pairs along both edges.

3. To start row 4 and all other rows, pick up two beads, and sew through the last pair of beads added on the previous row.

note As with any bead stitching technique, consistent tension is important. Tension should be tight enough that the beads fit together snugly, yet not so tight that the weaving warps or buckles. You should be able to feel the beads pop into place. Practice makes perfect.

ENDING AND ADDING THREAD

To **end a thread**, weave back into the beadwork, following the existing thread path, changing directions at least twice as you weave so the thread crosses itself. Be sure to pull fairly tightly so that your thread drops between the beads, not on top; you shouldn't see your thread. To **add a thread**, start several rows below the point where the last bead was added, follow the existing thread path and weave through the beadwork, changing direction at least twice, exiting where you left off and you'll be ready to add the first beads with the new thread. With this method, your threads will be secure without needing to make knots which tend to show or distort the work.

READING THE PATTERNS AND WORD CHARTS

Each project includes the bead list with Miyuki Delica color numbers and bead counts, and both a pattern and a word chart. The **pattern** is easy to follow— just remember that peyote stitch rows are offset when you pick up two beads and sew through the next two beads.

The **word chart** has (L) "left" or (R) "right" listed at the beginning of each row. The right and left designations refer to the direction in which you're *reading* the pattern—but when I work from the word chart, I find the designations helpful to remind me which direction I should be *stitching*. You should be working toward your tail thread on (R) rows and away from the tail on (L) rows. (L) rows are the

HALF-HITCH KNOT
Pass the needle under the thread between two beads. A loop will form as you pull the thread through. Cross over the thread between the beads, sew through the loop, and pull gently to draw the knot into the beadwork.

even-numbered rows; (R) rows are the odd. Pick up the listed number of beads (in pairs) as directed.

KEEPING ON TRACK

It's important that you keep track of each row as you finish it. There are several ways to do this. If using the word chart, place a Post-It Note just below the row you are working; before moving the note, tick or highlight the row to show you have finished it, and then place the note under the next row. (To avoid marking up your book, you can photocopy the patterns.) Another idea is to place the word chart in a plastic sheet protector and use a watercolor marker to cross off each row as you finish. When you're done with that page, simply wipe off your marks with a damp paper towel and you'll be ready to re-use the sheet protector. You might find that a desktop paper holder works well (the kind you'd have next to your computer when you are typing text from a page); simply slide the guide down after you finish a row. You can easily find them at your local office supply store or online.

If using the pattern, keep in mind that peyote stitch rows are offset. You can cut a Post-It Note with jagged "teeth" to show the current row and move it after each is finished. You could also use a ruler to follow along, ignoring the partial beads and working only with the whole beads in the pattern.

PROBLEM SOLVING

I've learned that part of beading involves the dreaded "frog stitch" (rip-it, rip-it). I used to come close to crying each time it happened, but I have accepted it as a necessary evil. It's important that you check your work every few rows, especially before ending a thread. It's a lot less anxiety-producing to undo a couple of rows than to have to cut off part of your work, undo a lot of what you've done, and then try to figure out where you are in the pattern or word chart. The most common problems I've made are: picking up the wrong number of beads (one or three beads instead of two); getting my thread caught on an "up" bead; going through only one of the two beads in the pair; and losing my place on the pattern and picking up the wrong color beads. Learn from my mistakes and keep an eye on your work as you go.

tip The time can fly by when you are engrossed in your beading; you might find that you get stiff or suffer from eye strain after you've been sitting in one position for a long time, focused on your beading. Consider setting a timer as a reminder to get up and stretch at regular intervals (perhaps every 30 minutes).

PROJECTS

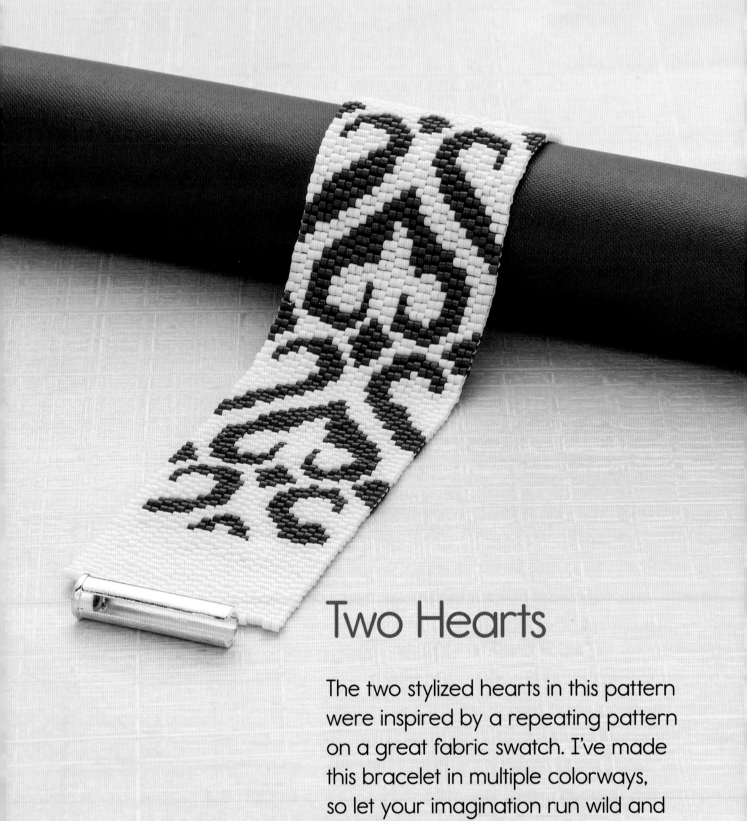

Two Hearts

The two stylized hearts in this pattern were inspired by a repeating pattern on a great fabric swatch. I've made this bracelet in multiple colorways, so let your imagination run wild and choose your favorite hues.

SUPPLIES

- 11º cylinder beads
  - 12g color A (Miyuki DB-1490, opaque bisque white)
  - 5g color B (Miyuki DB-2140, opaque anemone Duracoat)
- 4-loop tube clasp
- Beading needle, size 10, 11, or 12
- Fireline, 6-lb. test; use crystal color if you choose a light color background
- Scissors, thread snips, or thread burner

A   B

The bracelet measures approximately 1½ in. (3.8cm) wide, and the heart motif measures nearly 4½ in. (11.4cm) long; to adjust the bracelet's length, add or subtract the number of solid-color rows at each end, making sure to account for the length of your clasp. For example, to yield 6½ in. (16.5cm) of beadwork, weave 1 in. (2.5cm) of solid white before starting the motif; weave another 1 in. of solid white after you finish the motif.

MAKE THE BRACELET

1. Follow the pattern or word chart below to complete the piece (see two-drop peyote stitch, p. 9), leaving an 8–10-in. (20–25cm) tail for adding the clasp. Add and end thread as needed.
2. Attach a 4-loop tube clasp to each end of the bracelet (see p. 7).

Rows 1 and 2 (L): (28)A
Rows 3–40 (R–L): (14)A
Row 41 (R): (2)B, (12)A
Row 42 (L): (2)B, (4)A, (2)B, (5)A, (1)B
Row 43 (R): (2)B, (5)A, (2)B, (4)A, (1)B
Row 44 (L): (2)B, (4)A, (2)B, (6)A
Row 45 (R): (2)B, (2)A, (1)B, (1)A, (3)B, (1)A, (2)B, (2)A
Row 46 (L): (5)B, (1)A, (2)B, (2)A, (2)B, (2)A

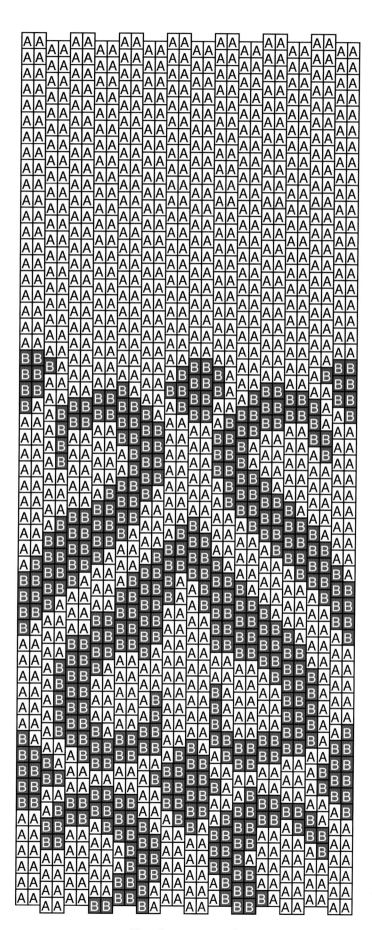

(Continues on p. 14)

Row 47 (R): (1)B, (1)A, (4)B, (1)A, (1)B, (2)A, (3)B, (1)A
Row 48 (L): (1)B, (1)A, (6)B, (1)A, (4)B, (1)A
Row 49 (R): (2)A, (4)B, (3)A, (4)B, (1)A
Row 50 (L): (4)A, (2)B, (2)A, (2)B, (2)A, (1)B, (1)A
Row 51 (R): (4)A, (2)B, (2)A, (2)B, (2)A, (2)B
Row 52 (L): (5)A, (1)B, (2)A, (2)B, (2)A, (1)B, (1)A
Row 53 (R): (5)A, (1)B, (2)A, (2)B, (3)A, (1)B
Row 54 (L): (5)A, (1)B, (2)A, (2)B, (2)A, (1)B, (1)A
Row 55 (R): (5)A, (1)B, (2)A, (2)B, (4)A
Row 56 (L): (4)A, (2)B, (2)A, (2)B, (4)A
Row 57 (R): (4)A, (2)B, (3)A, (2)B, (3)A
Row 58 (L): (4)A, (2)B, (3)A, (2)B, (3)A
Row 59 (R): (4)A, (2)B, (3)A, (3)B, (2)A
Row 60 (L): (3)A, (3)B, (4)A, (2)B, (2)A
Row 61 (R): (2)A, (4)B, (4)A, (2)B, (2)A
Row 62 (L): (2)A, (3)B, (2)A, (1)B, (2)A, (3)B, (1)A
Row 63 (R): (2)A, (3)B, (2)A, (1)B, (2)A, (3)B, (1)A
Row 64 (L): (2)A, (2)B, (2)A, (2)B, (2)A, (4)B
Row 65 (R): (2)A, (2)B, (2)A, (2)B, (3)A, (3)B
Row 66 (L): (2)A, (2)B, (2)A, (3)B, (2)A, (3)B
Row 67 (R): (1)A, (3)B, (2)A, (3)B, (3)A, (2)B
Row 68 (L): (1)A, (2)B, (3)A, (4)B, (2)A, (2)B
Row 69 (R): (3)B, (2)A, (2)B, (1)A, (2)B, (2)A, (2)B
Row 70 (L): (2)B, (3)A, (2)B, (1)A, (2)B, (2)A, (2)B
Row 71 (R): (2)B, (2)A, (3)B, (1)A, (2)B, (3)A, (1)B
Row 72 (L): (2)B, (2)A, (3)B, (1)A, (2)B, (3)A, (1)B
Row 73 (R): (2)B, (2)A, (2)B, (2)A, (3)B, (3)A
Row 74 (L): (2)B, (2)A, (2)B, (2)A, (4)B, (2)A
Row 75 (R): (1)B, (3)A, (2)B, (2)A, (4)B, (2)A
Row 76 (L): (1)B, (2)A, (3)B, (2)A, (4)B, (2)A
Row 77 (R): (2)A, (4)B, (2)A, (4)B, (2)A
Row 78 (L): (2)A, (4)B, (3)A, (3)B, (2)A
Row 79 (R): (2)A, (2)B, (6)A, (2)B, (2)A
Row 80 (L): (2)A, (2)B, (7)A, (2)B, (1)A
Row 81 (R): (2)A, (2)B, (7)A, (2)B, (1)A
Row 82 (L): (2)A, (2)B, (8)A, (1)B, (1)A
Row 83 (R): (2)A, (2)B, (4)A, (1)B, (3)A, (1)B, (1)A
Row 84 (L): (2)A, (2)B, (4)A, (1)B, (3)A, (1)B, (1)A
Row 85 (R): (2)A, (2)B, (4)A, (1)B, (3)A, (1)B, (1)A
Row 86 (L): (2)A, (2)B, (4)A, (1)B, (3)A, (1)B, (1)A
Row 87 (R): (2)A, (2)B, (4)A, (1)B, (3)A, (1)B, (1)A
Row 88 (L): (1)B, (1)A, (2)B, (4)A, (2)B, (1)A, (2)B, (1)A
Row 89 (R): (1)B, (1)A, (4)B, (2)A, (5)B, (1)A
Row 90 (L): (6)B, (1)A, (5)B, (2)A
Row 91 (R): (2)B, (1)A, (3)B, (1)A, (1)B, (1)A, (3)B, (2)A
Row 92 (L): (2)B, (2)A, (4)B, (2)A, (2)B, (1)A, (1)B
Row 93 (R): (2)B, (4)A, (2)B, (5)A, (1)B
Row 94 (L): (2)B, (4)A, (3)B, (3)A, (2)B
Row 95 (R): (2)B, (4)A, (3)B, (4)A, (1)B
Row 96 (L): (2)B, (2)A, (1)B, (1)A, (2)B, (2)A, (2)B, (2)A
Row 97 (R): (8)B, (2)A, (2)B, (2)A
Row 98 (L): (1)B, (1)A, (6)B, (2)A, (3)B, (1)A
Row 99 (R): (2)A, (4)B, (1)A, (1)B, (1)A, (4)B, (1)A
Row 100 (L): (2)A, (1)B, (1)A, (2)B, (1)A, (1)B, (1)A, (2)B, (1)A, (2)B
Row 101 (R): (4)A, (2)B, (2)A, (2)B, (2)A, (2)B
Row 102 (L): (4)A, (2)B, (2)A, (2)B, (2)A, (2)B

Row 103 (R): (5)A, (1)B, (2)A, (2)B, (3)A, (1)B
Row 104 (L): (5)A, (1)B, (2)A, (2)B, (4)A
Row 105 (R): (5)A, (1)B, (2)A, (2)B, (4)A
Row 106 (L): (4)A, (2)B, (2)A, (2)B, (4)A
Row 107 (R): (4)A, (2)B, (3)A, (1)B, (4)A
Row 108 (L): (4)A, (2)B, (3)A, (1)B, (4)A
Row 109 (R): (4)A, (2)B, (3)A, (2)B, (3)A
Row 110 (L): (4)A, (2)B, (3)A, (3)B, (2)A
Row 111 (R): (3)A, (3)B, (4)A, (2)B, (2)A
Row 112 (L): (3)A, (2)B, (5)A, (2)B, (2)A
Row 113 (R): (2)A, (3)B, (2)A, (1)B, (2)A, (2)B, (2)A
Row 114 (L): (2)A, (2)B, (3)A, (1)B, (2)A, (2)B, (2)A
Row 115 (R): (2)A, (2)B, (2)A, (2)B, (3)A, (2)B, (1)A
Row 116 (L): (2)A, (2)B, (2)A, (2)B, (2)A, (3)B, (1)A
Row 117 (R): (2)A, (2)B, (2)A, (3)B, (3)A, (2)B
Row 118 (L): (2)A, (2)B, (2)A, (3)B, (3)A, (2)B
Row 119 (R): (1)A, (3)B, (2)A, (4)B, (2)A, (2)B
Row 120 (L): (1)A, (1)B, (3)A, (5)B, (2)A, (2)B
Row 121 (R): (2)B, (3)A, (2)B, (1)A, (2)B, (2)A, (2)B
Row 122 (L): (2)B, (2)A, (3)B, (1)A, (2)B, (2)A, (2)B
Row 123 (R): (2)B, (2)A, (3)B, (1)A, (3)B, (2)A, (1)B
Row 124 (L): (2)B, (2)A, (2)B, (2)A, (3)B, (2)A, (1)B
Row 125 (R): (2)B, (2)A, (2)B, (2)A, (4)B, (2)A
Row 126 (L): (1)B, (3)A, (2)B, (2)A, (4)B, (2)A
Row 127 (R): (3)A, (3)B, (3)A, (3)B, (2)A
Row 128 (L): (3)A, (3)B, (2)A, (4)B, (2)A
Row 129 (R): (2)A, (4)B, (4)A, (2)B, (2)A
Row 130 (L): (2)A, (2)B, (6)A, (2)B, (2)A
Row 131 (R): (2)A, (2)B, (7)A, (2)B, (1)A
Row 132 (L): (2)A, (2)B, (7)A, (2)B, (1)A
Row 133 (R): (2)A, (2)B, (4)A, (1)B, (3)A, (1)B, (1)A
Row 134 (L): (2)A, (2)B, (4)A, (1)B, (3)A, (1)B, (1)A
Row 135 (R): (2)A, (2)B, (4)A, (1)B, (3)A, (1)B, (1)A
Row 136 (L): (2)A, (2)B, (4)A, (1)B, (3)A, (1)B, (1)A
Row 137 (R): (2)A, (2)B, (4)A, (1)B, (3)A, (1)B, (1)A
Row 138 (L): (2)A, (2)B, (4)A, (1)B, (2)A, (2)B, (1)A
Row 139 (R): (2)A, (2)B, (4)A, (2)B, (1)A, (2)B, (1)A
Row 140 (L): (1)B, (1)A, (4)B, (2)A, (4)B, (2)A
Row 141 (R): (6)B, (3)A, (3)B, (2)A
Row 142 (L): (6)B, (1)A, (1)B, (1)A, (3)B, (1)A, (1)B
Row 143 (R): (2)B, (2)A, (2)B, (1)A, (1)B, (2)A, (2)B, (2)A
Row 144 (L): (2)B, (4)A, (2)B, (4)A, (2)B
Row 145 (R): (2)B, (4)A, (3)B, (4)A, (1)B
Row 146 (L): (2)B, (4)A, (3)B, (4)A, (1)B
Row 147 (R): (2)B, (1)A, (2)B, (1)A, (2)B, (2)A, (2)B, (2)A
Row 148 (L): (1)B, (1)A, (6)B, (2)A, (2)B, (2)A
Row 149 (R): (1)B, (1)A, (4)B, (1)A, (1)B, (2)A, (3)B, (1)A
Row 150 (L): (2)A, (4)B, (1)A, (1)B, (1)A, (4)B, (1)A
Row 151 (R): (2)A, (1)B, (1)A, (2)B, (3)A, (2)B, (1)A, (2)B
Row 152 (L): (4)A, (2)B, (2)A, (2)B, (2)A, (1)B, (1)A
Row 153 (R): (5)A, (1)B, (3)A, (1)B, (3)A, (1)B
Row 154 (L): (4)A, (2)B, (2)A, (2)B, (2)A, (1)B, (1)A
Row 155 (R): (5)A, (1)B, (3)A, (1)B, (3)A, (1)B
Row 156 (L): (4)A, (2)B, (2)A, (2)B, (4)A
Row 157 (R): (5)A, (1)B, (3)A, (1)B, (4)A
Row 158 (L): (4)A, (2)B, (2)A, (2)B, (4)A
Row 159 (R): (4)A, (2)B, (3)A, (2)B, (3)A

Row 160 (L): (4)A, (2)B, (3)A, (2)B, (3)A
Row 161 (R): (2)A, (4)B, (4)A, (2)B, (2)A
Row 162 (L): (2)A, (3)B, (5)A, (3)B, (1)A
Row 163 (R): (2)A, (3)B, (5)A, (3)B, (1)A
Row 164 (L): (2)A, (2)B, (2)A, (2)B, (2)A, (4)B
Row 165 (R): (2)A, (2)B, (3)A, (2)B, (1)A, (4)B
Row 166 (L): (2)A, (2)B, (2)A, (2)B, (2)A, (4)B
Row 167 (R): (2)A, (2)B, (2)A, (4)B, (2)A, (2)B
Row 168 (L): (14)A
Row 169 (R): (6)A, (4)B, (4)A
Row 170 (L): (5)A, (1)B, (2)A, (1)B, (5)A
Rows 171–212 (R–L): (14)A

15

Some Like It Hot!

Are you a lover of spicy food? Yes?
Wear your love on your wrist. If you
prefer hot green peppers, change
up the colors.

SUPPLIES

- 11º cylinder beads
  - 9-10g color A (Miyuki DB-1490, opaque bisque white)
  - 1g color B (Miyuki DB-19, opaque vermillion red AB)
  - 4g color C (Miyuki DB-723, opaque red)
  - 1g color D (Miyuki DB-690 (silver-lined leaf green)
- 4-loop tube clasp
- Beading needle, size 10, 11, or 12
- Fireline, crystal, 6-lb. test
- Scissors, thread snips, or thread burner

A   B   C   D

The pepper measures 4½ in. (11.4cm) long; add rows of solid white at top and bottom to reach your desired length. For example, to yield 6½ in. (16.5cm) of beadwork, weave 1 in. (2.5cm) of solid white before starting the motif; weave another 1 in. (2.5 cm) of solid white after you finish the motif. The finished bracelet is 1½ in. (3.8cm) wide.

MAKE THE BRACELET

1. Follow the pattern or word chart below to complete the piece (see two-drop peyote stitch, p. 9), leaving an 8–10-in. (20–25cm) tail for adding the clasp. Add and end thread as needed.
2. Attach a 4-loop tube clasp to each end of the bracelet (see p. 7).

Rows 1 and 2 (L): (28)A
Rows 3–29 (R–L): (14)A
Row 30 (L): (11)A, (1)D, (2)A
Row 31 (R): (3)A, (1)D, (10)A
Row 32 (L): (14)A
Row 33 (R): (2)A, (2)D, (10)A
Row 34 (L): (14)A
Row 35 (R): (2)A, (2)D, (10)A
Row 36 (L): (14)A
Row 37 (R): (2)A, (2)D, (10)A

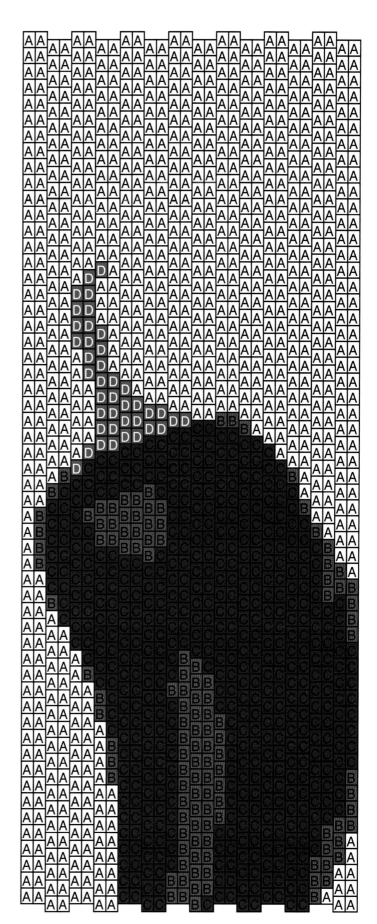

(Continues on p. 18)

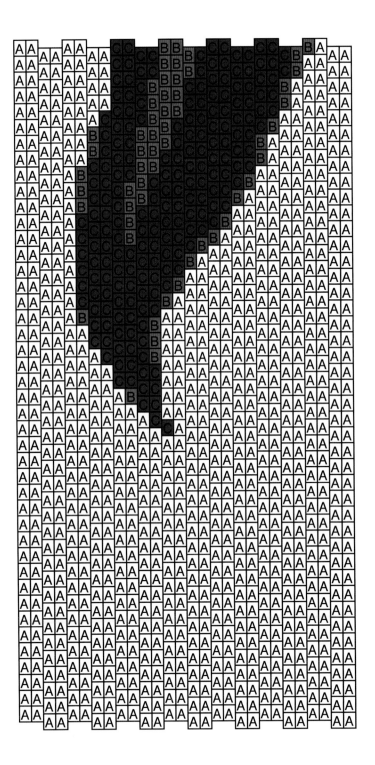

Row 38 (L): (11)A, (1)D, (2)A
Row 39 (R): (2)A, (2)D, (10)A
Row 40 (L): (11)A, (1)D, (2)A
Row 41 (R): (3)A, (1)D, (10)A
Row 42 (L): (11)A, (1)D, (2)A
Row 43 (R): (3)A, (1)D, (10)A
Row 44 (L): (10)A, (2)D, (2)A
Row 45 (R): (4)A, (1)D, (9)A
Row 46 (L): (10)A, (2)D, (2)A
Row 47 (R): (4)A, (2)D, (8)A
Row 48 (L): (8)A, (4)D, (2)A
Row 49 (R): (4)A, (4)D, (2)B, (4)A
Row 50 (L): (5)A, (1)B, (2)C, (4)D, (2)A
Row 51 (R): (4)A, (2)D, (4)C, (4)A
Row 52 (L): (4)A, (6)C, (2)D, (2)A
Row 53 (R): (3)A, (1)D, (7)C, (3)A
Row 54 (L): (4)A, (8)C, (2)A
Row 55 (R): (2)A, (1)D, (9)C, (2)A
Row 56 (L): (3)A, (1)B, (8)C, (1)B, (1)A
Row 57 (R): (2)A, (10)C, (2)A
Row 58 (L): (3)A, (6)C, (1)B, (3)C, (1)B
Row 59 (R): (2)A, (2)C, (2)B, (6)C, (2)A
Row 60 (L): (2)A, (1)B, (5)C, (4)B, (2)C
Row 61 (R): (1)A, (1)B, (1)C, (3)B, (6)C, (2)A
Row 62 (L): (2)A, (6)C, (4)B, (2)C
Row 63 (R): (1)A, (1)B, (2)C, (2)B, (6)C, (1)B, (1)A
Row 64 (L): (2)A, (6)C, (4)B, (2)C
Row 65 (R): (1)A, (1)B, (2)C, (2)B, (7)C, (1)B
Row 66 (L): (2)A, (7)C, (1)B, (4)C
Row 67 (R): (1)A, (1)B, (11)C, (1)B
Row 68 (L): (1)A, (1)B, (12)C
Row 69 (R): (2)A, (11)C, (1)B
Row 70 (L): (2)B, (12)C
Row 71 (R): (2)A, (11)C, (1)B
Row 72 (L): (1)B, (12)C, (1)B
Row 73 (R): (2)A, (12)C
Row 74 (L): (1)B, (12)C, (1)A
Row 75 (R): (2)A, (12)C
Row 76 (L): (1)B, (11)C, (2)A
Row 77 (R): (2)A, (12)C
Row 78 (L): (12)C, (2)A
Row 79 (R): (3)A, (4)C, (1)B, (6)C
Row 80 (L): (7)C, (1)B, (4)C, (2)A
Row 81 (R): (3)A, (1)B, (3)C, (1)B, (6)C
Row 82 (L): (6)C, (2)B, (4)C, (2)A
Row 83 (R): (4)A, (2)C, (2)B, (6)C
Row 84 (L): (6)C, (2)B, (3)C, (1)B, (2)A
Row 85 (R): (4)A, (3)C, (1)B, (6)C
Row 86 (L): (6)C, (2)B, (3)C, (1)B, (2)A
Row 87 (R): (4)A, (3)C, (2)B, (5)C
Row 88 (L): (6)C, (2)B, (3)C, (3)A
Row 89 (R): (4)A, (3)C, (2)B, (5)C
Row 90 (L): (6)C, (2)B, (2)C, (1)B, (3)A
Row 91 (R): (4)A, (3)C, (2)B, (5)C
Row 92 (L): (6)C, (2)B, (2)C, (1)B, (3)A
Row 93 (R): (4)A, (3)C, (2)B, (5)C
Row 94 (L): (1)B, (5)C, (2)B, (2)C, (1)B, (3)A

Row 95 (R): (4)A, (3)C, (2)B, (5)C
Row 96 (L): (1)B, (5)C, (2)B, (2)C, (4)A
Row 97 (R): (4)A, (3)C, (2)B, (5)C
Row 98 (L): (1)B, (5)C, (2)B, (2)C, (4)A
Row 99 (R): (4)A, (3)C, (2)B, (5)C
Row 100 (L): (2)B, (4)C, (2)B, (2)C, (4)A
Row 101 (R): (4)A, (3)C, (1)B, (5)C, (1)B
Row 102 (L): (1)A, (1)B, (4)C, (2)B, (2)C, (4)A
Row 103 (R): (4)A, (3)C, (1)B, (5)C, (1)B
Row 104 (L): (1)A, (1)B, (4)C, (2)B, (2)C, (4)A
Row 105 (R): (4)A, (3)C, (1)B, (4)C, (2)B
Row 106 (L): (2)A, (4)C, (2)B, (2)C, (4)A
Row 107 (R): (4)A, (2)C, (2)B, (4)C, (2)B
Row 108 (L): (2)A, (4)C, (2)B, (2)C, (4)A
Row 109 (R): (4)A, (2)C, (2)B, (4)C, (1)B, (1)A
Row 110 (L): (2)A, (5)C, (1)B, (2)C, (4)A
Row 111 (R): (4)A, (2)C, (2)B, (4)C, (1)B, (1)A
Row 112 (L): (2)A, (1)B, (4)C, (1)B, (2)C, (4)A
Row 113 (R): (4)A, (2)C, (2)B, (4)C, (2)A
Row 114 (L): (2)A, (1)B, (4)C, (1)B, (2)C, (4)A
Row 115 (R): (4)A, (2)C, (2)B, (4)C, (2)A
Row 116 (L): (3)A, (1)B, (4)C, (1)B, (1)C, (4)A
Row 117 (R): (4)A, (2)C, (2)B, (4)C, (2)A
Row 118 (L): (3)A, (1)B, (4)C, (1)B, (1)C, (4)A
Row 119 (R): (4)A, (2)C, (2)B, (4)C, (2)A
Row 120 (L): (4)A, (4)C, (1)B, (2)C, (3)A
Row 121 (R): (4)A, (2)C, (1)B, (4)C, (1)B, (2)A
Row 122 (L): (4)A, (4)C, (2)B, (1)C, (1)B, (2)A
Row 123 (R): (4)A, (2)C, (1)B, (3)C, (1)B, (3)A
Row 124 (L): (4)A, (4)C, (2)B, (1)C, (1)B, (2)A
Row 125 (R): (4)A, (6)C, (1)B, (3)A
Row 126 (L): (4)A, (4)C, (2)B, (2)C, (2)A
Row 127 (R): (3)A, (1)B, (6)C, (4)A
Row 128 (L): (4)A, (1)B, (4)C, (1)B, (2)C, (2)A
Row 129 (R): (3)A, (1)B, (1)C, (1)B, (4)C, (4)A
Row 130 (L): (5)A, (1)B, (3)C, (1)B, (2)C, (2)A

Row 131 (R): (3)A, (1)B, (1)C, (1)B, (4)C, (4)A
Row 132 (L): (6)A, (6)C, (2)A
Row 133 (R): (3)A, (2)C, (1)B, (3)C, (1)B, (4)A
Row 134 (L): (6)A, (6)C, (2)A
Row 135 (R): (3)A, (2)C, (1)B, (2)C, (1)B, (5)A
Row 136 (L): (6)A, (1)B, (5)C, (2)A
Row 137 (R): (3)A, (5)C, (6)A
Row 138 (L): (7)A, (1)B, (4)C, (2)A
Row 139 (R): (3)A, (5)C, (6)A
Row 140 (L): (8)A, (4)C, (2)A
Row 141 (R): (3)A, (4)C, (1)B, (6)A
Row 142 (L): (8)A, (4)C, (2)A
Row 143 (R): (3)A, (3)C, (1)B, (7)A
Row 144 (L): (8)A, (4)C, (2)A
Row 145 (R): (3)A, (1)B, (2)C, (8)A
Row 146 (L): (8)A, (1)B, (3)C, (2)A
Row 147 (R): (4)A, (2)C, (8)A
Row 148 (L): (8)A, (1)B, (3)C, (2)A
Row 149 (R): (4)A, (2)C, (8)A
Row 150 (L): (8)A, (1)B, (2)C, (3)A
Row 151 (R): (4)A, (2)C, (8)A
Row 152 (L): (8)A, (2)C, (4)A
Row 153 (R): (4)A, (2)C, (8)A
Row 154 (L): (8)A, (2)C, (4)A
Row 155 (R): (5)A, (1)B, (8)A
Row 156 (L): (8)A, (2)C, (4)A
Row 157 (R): (14)A
Row 158 (L): (8)A, (1)C, (5)A
Row 159 (R): (6)A, (1)C, (7)A
Rows 160–196 (L–R): (14)A

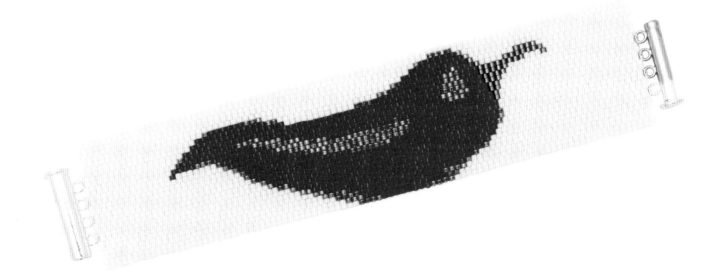

Treble Clef

This is perfect for all the musicians and music lovers in your life. I've made it in the traditional black on white, but use your imagination and choose your favorite colors.

note
The clef pattern begins on row 29 of the word chart. Adjust your bracelet size with that in mind.

SUPPLIES

- 11° cylinder beads
  - 10–11g color A (Miyuki DB-1490, opaque bisque white)
  - 3g color B (Miyuki DB-10, opaque black)
- 4-loop tube clasp
- Beading needle, size 10, 11, or 12
- Fireline, crystal, 6-lb. test
- Scissors, thread snips, or thread burner

A   B

The clef measures 3½ in. (8.9cm) long; to calculate how much solid color to weave at each end (top and bottom), subtract 3½ in. from your total desired length and divide by two. If you want the beaded portion of your bracelet to measure 6½ in. (16.5cm), you would weave 1½ in. (3.8cm) of solid white at each end (6½– 3½ = 3; 3 x ½ = 1.5). The finished bracelet is 1½ in. wide.

MAKE THE BRACELET

1. Follow the pattern or word chart below to complete the piece (see two-drop peyote stitch, p. 9), leaving an 8–10-in. (20–25cm) tail for adding the clasp. Add and end thread as needed.
2. Attach a 4-loop tube clasp to each end of the bracelet (see p. 7).

Rows 1 and 2: (L) (28)A
Rows 3–28: (14)A
Row 29: (R) (8)A, (2)B, (4)A
Row 30: (L) (5)A, (3)B, (6)A
Row 31: (R) (7)A, (3)B, (4)A
Row 32: (L) (4)A, (4)B, (6)A
Row 33: (R) (6)A, (4)B, (4)A
Row 34: (L) (4)A, (4)B, (6)A
Row 35: (R) (6)A, (5)B, (3)A
Row 36: (L) (4)A, (5)B, (5)A
Row 37: (R) (6)A, (6)B, (2)A
Row 38: (L) (4)A, (6)B, (4)A
Row 39: (R): (6)A, (2)B, (2)A, (2)B, (2)A
Row 40: (L) (4)A, (1)B, (2)A, (3)B, (4)A
Row 41: (R) (6)A, (2)B, (2)A, (2)B, (2)A

(Continues on p. 22)

Row 42: (L) (4)A, (1)B, (3)A, (2)B, (4)A
Row 43: (R) (6)A, (2)B, (2)A, (2)B, (2)A
Row 44: (L) (4)A, (2)B, (2)A, (2)B, (4)A
Row 45: (R) (6)A, (2)B, (2)A, (2)B, (2)A
Row 46: (L) (4)A, (2)B, (2)A, (2)B, (4)A
Row 47: (R) (6)A, (2)B, (2)A, (2)B, (2)A
Row 48: (L) (4)A, (2)B, (2)A, (2)B, (4)A
Row 49: (R) (6)A, (1)B, (2)A, (2)B, (3)A
Row 50: (L) (4)A, (2)B, (2)A, (2)B, (4)A
Row 51: (R) (6)A, (1)B, (2)A, (2)B, (3)A
Row 52: (L) (4)A, (2)B, (2)A, (2)B, (4)A
Row 53: (R) (6)A, (1)B, (1)A, (3)B, (3)A
Row 54: (L) (4)A, (3)B, (1)A, (2)B, (4)A
Row 55: (R) (6)A, (1)B, (1)A, (2)B, (4)A
Row 56: (L) (4)A, (5)B, (5)A
Row 57: (R) (6)A, (4)B, (4)A
Row 58: (L) (4)A, (5)B, (5)A
Row 59: (R) (6)A, (4)B, (4)A
Row 60: (L) (5)A, (4)B, (5)A
Row 61: (R) (6)A, (4)B, (4)A
Row 62: (L) (6)A, (4)B, (4)A
Row 63: (R) (6)A, (4)B, (4)A
Row 64: (L) (6)A, (4)B, (4)A
Row 65: (R) (5)A, (4)B, (5)A
Row 66: (L) (6)A, (4)B, (4)A
Row 67: (R) (4)A, (4)B, (6)A
Row 68: (L) (6)A, (5)B, (3)A
Row 69: (R) (4)A, (4)B, (6)A
Row 70: (L) (7)A, (5)B, (2)A
Row 71: (R) (3)A, (5)B, (6)A
Row 72: (L) (7)A, (5)B, (2)A
Row 73: (R) (2)A, (6)B, (6)A
Row 74: (L) (7)A, (5)B, (2)A
Row 75: (R) (2)A, (4)B, (1)A, (1)B, (6)A
Row 76: (L) (6)A, (2)B, (1)A, (4)B, (1)A
Row 77: (R) (2)A, (4)B, (1)A, (1)B, (6)A
Row 78: (L) (6)A, (2)B, (2)A, (3)B, (1)A
Row 79: (R) (2)A, (3)B, (2)A, (3)B, (4)A
Row 80: (L) (4)A, (4)B, (2)A, (4)B
Row 81: (R) (2)A, (2)B, (2)A, (6)B, (2)A
Row 82: (L) (3)A, (6)B, (1)A, (4)B
Row 83: (R) (2)A, (2)B, (2)A, (6)B, (2)A
Row 84: (L) (2)A, (8)B, (1)A, (3)B
Row 85: (R) (1)A, (3)B, (2)A, (7)B, (1)A
Row 86: (L) (2)A, (8)B, (2)A, (2)B
Row 87: (R) (1)A, (3)B, (1)A, (4)B, (1)A, (4)B
Row 88: (L) (2)A, (2)B, (2)A, (4)B, (2)A, (2)B
Row 89: (R) (1)A, (3)B, (1)A, (5)B, (1)A, (3)B
Row 90: (L) (1)A, (3)B, (2)A, (1)B, (1)A, (2)B, (2)A, (2)B
Row 91: (R) (1)A, (3)B, (1)A, (2)B, (1)A, (2)B, (1)A, (3)B
Row 92: (L) (1)A, (3)B, (2)A, (1)B, (1)A, (2)B, (2)A, (2)B
Row 93: (R) (2)A, (2)B, (1)A, (1)B, (2)A, (2)B, (2)A, (2)B
Row 94: (L) (1)A, (3)B, (4)A, (2)B, (2)A, (2)B
Row 95: (R) (2)A, (2)B, (1)A, (1)B, (2)A, (2)B, (2)A, (2)B
Row 96: (L) (1)A, (3)B, (1)A, (1)B, (2)A, (2)B, (2)A, (2)B
Row 97: (R) (2)A, (2)B, (2)A, (1)B, (1)A, (2)B, (2)A, (2)B
Row 98: (L) (1)A, (3)B, (1)A, (1)B, (2)A, (2)B, (1)A, (2)B, (1)A

Row 99: (R) (2)A, (2)B, (2)A, (4)B, (1)A, (3)B
Row 100: (L) (2)A, (2)B, (1)A, (1)B, (1)A, (2)B, (1)A, (2)B, (2)A
Row 101: (R) (2)A, (3)B, (1)A, (2)B, (1)A, (1)B, (1)A, (2)B, (1)A
Row 102: (L) (2)A, (2)B, (1)A, (3)B, (2)A, (2)B, (2)A
Row 103: (R) (3)A, (3)B, (3)A, (3)B, (2)A
Row 104: (L) (3)A, (3)B, (3)A, (3)B, (2)A
Row 105: (R) (4)A, (2)B, (2)A, (4)B, (2)A
Row 106: (L) (4)A, (7)B, (3)A
Row 107: (R) (4)A, (8)B, (2)A
Row 108: (L) (4)A, (6)B, (4)A
Row 109: (R) (6)A, (5)B, (3)A
Row 110: (L) (4)A, (4)B, (6)A
Row 111: (R) (10)A, (1)B, (3)A
Row 112: (L) (4)A, (2)B, (8)A
Row 113: (R) (10)A, (1)B, (3)A
Row 114: (L) (4)A, (1)B, (9)A
Row 115: (R) (10)A, (1)B, (3)A
Row 116: (L) (4)A, (1)B, (3)A, (2)B, (4)A
Row 117: (R) (4)A, (4)B, (2)A, (2)B, (2)A
Row 118: (L) (4)A, (1)B, (2)A, (3)B, (4)A
Row 119: (R) (4)A, (4)B, (2)A, (2)B, (2)A
Row 120: (L) (4)A, (1)B, (2)A, (4)B, (3)A
Row 121: (R) (4)A, (4)B, (2)A, (2)B, (2)A
Row 122: (L) (4)A, (1)B, (1)A, (5)B, (3)A
Row 123: (R) (4)A, (4)B, (2)A, (2)B, (2)A
Row 124: (L) (4)A, (7)B, (3)A
Row 125: (R) (4)A, (4)B, (2)A, (2)B, (2)A
Row 126: (L) (4)A, (2)B, (1)A, (4)B, (3)A
Row 127: (R) (4)A, (4)B, (1)A, (2)B, (3)A
Row 128: (L) (4)A, (2)B, (2)A, (2)B, (4)A
Row 129: (R) (4)A, (6)B, (4)A
Row 130: (L) (4)A, (6)B, (4)A
Row 131: (R) (6)A, (4)B, (4)A
Row 132: (L) (6)A, (2)B, (6)A
Row 133–196: (or end of bracelet): (14)A

project idea

If you prefer to hang this instead of wearing it as a bracelet, omit the clasp and either frame it or add a hanging loop of beads. It makes a lovely gift for a music teacher. You could also sew closed jump rings to each top corner and then use open jump rings to attach a chain or rope.

Crosshatch

An easy-to-make design doesn't have
to be boring, even with a repetitive
pattern. One of my favorite things
about this design is the endless color
combinations you can use, whether
you prefer a dramatic or subtle effect.

SUPPLIES

- 11º cylinder beads
  - 9g color A (Miyuki DB-391, opaque olive satin)
  - 6g color B (Miyuki DB-1510, matte opaque bisque white)
- 4-loop tube clasp
- Beading needle, size 10, 11, or 12
- Fireline, crystal or smoke (depending on your bead colors), 6-lb. test
- Scissors, thread snips, or thread burner

A   B

This bracelet measures 1½ in. (3.8cm) wide and 7 in. (18cm) long, not including the clasp.

MAKE THE BRACELET

1. Follow the pattern or word chart below to complete the piece (see two-drop peyote stitch, p. 9), leaving an 8–10-in. (20–25cm) tail for adding the clasp. Add and end thread as needed.
2. Attach a 4-loop tube clasp to each end of the bracelet (see p. 7).

Rows 1 and 2 (L): (1)A, (13)B, (4)A, (5)B, (5)A
Row 3 (R): (3)A, (3)B, (8)A
Row 4 (L): (10)A, (2)B, (2)A
Row 5 (R): (3)A, (3)B, (8)A
Row 6 (L): (10)A, (2)B, (2)A
Row 7 (R): (3)A, (3)B, (8)A
Row 8 (L): (10)A, (2)B, (2)A
Row 9 (R): (10)A, (2)B, (2)A
Row 10 (L): (3)A, (3)B, (8)A
Row 11 (R): (10)A, (2)B, (2)A
Row 12 (L): (3)A, (3)B, (8)A
Row 13 (R): (10)A, (2)B, (2)A
Row 14 (L): (3)A, (3)B, (8)A
Row 15 (R): (1)A, (7)B, (2)A, (2)B, (2)A
Row 16 (L): (3)A, (3)B, (2)A, (6)B
Row 17 (R): (1)A, (7)B, (2)A, (2)B, (2)A
Row 18 (L): (1)B, (2)A, (3)B, (2)A, (6)B
Row 19 (R): (1)A, (7)B, (2)A, (2)B, (2)A

(Continues on p. 26)

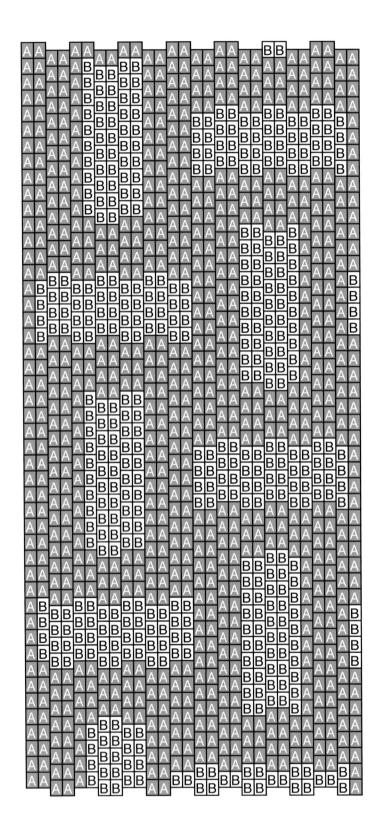

Row 20 (L): (1)B, (2)A, (3)B, (2)A, (6)B
Row 21 (R): (1)A, (7)B, (2)A, (2)B, (2)A
Row 22 (L): (1)B, (2)A, (3)B, (2)A, (6)B
Row 23 (R): (10)A, (2)B, (2)A
Row 24 (L): (3)A, (3)B, (8)A
Row 25 (R): (10)A, (2)B, (2)A
Row 26 (L): (3)A, (3)B, (8)A
Row 27 (R): (10)A, (2)B, (2)A
Row 28 (L): (3)A, (3)B, (8)A
Row 29 (R): (14)A
Row 30 (L): (10)A, (2)B, (2)A
Row 31 (R): (3)A, (3)B, (8)A
Row 32 (L): (10)A, (2)B, (2)A
Row 33 (R): (3)A, (3)B, (8)A
Row 34 (L): (10)A, (2)B, (2)A
Row 35 (R): (3)A, (3)B, (8)A
Row 36 (L): (1)A, (7)B, (2)A, (2)B, (2)A
Row 37 (R): (3)A, (3)B, (2)A, (6)B
Row 38 (L): (1)A, (7)B, (2)A, (2)B, (2)A
Row 39 (R): (3)A, (3)B, (2)A, (6)B
Row 40 (L): (1)A, (7)B, (2)A, (2)B, (2)A
Row 41 (R): (3)A, (3)B, (2)A, (6)B
Row 42 (L): (1)A, (7)B, (2)A, (2)B, (2)A
Row 43 (R): (3)A, (3)B, (2)A, (6)B
Row 44 (L): (10)A, (2)B, (2)A
Row 45 (R): (3)A, (3)B, (8)A
Row 46 (L): (10)A, (2)B, (2)A
Row 47 (R): (3)A, (3)B, (8)A
Row 48 (L): (10)A, (2)B, (2)A
Row 49 (R): (3)A, (3)B, (8)A
Row 50 (L): (14)A
Row 51 (R): (10)A, (2)B, (2)A
Row 52 (L): (3)A, (3)B, (8)A
Row 53 (R): (10)A, (2)B, (2)A
Row 54 (L): (3)A, (3)B, (8)A
Row 55 (R): (10)A, (2)B, (2)A
Row 56 (L): (3)A, (3)B, (8)A
Row 57 (R): (1)A, (7)B, (2)A, (2)B, (2)A
Row 58 (L): (1)B, (2)A, (3)B, (2)A, (6)B
Row 59 (R): (1)A, (7)B, (2)A, (2)B, (2)A
Row 60 (L): (1)B, (2)A, (3)B, (2)A, (6)B
Row 61 (R): (1)A, (7)B, (2)A, (2)B, (2)A
Row 62 (L): (1)B, (2)A, (3)B, (2)A, (6)B
Row 63 (R): (1)A, (7)B, (2)A, (2)B, (2)A
Row 64 (L): (3)A, (3)B, (2)A, (6)B
Row 65 (R): (10)A, (2)B, (2)A
Row 66 (L): (3)A, (3)B, (8)A
Row 67 (R): (10)A, (2)B, (2)A
Row 68 (L): (3)A, (3)B, (8)A
Row 69 (R): (10)A, (2)B, (2)A
Row 70 (L): (3)A, (3)B, (8)A
Row 71 (R): (14)A
Row 72 (L): (10)A, (2)B, (2)A
Row 73 (R): (3)A, (3)B, (8)A
Row 74 (L): (10)A, (2)B, (2)A
Row 75 (R): (3)A, (3)B, (8)A
Row 76 (L): (10)A, (2)B, (2)A

Row 77 (R): (3)A, (3)B, (2)A, (6)B
Row 78 (L): (1)A, (7)B, (2)A, (2)B, (2)A
Row 79 (R): (3)A, (3)B, (2)A, (6)B
Row 80 (L): (1)A, (7)B, (2)A, (2)B, (2)A
Row 81 (R): (3)A, (3)B, (2)A, (6)B
Row 82 (L): (1)A, (7)B, (2)A, (2)B, (2)A
Row 83 (R): (3)A, (3)B, (2)A, (6)B
Row 84 (L): (1)A, (7)B, (2)A, (2)B, (2)A
Row 85 (R): (3)A, (3)B, (2)A, (6)B
Row 86 (L): (10)A, (2)B, (2)A
Row 87 (R): (3)A, (3)B, (8)A
Row 88 (L): (10)A, (2)B, (2)A
Row 89 (R): (3)A, (3)B, (8)A
Row 90 (L): (10)A, (2)B, (2)A
Row 91 (R): (3)A, (3)B, (8)A
Row 92 (L): (3)A, (3)B, (8)A
Row 93 (R): (10)A, (2)B, (2)A
Row 94 (L): (3)A, (3)B, (8)A
Row 95 (R): (10)A, (2)B, (2)A
Row 96 (L): (3)A, (3)B, (8)A
Row 97 (R): (10)A, (2)B, (2)A
Row 98 (L): (3)A, (3)B, (2)A, (6)B
Row 99 (R): (1)A, (7)B, (2)A, (2)B, (2)A
Row 100 (L): (1)B, (2)A, (3)B, (2)A, (6)B
Row 101 (R): (1)A, (7)B, (2)A, (2)B, (2)A
Row 102 (L): (1)B, (2)A, (3)B, (2)A, (6)B
Row 103 (R): (1)A, (7)B, (2)A, (2)B, (2)A
Row 104 (L): (1)B, (2)A, (3)B, (2)A, (6)B
Row 105 (R): (1)A, (7)B, (2)A, (2)B, (2)A
Row 106 (L): (3)A, (3)B, (2)A, (6)B
Row 107 (R): (10)A, (2)B, (2)A
Row 108 (L): (3)A, (3)B, (8)A
Row 109 (R): (10)A, (2)B, (2)A
Row 110 (L): (3)A, (3)B, (8)A
Row 111 (R): (10)A, (2)B, (2)A
Row 112 (L): (14)A
Row 113 (R): (3)A, (3)B, (8)A
Row 114 (L): (10)A, (2)B, (2)A
Row 115 (R): (3)A, (3)B, (8)A
Row 116 (L): (10)A, (2)B, (2)A
Row 117 (R): (3)A, (3)B, (8)A
Row 118 (L): (10)A, (2)B, (2)A
Row 119 (R): (3)A, (3)B, (2)A, (6)B
Row 120 (L): (1)A, (7)B, (2)A, (2)B, (2)A
Row 121 (R): (3)A, (3)B, (2)A, (6)B
Row 122 (L): (1)A, (7)B, (2)A, (2)B, (2)A
Row 123 (R): (3)A, (3)B, (2)A, (6)B
Row 124 (L): (1)A, (7)B, (2)A, (2)B, (2)A
Row 125 (R): (3)A, (3)B, (2)A, (6)B
Row 126 (L): (1)A, (7)B, (2)A, (2)B, (2)A
Row 127 (R): (3)A, (3)B, (8)A
Row 128 (L): (10)A, (2)B, (2)A
Row 129 (R): (3)A, (3)B, (8)A
Row 130 (L): (10)A, (2)B, (2)A
Row 131 (R): (3)A, (3)B, (8)A
Row 132 (L): (10)A, (2)B, (2)A
Row 133 (R): (14)A

Row 134 (L): (3)A, (3)B, (8)A
Row 135 (R): (10)A, (2)B, (2)A
Row 136 (L): (3)A, (3)B, (8)A
Row 137 (R): (10)A, (2)B, (2)A
Row 138 (L): (3)A, (3)B, (8)A
Row 139 (R): (10)A, (2)B, (2)A
Row 140 (L): (1)B, (2)A, (3)B, (2)A, (6)B
Row 141 (R): (1)A, (7)B, (2)A, (2)B, (2)A
Row 142 (L): (1)B, (2)A, (3)B, (2)A, (6)B
Row 143 (R): (1)A, (7)B, (2)A, (2)B, (2)A
Row 144 (L): (1)B, (2)A, (3)B, (2)A, (6)B
Row 145 (R): (1)A, (7)B, (2)A, (2)B, (2)A
Row 146 (L): (1)B, (2)A, (3)B, (2)A, (6)B
Row 147 (R): (1)A, (7)B, (2)A, (2)B, (2)A
Row 148 (L): (3)A, (3)B, (8)A
Row 149 (R): (10)A, (2)B, (2)A
Row 150 (L): (3)A, (3)B, (8)A
Row 151 (R): (10)A, (2)B, (2)A
Row 152 (L): (3)A, (3)B, (8)A
Row 153 (R): (10)A, (2)B, (2)A
Row 154 (L): (14)A
Row 155 (R): (3)A, (3)B, (8)A
Row 156 (L): (10)A, (2)B, (2)A
Row 157 (R): (3)A, (3)B, (8)A
Row 158 (L): (10)A, (2)B, (2)A
Row 159 (R): (3)A, (3)B, (8)A
Row 160 (L): (10)A, (2)B, (2)A
Row 161 (R): (3)A, (3)B, (2)A, (6)B
Row 162 (L): (1)A, (7)B, (2)A, (2)B, (2)A
Row 163 (R): (3)A, (3)B, (2)A, (6)B
Row 164 (L): (1)A, (7)B, (2)A, (2)B, (2)A
Row 165 (R): (3)A, (3)B, (2)A, (6)B
Row 166 (L): (1)A, (7)B, (2)A, (2)B, (2)A
Row 167 (R): (3)A, (3)B, (2)A, (6)B
Row 168 (L): (1)A, (7)B, (2)A, (2)B, (2)A
Row 169 (R): (3)A, (3)B, (8)A
Row 170 (L): (10)A, (2)B, (2)A
Row 171 (R): (3)A, (3)B, (8)A
Row 172 (L): (10)A, (2)B, (2)A
Row 173 (R): (3)A, (3)B, (8)A
Row 174 (L): (10)A, (2)B, (2)A
Row 175 (R): (10)A, (2)B, (2)A
Row 176 (L): (3)A, (3)B, (8)A
Row 177 (R): (10)A, (2)B, (2)A
Row 178 (L): (3)A, (3)B, (8)A
Row 179 (R): (10)A, (2)B, (2)A
Row 180 (L): (3)A, (3)B, (8)A
Row 181 (R): (1)A, (7)B, (2)A, (2)B, (2)A
Row 182 (L): (1)B, (2)A, (3)B, (2)A, (6)B
Row 183 (R): (1)A, (7)B, (2)A, (2)B, (2)A
Row 184 (L): (1)B, (2)A, (3)B, (2)A, (6)B
Row 185 (R): (1)A, (7)B, (2)A, (2)B, (2)A
Row 186 (L): (1)B, (2)A, (3)B, (2)A, (6)B
Row 187 (R): (1)A, (7)B, (2)A, (2)B, (2)A
Row 188 (L): (1)B, (2)A, (3)B, (2)A, (6)B
Row 189 (R): (10)A, (2)B, (2)A
Row 190 (L): (3)A, (3)B, (8)A

Row 191 (R): (10)A, (2)B, (2)A
Row 192 (L): (3)A, (3)B, (8)A
Row 193 (R): (10)A, (2)B, (2)A
Row 194 (L): (3)A, (3)B, (8)A
Row 195 (R): (14)A
Row 196 (L): (10)A, (2)B, (2)A
Row 197 (R): (3)A, (3)B, (8)A
Row 198 (L): (10)A, (2)B, (2)A
Row 199 (R): (3)A, (3)B, (8)A
Row 200 (L): (10)A, (2)B, (2)A
Row 201 (R): (3)A, (3)B, (8)A
Row 202 (L): (1)A, (7)B, (2)A, (2)B, (2)A
Row 203 (R): (3)A, (11)B
Row 204 (L): (1)A, (7)B, (2)A, (2)B, (2)A

Tessellation

Tessellation is an arrangement of shapes closely fitted together in a repeated pattern without gaps or overlapping. Math geekiness aside, I simply find the design visually appealing, regardless of the technical specifications.

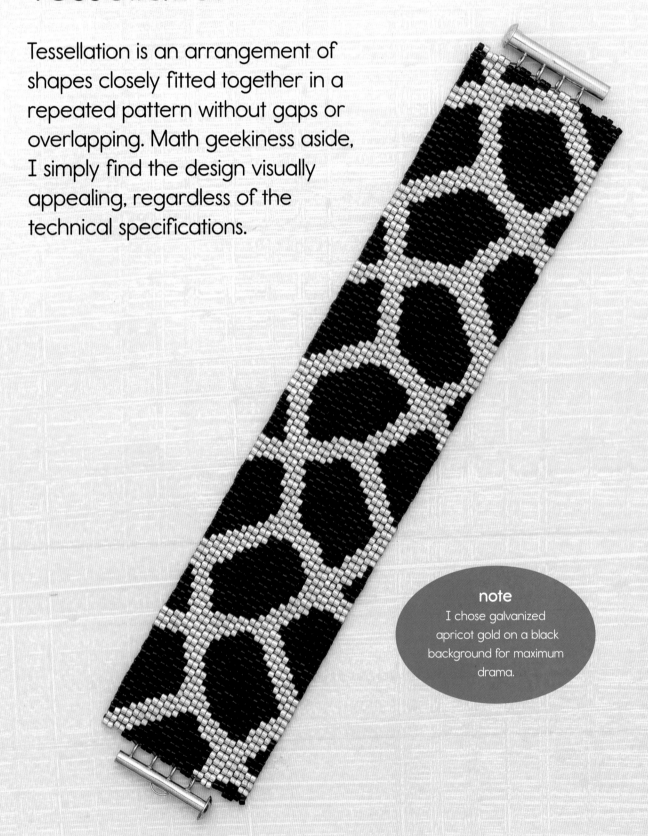

note
I chose galvanized apricot gold on a black background for maximum drama.

SUPPLIES

- 11º cylinder beads
  - 9g color A (Miyuki DB-10, opaque black)
  - 7g color B (Miyuki DB-411, galvanized apricot gold)
- 4-loop tube clasp (rose gold)
- Beading needle, size 10, 11, or 12
- Fireline, crystal or smoke (depending on your bead colors), 6-lb. test
- Scissors, thread snips, or thread burner

A   B

This bracelet measures 1½ in. (3.8cm) wide and 7 in. (18cm) long, not including the clasp.

MAKE THE BRACELET

1. Follow the pattern or word chart below to complete the piece (see two-drop peyote stitch, p. 9), leaving an 8–10-in. (20–25cm) tail for adding the clasp. Add and end thread as needed.
2. Attach a 4-loop tube clasp to each end of the bracelet (see p. 7).

Rows 1 and 2 (L): (8)A, (6)B, (8)A, (5)B, (1)A
Row 3 (R): (2)A, (2)B, (2)A, (5)B, (3)A
Row 4 (L): (4)A, (6)B, (2)A, (2)B
Row 5 (R): (2)A, (10)B, (2)A
Row 6 (L): (3)A, (10)B, (1)A
Row 7 (R): (2)A, (6)B, (2)A, (2)B, (2)A
Row 8 (L): (2)A, (3)B, (3)A, (4)B, (2)A
Row 9 (R): (2)A, (4)B, (4)A, (3)B, (1)A
Row 10 (L): (2)A, (2)B, (6)A, (4)B
Row 11 (R): (1)A, (4)B, (6)A, (3)B
Row 12 (L): (1)A, (3)B, (6)A, (4)B
Row 13 (R): (5)B, (7)A, (2)B
Row 14 (L): (3)B, (7)A, (4)B
Row 15 (R): (2)B, (2)A, (2)B, (6)A, (2)B
Row 16 (L): (2)B, (8)A, (2)B, (1)A, (1)B
Row 17 (R): (2)B, (2)A, (2)B, (7)A, (1)B
Row 18 (L): (2)B, (7)A, (2)B, (3)A
Row 19 (R): (4)A, (2)B, (8)A

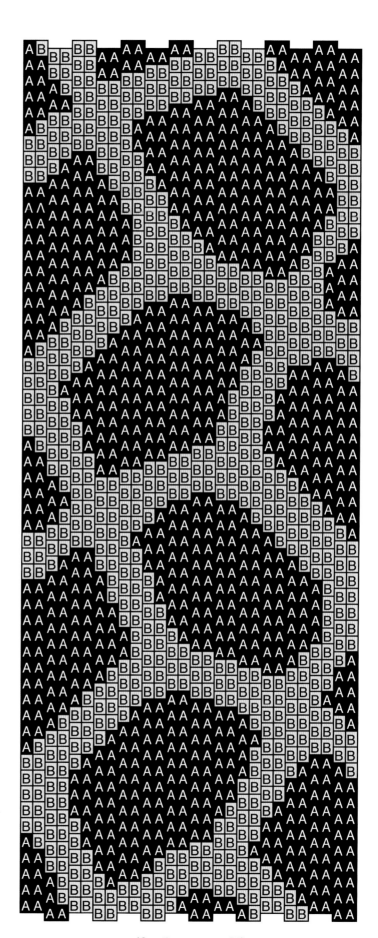

(Continues on p. 30)

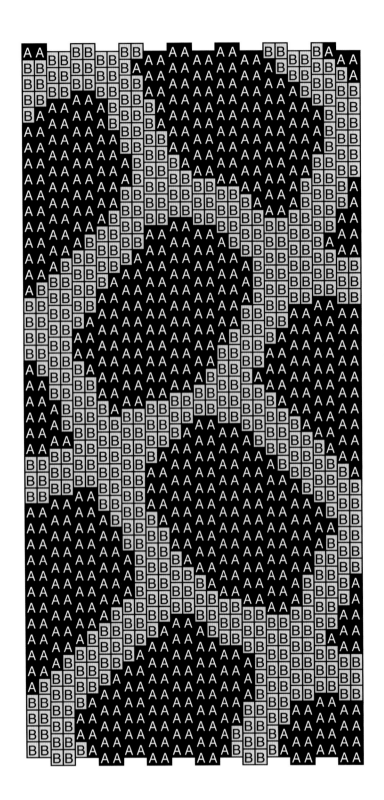

Row 20 (L): (2)B, (6)A, (2)B, (4)A
Row 21 (R): (4)A, (2)B, (8)A
Row 22 (L): (2)B, (6)A, (2)B, (4)A
Row 23 (R): (5)A, (2)B, (6)A, (1)B
Row 24 (L): (2)B, (6)A, (2)B, (4)A
Row 25 (R): (5)A, (3)B, (4)A, (2)B
Row 26 (L): (1)A, (1)B, (5)A, (3)B, (4)A
Row 27 (R): (5)A, (3)B, (4)A, (2)B
Row 28 (L): (2)A, (1)B, (3)A, (4)B, (4)A
Row 29 (R): (4)A, (6)B, (2)A, (1)B, (1)A
Row 30 (L): (2)A, (9)B, (3)A
Row 31 (R): (4)A, (9)B, (1)A
Row 32 (L): (2)A, (10)B, (2)A
Row 33 (R): (3)A, (3)B, (2)A, (5)B, (1)A
Row 34 (L): (2)A, (4)B, (4)A, (2)B, (2)A
Row 35 (R): (2)A, (3)B, (5)A, (4)B
Row 36 (L): (5)B, (5)A, (3)B, (1)A
Row 37 (R): (2)A, (2)B, (6)A, (4)B
Row 38 (L): (4)B, (7)A, (3)B
Row 39 (R): (1)A, (3)B, (6)A, (4)B
Row 40 (L): (5)B, (7)A, (2)B
Row 41 (R): (3)B, (7)A, (2)B, (2)A
Row 42 (L): (1)B, (3)A, (2)B, (6)A, (2)B
Row 43 (R): (2)B, (8)A, (2)B, (2)A
Row 44 (L): (4)A, (2)B, (7)A, (1)B
Row 45 (R): (2)B, (7)A, (2)B, (3)A
Row 46 (L): (4)A, (2)B, (6)A, (2)B
Row 47 (R): (2)B, (7)A, (2)B, (3)A
Row 48 (L): (4)A, (2)B, (6)A, (2)B
Row 49 (R): (3)B, (5)A, (2)B, (4)A
Row 50 (L): (4)A, (2)B, (6)A, (2)B
Row 51 (R): (1)A, (2)B, (5)A, (2)B, (4)A
Row 52 (L): (4)A, (4)B, (4)A, (2)B
Row 53 (R): (2)A, (2)B, (2)A, (5)B, (3)A
Row 54 (L): (4)A, (6)B, (2)A, (2)B
Row 55 (R): (2)A, (10)B, (2)A
Row 56 (L): (3)A, (10)B, (1)A
Row 57 (R): (2)A, (10)B, (2)A
Row 58 (L): (2)A, (4)B, (2)A, (4)B, (2)A
Row 59 (R): (2)A, (4)B, (4)A, (3)B, (1)A
Row 60 (L): (2)A, (3)B, (4)A, (4)B, (1)A
Row 61 (R): (2)A, (4)B, (4)A, (4)B
Row 62 (L): (1)A, (3)B, (6)A, (4)B
Row 63 (R): (5)B, (6)A, (3)B
Row 64 (L): (4)B, (6)A, (4)B
Row 65 (R): (2)B, (2)A, (2)B, (6)A, (2)B
Row 66 (L): (3)B, (7)A, (2)B, (1)A, (1)B
Row 67 (R): (2)B, (2)A, (2)B, (6)A, (2)B
Row 68 (L): (2)B, (7)A, (2)B, (3)A
Row 69 (R): (4)A, (2)B, (7)A, (1)B
Row 70 (L): (2)B, (7)A, (2)B, (3)A
Row 71 (R): (4)A, (2)B, (7)A, (1)B
Row 72 (L): (2)B, (6)A, (2)B, (4)A
Row 73 (R): (4)A, (2)B, (7)A, (1)B
Row 74 (L): (2)B, (6)A, (2)B, (4)A
Row 75 (R): (5)A, (2)B, (6)A, (1)B
Row 76 (L): (2)B, (6)A, (2)B, (4)A

Row 77 (R): (5)A, (3)B, (4)A, (2)B
Row 78 (L): (1)A, (2)B, (3)A, (4)B, (4)A
Row 79 (R): (4)A, (6)B, (2)A, (2)B
Row 80 (L): (2)A, (9)B, (3)A
Row 81 (R): (4)A, (10)B
Row 82 (L): (2)A, (10)B, (2)A
Row 83 (R): (3)A, (3)B, (2)A, (5)B, (1)A
Row 84 (L): (2)A, (4)B, (4)A, (2)B, (2)A
Row 85 (R): (2)A, (3)B, (5)A, (4)B
Row 86 (L): (1)A, (4)B, (5)A, (3)B, (1)A
Row 87 (R): (2)A, (2)B, (6)A, (4)B
Row 88 (L): (4)B, (7)A, (3)B
Row 89 (R): (1)A, (3)B, (6)A, (4)B
Row 90 (L): (5)B, (7)A, (2)B
Row 91 (R): (3)B, (7)A, (2)B, (2)A
Row 92 (L): (1)B, (2)A, (2)B, (7)A, (2)B
Row 93 (R): (2)B, (8)A, (2)B, (2)A
Row 94 (L): (4)A, (2)B, (6)A, (2)B
Row 95 (R): (2)B, (8)A, (2)B, (2)A
Row 96 (L): (4)A, (2)B, (6)A, (2)B
Row 97 (R): (2)B, (7)A, (2)B, (3)A
Row 98 (L): (4)A, (2)B, (6)A, (2)B
Row 99 (R): (3)B, (5)A, (2)B, (4)A
Row 100 (L): (4)A, (2)B, (6)A, (2)B
Row 101 (R): (1)A, (2)B, (5)A, (2)B, (4)A
Row 102 (L): (5)A, (3)B, (4)A, (2)B
Row 103 (R): (2)A, (2)B, (2)A, (4)B, (4)A
Row 104 (L): (4)A, (5)B, (3)A, (2)B
Row 105 (R): (2)A, (2)B, (2)A, (5)B, (3)A
Row 106 (L): (4)A, (6)B, (1)A, (2)B, (1)A
Row 107 (R): (2)A, (10)B, (2)A
Row 108 (L): (3)A, (3)B, (2)A, (5)B, (1)A
Row 109 (R): (2)A, (5)B, (3)A, (2)B, (2)A
Row 110 (L): (2)A, (3)B, (3)A, (4)B, (2)A
Row 111 (R): (2)A, (4)B, (4)A, (3)B, (1)A
Row 112 (L): (2)A, (2)B, (6)A, (4)B
Row 113 (R): (5)B, (6)A, (3)B
Row 114 (L): (1)A, (3)B, (6)A, (4)B
Row 115 (R): (6)B, (6)A, (2)B
Row 116 (L): (3)B, (7)A, (4)B
Row 117 (R): (2)B, (2)A, (2)B, (6)A, (2)B
Row 118 (L): (2)B, (7)A, (2)B, (3)A
Row 119 (R): (1)B, (3)A, (2)B, (/)A, (1)B
Row 120 (L): (2)B, (7)A, (2)B, (3)A
Row 121 (R): (4)A, (2)B, (7)A, (1)B
Row 122 (L): (2)B, (6)A, (2)B, (4)A
Row 123 (R): (4)A, (2)B, (7)A, (1)B
Row 124 (L): (2)B, (6)A, (2)B, (4)A
Row 125 (R): (5)A, (2)B, (5)A, (2)B
Row 126 (L): (2)B, (6)A, (2)B, (4)A
Row 127 (R): (5)A, (3)B, (4)A, (2)B
Row 128 (L): (1)A, (2)B, (3)A, (4)B, (4)A
Row 129 (R): (4)A, (6)B, (2)A, (2)B
Row 130 (L): (1)A, (2)B, (2)A, (5)B, (4)A
Row 131 (R): (4)A, (6)B, (2)A, (2)B
Row 132 (L): (2)A, (9)B, (3)A
Row 133 (R): (4)A, (2)B, (2)A, (6)B

Row 134 (L): (2)A, (4)B, (4)A, (2)B, (2)A
Row 135 (R): (3)A, (3)B, (3)A, (4)B, (1)A
Row 136 (L): (2)A, (4)B, (4)A, (2)B, (2)A
Row 137 (R): (2)A, (3)B, (5)A, (4)B
Row 138 (L): (5)B, (5)A, (3)B, (1)A
Row 139 (R): (2)A, (2)B, (6)A, (4)B
Row 140 (L): (5)B, (6)A, (3)B
Row 141 (R): (1)A, (3)B, (6)A, (4)B
Row 142 (L): (5)B, (7)A, (2)B
Row 143 (R): (4)B, (6)A, (2)B, (2)A
Row 144 (L): (4)A, (2)B, (6)A, (2)B
Row 145 (R): (3)B, (7)A, (2)B, (2)A
Row 146 (L): (4)A, (2)B, (6)A, (2)B
Row 147 (R): (2)B, (7)A, (2)B, (3)A
Row 148 (L): (4)A, (2)B, (6)A, (2)B
Row 149 (R): (2)B, (6)A, (2)B, (4)A
Row 150 (L): (4)A, (2)B, (6)A, (2)B
Row 151 (R): (1)A, (2)B, (5)A, (2)B, (4)A
Row 152 (L): (5)A, (2)B, (5)A, (2)B
Row 153 (R): (2)A, (2)B, (4)A, (2)B, (4)A
Row 154 (L): (4)A, (4)B, (4)A, (2)B
Row 155 (R): (2)A, (2)B, (2)A, (5)B, (3)A
Row 156 (L): (4)A, (6)B, (1)A, (2)B, (1)A
Row 157 (R): (2)A, (10)B, (2)A
Row 158 (L): (3)A, (3)B, (2)A, (5)B, (1)A
Row 159 (R): (2)A, (5)B, (3)A, (2)B, (2)A
Row 160 (L): (2)A, (3)B, (3)A, (4)B, (2)A
Row 161 (R): (2)A, (4)B, (4)A, (3)B, (1)A
Row 162 (L): (2)A, (2)B, (5)A, (5)B
Row 163 (R): (6)B, (5)A, (3)B
Row 164 (L): (1)A, (3)B, (6)A, (4)B
Row 165 (R): (6)B, (6)A, (2)B
Row 166 (L): (3)B, (7)A, (4)B
Row 167 (R): (2)B, (2)A, (2)B, (6)A, (2)B
Row 168 (L): (2)B, (8)A, (2)B, (2)A
Row 169 (R): (4)A, (2)B, (7)A, (1)B
Row 170 (L): (2)B, (7)A, (2)B, (3)A
Row 171 (R): (4)A, (2)B, (8)A
Row 172 (L): (2)B, (6)A, (2)B, (4)A
Row 173 (R): (4)A, (2)B, (7)A, (1)B
Row 174 (L): (2)B, (6)A, (2)B, (4)A
Row 175 (R): (5)A, (2)B, (5)A, (2)B
Row 176 (L): (2)B, (6)A, (2)B, (4)A
Row 177 (R): (5)A, (3)B, (4)A, (2)B
Row 178 (L): (1)A, (2)B, (4)A, (3)B, (4)A
Row 179 (R): (5)A, (3)B, (4)A, (2)B
Row 180 (L): (1)A, (2)B, (3)A, (4)B, (4)A
Row 181 (R): (4)A, (6)B, (2)A, (2)B
Row 182 (L): (2)A, (9)B, (3)A
Row 183 (R): (4)A, (2)B, (2)A, (6)B
Row 184 (L): (2)A, (5)B, (2)A, (3)B, (2)A
Row 185 (R): (3)A, (3)B, (2)A, (5)B, (1)A
Row 186 (L): (2)A, (4)B, (4)A, (2)B, (2)A
Row 187 (R): (2)A, (3)B, (5)A, (4)B
Row 188 (L): (5)B, (5)A, (3)B, (1)A
Row 189 (R): (2)A, (2)B, (6)A, (4)B
Row 190 (L): (5)B, (6)A, (3)B

Row 191 (R): (1)A, (3)B, (6)A, (4)B
Row 192 (L): (5)B, (7)A, (2)B
Row 193 (R): (3)B, (7)A, (2)B, (2)A
Row 194 (L): (4)A, (2)B, (6)A, (2)B
Row 195 (R): (2)B, (8)A, (2)B, (2)A
Row 196 (L): (4)A, (2)B, (6)A, (2)B
Row 197 (R): (2)B, (7)A, (2)B, (3)A
Row 198 (L): (4)A, (2)B, (6)A, (2)B
Row 199 (R): (3)B, (6)A, (2)B, (3)A
Row 200 (L): (4)A, (2)B, (6)A, (2)B

Trapezoids

Yes, I loved geometry class in high school, and part of that love was the variety of shapes and forms we studied. Who knew that my math nerdiness would carry over to my designs?

note

The color choice is up to you; for the bracelet pictured here, I opted for black and white, a color combination that goes with so many outfits.

SUPPLIES

- 11º cylinder beads
  - 6g color A (Miyuki DB-1490, opaque bisque white)
  - 6g color B (Miyuki DB-10, opaque black)
- 4-loop tube clasp
- Beading needle, size 10, 11, or 12
- Fireline, crystal or smoke (depending on your bead colors), 6-lb. test
- Scissors, thread snips, or thread burner

A   B

The bracelet is a bit narrower than the majority of those in the book. It measures 1¼ in. (3.2cm) wide and 6½ in. (16.5cm) long, not including clasp. For a wider 2-in. (5cm) version, use 11º hex-cut beads (the example on p. 35 uses Miyuki MR11C-451 in gunmetal and MR11C-2425 in silver-lined teal).

MAKE THE BRACELET

1. Follow the pattern or word chart below to complete the piece (see two-drop peyote stitch, p. 9), leaving an 8–10-in. (20–25cm) tail for adding the clasp. Add and end thread as needed.
2. Attach a 4-loop tube clasp to each end of the bracelet (see p. 7).

Rows 1 and 2 (L): (1)B, (11)A, (11)B, (1)A
Row 3 (R): (1)A, (5)B, (6)A
Row 4 (L): (1)B, (5)A, (6)B
Row 5 (R): (1)A, (5)B, (6)A
Row 6 (L): (1)B, (5)A, (6)B
Row 7 (R): (1)A, (5)B, (6)A
Row 8 (L): (1)B, (5)A, (6)B
Row 9 (R): (1)A, (5)B, (6)A
Row 10 (L): (1)B, (5)A, (6)B
Row 11 (R): (1)A, (6)B, (5)A
Row 12 (L): (1)B, (6)A, (5)B

(Continues on p. 34)

Row 13 (R): (1)A, (7)B, (4)A
Row 14 (L): (1)B, (4)A, (1)B, (2)A, (4)B
Row 15 (R): (1)A, (4)B, (1)A, (2)B, (4)A
Row 16 (L): (1)B, (3)A, (2)B, (2)A, (4)B
Row 17 (R): (1)A, (3)B, (2)A, (3)B, (3)A
Row 18 (L): (1)B, (3)A, (2)B, (3)A, (3)B
Row 19 (R): (1)A, (3)B, (2)A, (4)B, (2)A
Row 20 (L): (1)B, (2)A, (3)B, (4)A, (2)B
Row 21 (R): (1)A, (2)B, (3)A, (4)B, (2)A
Row 22 (L): (1)B, (1)A, (4)B, (4)A, (2)B
Row 23 (R): (1)A, (1)B, (4)A, (5)B, (1)A
Row 24 (L): (1)B, (1)A, (4)B, (5)A, (1)B
Row 25 (R): (1)A, (1)B, (4)A, (6)B
Row 26 (L): (1)A, (5)B, (6)A
Row 27 (R): (1)B, (5)A, (6)B
Row 28 (L): (1)A, (5)B, (6)A
Row 29 (R): (1)B, (5)A, (6)B
Row 30 (L): (1)A, (5)B, (6)A
Row 31 (R): (1)B, (5)A, (6)B
Row 32 (L): (1)A, (5)B, (6)A
Row 33 (R): (1)B, (5)A, (6)B
Row 34 (L): (1)A, (5)B, (6)A
Row 35 (R): (1)B, (5)A, (6)B
Row 36 (L): (1)A, (5)B, (6)A
Row 37 (R): (1)B, (5)A, (6)B
Row 38 (L): (1)A, (5)B, (6)A
Row 39 (R): (1)B, (5)A, (6)B
Row 40 (L): (1)A, (5)B, (6)A
Row 41 (R): (1)B, (5)A, (6)B
Row 42 (L): (1)A, (5)B, (6)A
Row 43 (R): (1)B, (5)A, (6)B
Row 44 (L): (1)A, (5)B, (6)A
Row 45 (R): (1)B, (5)A, (6)B
Row 46 (L): (1)A, (5)B, (6)A
Row 47 (R): (1)B, (5)A, (6)B
Row 48 (L): (1)A, (5)B, (6)A
Row 49 (R): (1)B, (5)A, (6)B
Row 50 (L): (1)A, (5)B, (6)A
Row 51 (R): (1)B, (5)A, (6)B
Row 52 (L): (1)A, (5)B, (6)A
Row 53 (R): (1)B, (5)A, (6)B
Row 54 (L): (1)A, (5)B, (6)A
Row 55 (R): (1)B, (5)A, (6)B
Row 56 (L): (1)A, (5)B, (6)A
Row 57 (R): (1)B, (5)A, (6)B
Row 58 (L): (1)A, (5)B, (6)A
Row 59 (R): (1)B, (5)A, (6)B
Row 60 (L): (1)A, (5)B, (6)A
Row 61 (R): (1)A, (1)B, (4)A, (6)B
Row 62 (L): (1)B, (1)A, (4)B, (5)A, (1)B
Row 63 (R): (1)A, (1)B, (4)A, (5)B, (1)A
Row 64 (L): (1)B, (1)A, (4)B, (4)A, (2)B
Row 65 (R): (1)A, (2)B, (3)A, (4)B, (2)A
Row 66 (L): (1)B, (2)A, (3)B, (4)A, (2)B
Row 67 (R): (1)A, (3)B, (2)A, (4)B, (2)A
Row 68 (L): (1)B, (3)A, (2)B, (3)A, (3)B
Row 69 (R): (1)A, (3)B, (2)A, (3)B, (3)A

Row 70 (L): (1)B, (3)A, (2)B, (2)A, (4)B
Row 71 (R): (1)A, (4)B, (1)A, (2)B, (4)A
Row 72 (L): (1)B, (4)A, (1)B, (2)A, (4)B
Row 73 (R): (1)A, (7)B, (4)A
Row 74 (L): (1)B, (6)A, (5)B
Row 75 (R): (1)A, (6)B, (5)A
Row 76 (L): (1)B, (5)A, (6)B
Row 77 (R): (1)A, (5)B, (6)A
Row 78 (L): (1)B, (5)A, (6)B
Row 79 (R): (1)A, (5)B, (6)A
Row 80 (L): (1)B, (5)A, (6)B
Row 81 (R): (1)A, (5)B, (6)A
Row 82 (L): (1)B, (5)A, (6)B
Row 83 (R): (1)A, (5)B, (6)A
Row 84 (L): (1)B, (5)A, (6)B
Row 85 (R): (1)A, (5)B, (6)A
Row 86 (L): (1)B, (5)A, (6)B
Row 87 (R): (1)A, (5)B, (6)A
Row 88 (L): (1)B, (5)A, (6)B
Row 89 (R): (1)A, (5)B, (6)A
Row 90 (L): (1)B, (5)A, (6)B
Row 91 (R): (1)A, (5)B, (6)A
Row 92 (L): (1)B, (5)A, (6)B
Row 93 (R): (1)A, (5)B, (6)A
Row 94 (L): (1)B, (5)A, (6)B
Row 95 (R): (1)A, (5)B, (6)A
Row 96 (L): (1)B, (5)A, (6)B
Row 97 (R): (1)A, (5)B, (6)A
Row 98 (L): (1)B, (5)A, (6)B
Row 99 (R): (1)A, (5)B, (6)A
Row 100 (L): (1)B, (5)A, (6)B
Row 101 (R): (1)A, (5)B, (6)A
Row 102 (L): (1)B, (5)A, (6)B
Row 103 (R): (1)A, (5)B, (6)A
Row 104 (L): (1)B, (5)A, (6)B
Row 105 (R): (1)A, (5)B, (6)A
Row 106 (L): (1)B, (5)A, (6)B
Row 107 (R): (1)A, (6)B, (5)A
Row 108 (L): (1)B, (6)A, (5)B
Row 109 (R): (1)A, (7)B, (4)A
Row 110 (L): (1)B, (4)A, (1)B, (2)A, (4)B
Row 111 (R): (1)A, (4)B, (1)A, (2)B, (4)A
Row 112 (L): (1)B, (3)A, (2)B, (2)A, (4)B
Row 113 (R): (1)A, (3)B, (2)A, (3)B, (3)A
Row 114 (L): (1)B, (3)A, (2)B, (3)A, (3)B
Row 115 (R): (1)A, (3)B, (2)A, (4)B, (2)A
Row 116 (L): (1)B, (2)A, (3)B, (4)A, (2)B
Row 117 (R): (1)A, (2)B, (3)A, (4)B, (2)A
Row 118 (L): (1)B, (1)A, (4)B, (4)A, (2)B
Row 119 (R): (1)A, (1)B, (4)A, (5)B, (1)A
Row 120 (L): (1)B, (1)A, (4)B, (5)A, (1)B
Row 121 (R): (1)A, (1)B, (4)A, (6)B
Row 122 (L): (1)A, (5)B, (6)A
Row 123 (R): (1)B, (5)A, (6)B
Row 124 (L): (1)A, (5)B, (6)A
Row 125 (R): (1)B, (5)A, (6)B
Row 126 (L): (1)A, (5)B, (6)A

Row 127 (R): (1)B, (5)A, (6)B
Row 128 (L): (1)A, (5)B, (6)A
Row 129 (R): (1)B, (5)A, (6)B
Row 130 (L): (1)A, (5)B, (6)A
Row 131 (R): (1)B, (5)A, (6)B
Row 132 (L): (1)A, (5)B, (6)A
Row 133 (R): (1)B, (5)A, (6)B
Row 134 (L): (1)A, (5)B, (6)A
Row 135 (R): (1)B, (5)A, (6)B
Row 136 (L): (1)A, (5)B, (6)A
Row 137 (R): (1)B, (5)A, (6)B
Row 138 (L): (1)A, (5)B, (6)A
Row 139 (R): (1)B, (5)A, (6)B
Row 140 (L): (1)A, (5)B, (6)A
Row 141 (R): (1)B, (5)A, (6)B
Row 142 (L): (1)A, (5)B, (6)A
Row 143 (R): (1)B, (5)A, (6)B
Row 144 (L): (1)A, (5)B, (6)A
Row 145 (R): (1)B, (5)A, (6)B
Row 146 (L): (1)A, (5)B, (6)A
Row 147 (R): (1)B, (5)A, (6)B
Row 148 (L): (1)A, (5)B, (6)A
Row 149 (R): (1)B, (5)A, (6)B
Row 150 (L): (1)A, (5)B, (6)A
Row 151 (R): (1)B, (5)A, (6)B
Row 152 (L): (1)A, (5)B, (6)A
Row 153 (R): (1)B, (5)A, (6)B
Row 154 (L): (1)A, (5)B, (6)A
Row 155 (R): (1)B, (5)A, (6)B
Row 156 (L): (1)A, (5)B, (6)A
Row 157 (R): (1)A, (1)B, (4)A, (6)B
Row 158 (L): (1)B, (1)A, (4)B, (5)A, (1)B
Row 159 (R): (1)A, (1)B, (4)A, (5)B, (1)A
Row 160 (L): (1)B, (1)A, (4)B, (4)A, (2)B
Row 161 (R): (1)A, (2)B, (3)A, (4)B, (2)A
Row 162 (L): (1)B, (2)A, (3)B, (4)A, (2)B
Row 163 (R): (1)A, (3)B, (2)A, (4)B, (2)A
Row 164 (L): (1)B, (3)A, (2)B, (3)A, (3)B
Row 165 (R): (1)A, (3)B, (2)A, (3)B, (3)A
Row 166 (L): (1)B, (3)A, (2)B, (2)A, (4)B
Row 167 (R): (1)A, (4)B, (1)A, (2)B, (4)A
Row 168 (L): (1)B, (4)A, (1)B, (2)A, (4)B
Row 169 (R): (1)A, (7)B, (4)A
Row 170 (L): (1)B, (6)A, (5)B
Row 171 (R): (1)A, (6)B, (5)A
Row 172 (L): (1)B, (5)A, (6)B
Row 173 (R): (1)A, (5)B, (6)A
Row 174 (L): (1)B, (5)A, (6)B
Row 175 (R): (1)A, (5)B, (6)A
Row 176 (L): (1)B, (5)A, (6)B
Row 177 (R): (1)A, (5)B, (6)A
Row 178 (L): (1)B, (5)A, (6)B
Row 179 (R): (1)A, (5)B, (6)A
Row 180 (L): (1)B, (5)A, (6)B
Row 181 (R): (1)A, (5)B, (6)A
Row 182 (L): (1)B, (5)A, (6)B
Row 183 (R): (1)A, (5)B, (6)A

Row 184 (L): (1)B, (5)A, (6)B
Row 185 (R): (1)A, (5)B, (6)A
Row 186 (L): (1)B, (5)A, (6)B
Row 187 (R): (1)A, (5)B, (6)A
Row 188 (L): (1)B, (5)A, (6)B
Row 189 (R): (1)A, (5)B, (6)A
Row 190 (L): (1)B, (5)A, (6)B
Row 191 (R): (1)A, (5)B, (6)A
Row 192 (L): (1)B, (5)A, (6)B
Row 193 (R): (1)A, (5)B, (6)A
Row 194 (L): (1)B, (5)A, (6)B
Row 195 (R): (1)A, (5)B, (6)A
Row 196 (L): (1)B, (5)A, (6)B
Row 197 (R): (1)A, (5)B, (6)A
Row 198 (L): (1)B, (5)A, (6)B
Row 199 (R): (1)A, (5)B, (6)A
Row 200 (L): (1)B, (5)A, (6)B

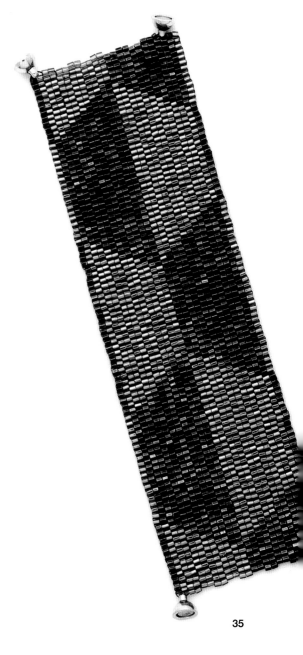

Chevrons

This is a fairly simple design, but depending on your color choices, it can be dramatic or subtle, bright or pastel.

note

If you change the colors, smoke Fireline or green Wildfire might be a more appropriate thread choice.

SUPPLIES

- 11º cylinder beads
  - 6g color A (Miyuki DB-203, cream ceylon)
  - 5g color B (Miyuki DB-661, opaque bright purple)
  - 4g color C (Miyuki DB-2138, opaque columbine Duracoat)
- 4-loop tube clasp
- Beading needle, size 10, 11, or 12
- Fireline, crystal, 6-lb. test
- Scissors, thread snips, or thread burner

A   B   C

The finished bracelet will measure 1½ in. (3.8cm) across and 6¾ in. (17.1cm) long, not including the clasp.

MAKE THE BRACELET

1. Follow the pattern or word chart below to complete the piece (see two-drop peyote stitch, p. 9), leaving an 8–10-in. (20–25cm) tail for adding the clasp. Add and end thread as needed.

2. Attach a 4-loop tube clasp to each end of the bracelet (see p. 7).

Rows 1 and 2: (L) (4)A, (9)B, (3)C, (8)B, (4)A
Row 3: (R) (2)A, (4)B, (2)C, (4)B, (2)A
Row 4: (L) (3)A, (4)B, (1)C, (4)B, (2)A
Row 5: (R) (3)A, (4)B, (1)C, (4)B, (2)A
Row 6: (L) (4)A, (8)B, (2)A
Row 7: (R) (4)A, (8)B, (2)A
Row 8: (L) (4)A, (8)B, (2)A
Row 9: (R) (4)A, (7)B, (3)A
Row 10: (L) (4)A, (7)B, (3)A
Row 11: (R) (4)A, (7)B, (3)A
Row 12: (L) (1)B, (3)A, (7)B, (3)A
Row 13: (R) (1)B, (3)A, (6)B, (4)A
Row 14: (L) (2)B, (2)A, (6)B, (4)A
Row 15: (R) (2)B, (2)A, (6)B, (4)A
Row 16: (L) (2)B, (3)A, (5)B, (3)A, (1)B

(Continues on p. 38)

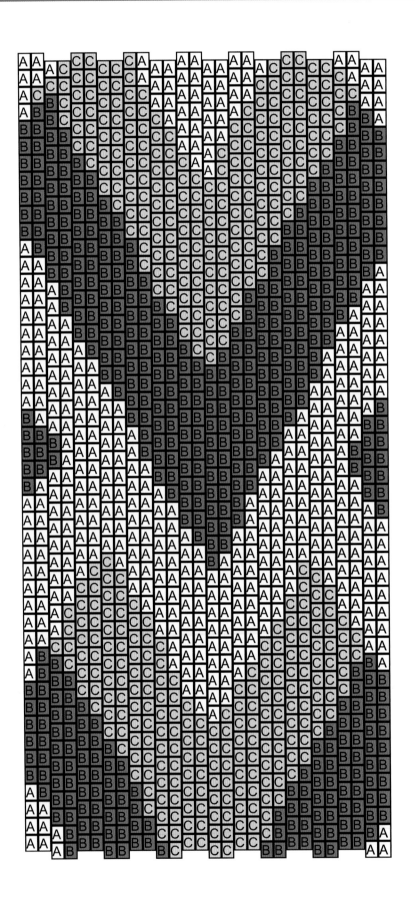

Row 17: (R) (2)B, (3)A, (5)B, (3)A, (1)B
Row 18: (L) (2)B, (4)A, (4)B, (3)A, (1)B
Row 19: (R) (2)B, (4)A, (4)B, (3)A, (1)B
Row 20: (L) (2)B, (4)A, (4)B, (4)A
Row 21: (R) (1)B, (5)A, (3)B, (5)A
Row 22: (L) (2)B, (4)A, (3)B, (5)A
Row 23: (R) (6)A, (2)B, (6)A
Row 24: (L) (1)B, (5)A, (2)B, (6)A
Row 25: (R) (6)A, (2)B, (6)A
Row 26: (L) (7)A, (1)B, (6)A
Row 27: (R) (7)A, (1)B, (6)A
Row 28: (L) (7)A, (1)B, (6)A
Row 29: (R) (3)A, (1)C, (7)A, (1)C, (2)A
Row 30: (L) (11)A, (1)C, (2)A
Row 31: (R) (2)A, (2)C, (6)A, (2)C, (2)A
Row 32: (L) (3)A, (1)C, (6)A, (2)C, (2)A
Row 33: (R) (2)A, (2)C, (6)A, (2)C, (2)A
Row 34: (L) (2)A, (3)C, (5)A, (3)C, (1)A
Row 35: (R) (2)A, (3)C, (5)A, (2)C, (2)A
Row 36: (L) (2)A, (4)C, (4)A, (4)C
Row 37: (R) (2)A, (3)C, (5)A, (3)C, (1)A
Row 38: (L) (2)A, (4)C, (4)A, (4)C
Row 39: (R) (1)A, (5)C, (3)A, (5)C
Row 40: (L) (2)A, (4)C, (4)A, (4)C
Row 41: (R) (2)B, (4)C, (3)A, (4)C, (1)B
Row 42: (L) (1)A, (1)B, (4)C, (3)A, (4)C, (1)B
Row 43: (R) (2)B, (4)C, (2)A, (4)C, (2)B
Row 44: (L) (2)B, (4)C, (2)A, (4)C, (2)B
Row 45: (R) (2)B, (4)C, (2)A, (4)C, (2)B
Row 46: (L) (3)B, (4)C, (1)A, (4)C, (2)B
Row 47: (R) (3)B, (4)C, (1)A, (4)C, (2)B
Row 48: (L) (3)B, (9)C, (2)B
Row 49: (R) (4)B, (8)C, (2)B
Row 50: (L) (4)B, (8)C, (2)B
Row 51: (R) (4)B, (7)C, (3)B
Row 52: (L) (4)B, (7)C, (3)B
Row 53: (R) (4)B, (7)C, (3)B
Row 54: (L) (4)B, (7)C, (3)B
Row 55: (R) (4)B, (6)C, (4)B
Row 56: (L) (4)B, (6)C, (4)B
Row 57: (R) (5)B, (5)C, (4)B
Row 58: (L) (1)A, (4)B, (5)C, (4)B
Row 59: (R) (1)A, (4)B, (5)C, (4)B
Row 60: (L) (1)A, (5)B, (4)C, (4)B
Row 61: (R) (2)A, (4)B, (4)C, (4)B
Row 62: (L) (2)A, (4)B, (4)C, (3)B, (1)A
Row 63: (R) (2)A, (4)B, (3)C, (4)B, (1)A
Row 64: (L) (2)A, (4)B, (3)C, (4)B, (1)A
Row 65: (R) (2)A, (4)B, (2)C, (5)B, (1)A
Row 66: (L) (2)A, (4)B, (2)C, (4)B, (2)A
Row 67: (R) (2)A, (4)B, (2)C, (4)B, (2)A
Row 68: (L) (2)A, (5)B, (1)C, (4)B, (2)A
Row 69: (R) (3)A, (3)B, (2)C, (4)B, (2)A
Row 70: (L) (3)A, (4)B, (1)C, (4)B, (2)A
Row 71: (R) (4)A, (3)B, (1)C, (4)B, (2)A
Row 72: (L) (4)A, (8)B, (2)A
Row 73: (R) (4)A, (8)B, (2)A

Row 74: (L) (4)A, (7)B, (3)A
Row 75: (R) (4)A, (7)B, (3)A
Row 76: (L) (1)B, (3)A, (7)B, (3)A
Row 77: (R) (1)B, (3)A, (6)B, (4)A
Row 78: (L) (2)B, (2)A, (6)B, (4)A
Row 79: (R) (2)B, (2)A, (6)B, (4)A
Row 80: (L) (2)B, (3)A, (5)B, (3)A, (1)B
Row 81: (R) (2)B, (3)A, (5)B, (3)A, (1)B
Row 82: (L) (2)B, (3)A, (5)B, (3)A, (1)B
Row 83: (R) (2)B, (4)A, (4)B, (3)A, (1)B
Row 84: (L) (2)B, (4)A, (4)B, (4)A
Row 85: (R) (1)B, (5)A, (4)B, (4)A
Row 86: (L) (2)B, (4)A, (3)B, (5)A
Row 87: (R) (6)A, (3)B, (5)A
Row 88: (L) (1)B, (5)A, (2)B, (6)A
Row 89: (R) (6)A, (2)B, (6)A
Row 90: (L) (6)A, (2)B, (6)A
Row 91: (R) (7)A, (1)B, (6)A
Row 92: (L) (7)A, (1)B, (6)A
Row 93: (R) (3)A, (1)C, (10)A
Row 94: (L) (3)A, (1)C, (7)A, (1)C, (2)A
Row 95: (R) (2)A, (2)C, (7)A, (1)C, (2)A
Row 96: (L) (3)A, (1)C, (6)A, (2)C, (2)A
Row 97: (R) (2)A, (2)C, (6)A, (2)C, (2)A
Row 98: (L) (2)A, (2)C, (6)A, (3)C, (1)A
Row 99: (R) (2)A, (3)C, (5)A, (2)C, (2)A
Row 100: (L) (2)A, (3)C, (5)A, (3)C, (1)A
Row 101: (R) (2)A, (3)C, (5)A, (3)C, (1)A
Row 102: (L) (2)A, (4)C, (4)A, (4)C
Row 103: (R) (1)A, (5)C, (4)A, (4)C
Row 104: (L) (2)A, (4)C, (4)A, (3)C, (1)B
Row 105: (R) (1)A, (1)B, (4)C, (3)A, (4)C, (1)B
Row 106: (L) (1)A, (1)B, (4)C, (3)A, (4)C, (1)B
Row 107: (R) (2)B, (4)C, (2)A, (5)C, (1)B
Row 108: (L) (2)B, (4)C, (2)A, (4)C, (2)B
Row 109: (R) (2)B, (4)C, (2)A, (4)C, (2)B
Row 110: (L) (2)B, (5)C, (1)A, (4)C, (2)B
Row 111: (R) (3)B, (4)C, (1)A, (4)C, (2)B
Row 112: (L) (3)B, (4)C, (1)A, (4)C, (2)B
Row 113: (R) (4)B, (8)C, (2)B
Row 114: (L) (4)B, (8)C, (2)B
Row 115: (R) (4)B, (8)C, (2)B
Row 116: (L) (4)B, (7)C, (3)B
Row 117: (R) (4)B, (7)C, (3)B
Row 118: (L) (4)B, (6)C, (4)B
Row 119: (R) (4)B, (6)C, (4)B
Row 120: (L) (4)B, (6)C, (4)B
Row 121: (R) (1)A, (4)B, (5)C, (4)B
Row 122: (L) (5)B, (5)C, (4)B
Row 123: (R) (2)A, (3)B, (5)C, (4)B
Row 124: (L) (1)A, (4)B, (5)C, (4)B
Row 125: (R) (2)A, (4)B, (4)C, (4)B
Row 126: (L) (2)A, (4)B, (4)C, (3)B, (1)A
Row 127: (R) (2)A, (4)B, (3)C, (5)B
Row 128: (L) (2)A, (4)B, (3)C, (4)B, (1)A
Row 129: (R) (2)A, (4)B, (3)C, (4)B, (1)A
Row 130: (L) (2)A, (4)B, (2)C, (4)B, (2)A

Row 131: (R) (2)A, (4)B, (2)C, (4)B, (2)A
Row 132: (L) (2)A, (4)B, (2)C, (4)B, (2)A
Row 133: (R) (3)A, (4)B, (1)C, (4)B, (2)A
Row 134: (L) (3)A, (4)B, (1)C, (4)B, (2)A
Row 135: (R) (4)A, (8)B, (2)A
Row 136: (L) (3)A, (9)B, (2)A
Row 137: (R) (4)A, (8)B, (2)A
Row 138: (L) (4)A, (7)B, (3)A
Row 139: (R) (4)A, (8)B, (2)A
Row 140: (L) (1)B, (3)A, (6)B, (4)A
Row 141: (R) (1)B, (3)A, (7)B, (3)A
Row 142: (L) (2)B, (2)A, (6)B, (4)A
Row 143: (R) (2)B, (3)A, (5)B, (4)A
Row 144: (L) (2)B, (2)A, (6)B, (3)A, (1)B
Row 145: (R) (2)B, (3)A, (5)B, (3)A, (1)B
Row 146: (L) (2)B, (3)A, (5)B, (3)A, (1)B
Row 147: (R) (2)B, (4)A, (4)B, (3)A, (1)B
Row 148: (L) (2)B, (4)A, (4)B, (4)A
Row 149: (R) (1)B, (5)A, (4)B, (4)A
Row 150: (L) (2)B, (4)A, (3)B, (5)A
Row 151: (R) (6)A, (3)B, (5)A
Row 152: (L) (1)B, (5)A, (2)B, (6)A
Row 153: (R) (6)A, (3)B, (5)A
Row 154: (L) (6)A, (2)B, (6)A
Row 155: (R) (7)A, (1)B, (6)A
Row 156: (L) (6)A, (2)B, (6)A
Row 157: (R) (14)A
Row 158: (L) (7)A, (1)B, (3)A, (1)C, (2)A
Row 159: (R) (3)A, (1)C, (7)A, (1)C, (2)A
Row 160: (L) (3)A, (1)C, (6)A, (2)C, (2)A
Row 161: (R) (2)A, (2)C, (7)A, (1)C, (2)A
Row 162: (L) (2)A, (2)C, (6)A, (2)C, (2)A
Row 163: (R) (2)A, (3)C, (5)A, (2)C, (2)A
Row 164: (L) (2)A, (2)C, (6)A, (3)C, (1)A
Row 165: (R) (2)A, (4)C, (4)A, (3)C, (1)A
Row 166: (L) (2)A, (3)C, (5)A, (3)C, (1)A
Row 167: (R) (2)A, (4)C, (4)A, (4)C
Row 168: (L) (2)A, (4)C, (3)A, (5)C
Row 169: (R) (1)A, (1)B, (4)C, (4)A, (4)C
Row 170: (L) (1)A, (1)B, (4)C, (3)A, (4)C, (1)B
Row 171: (R) (1)A, (1)B, (4)C, (3)A, (4)C, (1)B
Row 172: (L) (2)B, (4)C, (2)A, (4)C, (2)B
Row 173: (R) (2)B, (4)C, (2)A, (5)C, (1)B
Row 174: (L) (2)B, (4)C, (2)A, (4)C, (2)B
Row 175: (R) (3)B, (4)C, (1)A, (4)C, (2)B
Row 176: (L) (2)B, (5)C, (1)A, (4)C, (2)B
Row 177: (R) (4)B, (8)C, (2)B
Row 178: (L) (3)B, (9)C, (2)B
Row 179: (R) (4)B, (8)C, (2)B
Row 180: (L) (4)B, (7)C, (3)B
Row 181: (R) (4)B, (8)C, (2)B
Row 182: (L) (4)B, (6)C, (4)B
Row 183: (R) (4)B, (7)C, (3)B
Row 184: (L) (4)B, (6)C, (4)B
Row 185: (R) (1)A, (4)B, (5)C, (4)B
Row 186: (L) (4)B, (6)C, (4)B
Row 187: (R) (2)A, (3)B, (5)C, (4)B

Row 188: (L) (5)B, (5)C, (4)B
Row 189: (R) (2)A, (4)B, (4)C, (4)B
Row 190: (L) (1)A, (4)B, (5)C, (3)B, (1)A
Row 191: (R) (2)A, (4)B, (4)C, (4)B
Row 192: (L) (2)A, (4)B, (3)C, (4)B, (1)A

Sunflowers

There's something about sunflowers that makes me happy; it's hard to look at them without smiling. They grow so big and tall, with bright, sunny colors. This is the perfect bracelet to wear on a sunny day or when you need a bit of cheering up.

SUPPLIES

- 11º cylinder beads
  - 8–9g color A (Miyuki DB-1490, opaque bisque white)
  - 2g color B (Miyuki DB-272, goldenrod lined topaz AB)
  - 5g color C (Miyuki DB-1582, matte opaque canary)
  - 1g color D (Miyuki DB-654, opaque maroon)
  - 2g color E (Miyuki DB-312, matte metallic dark raspberry)
- Beading needle, size 10, 11, or 12
- Fireline, crystal, 6-lb. test
- 3- or 4-loop clasp
- Scissors, thread snips, or thread burner

A   B   C   D   E

The bracelet measures 1½ in. (3.8cm) wide, and the sunflower portion measures 4 in. (10cm) long. To calculate how much solid white to bead at each end, subtract 4 in. from the total desired length of your bracelet (not including the clasp), and divide that number by 2. The bracelet shown is 6½ in. (16.5cm) long, not including the clasp, with 1¼ in. (3.2cm) of solid white at each end.

MAKE THE BRACELET

1. Follow the pattern or word chart below to complete the piece (see two-drop peyote stitch, p. 9), leaving an 8–10-in. (20–25cm) tail for adding the clasp. NOTE: If you are making the bracelet a different length, be sure to start the sunflower motif on an even-numbered row (working away from your tail thread). Add and end thread as needed.

2. Attach a 4-loop tube clasp to each end of the bracelet (see p. 7).

(Continues on p. 42)

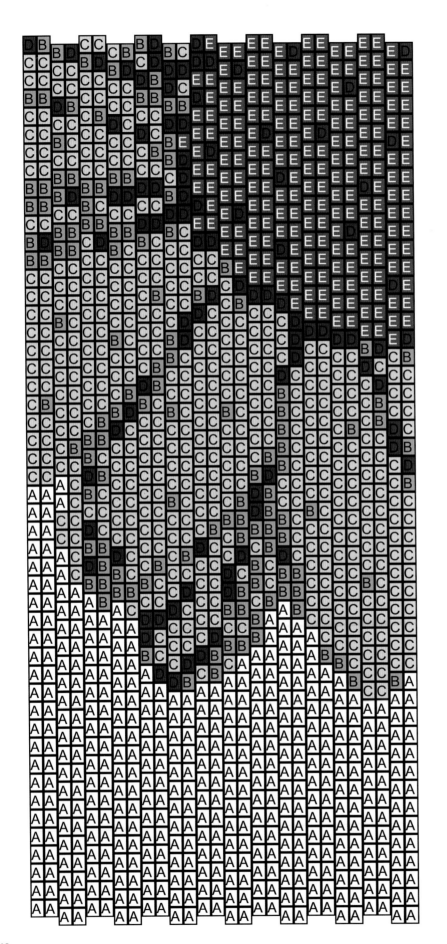

Rows 1 and 2 (L): (28)A

Rows 3–49: (14)A

Row 50 (L): (7)A, (1)B, (6)A

Row 51 (R): (7)A, (1)B, (4)A, (1)C, (1)B

Row 52 (L): (2)C, (1)B, (3)A, (2)C, (6)A

Row 53 (R): (6)A, (1)B, (1)C, (1)B, (1)C, (2)A, (2)C

Row 54 (L): (2)B, (2)C, (2)A, (2)C, (6)A

Row 55 (R): (6)A, (4)C, (1)A, (1)B, (2)C

Row 56 (L): (4)C, (1)A, (3)C, (6)A

Row 57 (R): (6)A, (3)C, (3)B, (2)C

Row 58 (L): (1)B, (1)C, (1)B, (1)C, (1)B, (3)C, (1)B, (5)A

Row 59 (R): (6)A, (4)C, (1)D, (1)B, (2)C

Row 60 (L): (1)B, (7)C, (1)B, (5)A

Row 61 (R): (2)B, (4)A, (4)C, (1)D, (3)C

Row 62 (L): (5)C, (2)B, (2)C, (3)A, (1)B, (1)C

Row 63 (R): (4)C, (2)A, (5)C, (1)B, (2)C

Row 64 (L): (4)C, (1)B, (4)C, (2)A, (3)C

Row 65 (R): (4)C, (2)A, (5)C, (1)B, (2)C

Row 66 (L): (3)C, (1)B, (1)D, (4)C, (1)A, (4)C

Row 67 (R): (10)C, (1)B, (2)C, (1)B

Row 68 (L): (3)C, (1)D, (1)C, (1)B, (2)C, (1)B, (1)D, (4)C

Row 69 (R): (2)C, (1)B, (5)C, (1)B, (1)C, (1)D, (3)C

Row 70 (L): (2)C, (1)B, (5)C, (1)D, (5)C

Row 71 (R): (1)B, (5)C, (1)B, (3)C, (1)D, (1)B, (2)C

Row 72 (L): (2)C, (1)B, (5)C, (1)B, (1)C, (1)B, (3)C

Row 73 (R): (6)C, (1)B, (4)C, (1)D, (1)B, (1)C

Row 74 (L): (4)C, (1)B, (9)C

Row 75 (R): (2)B, (4)C, (1)B, (1)D, (3)C, (1)B, (1)D, (1)C

Row 76 (L): (7)C, (1)D, (6)C

Row 77 (R): (1)C, (1)D, (9)C, (1)D, (1)B, (1)D

Row 78 (L): (7)C, (1)B, (4)C, (1)B, (1)D

Row 79 (R): (5)C, (1)B, (7)C, (1)B

Row 80 (L): (1)C, (1)B, (1)C, (1)B, (2)C, (1)B, (1)D, (4)C, (1)B, (1)C

Row 81 (R): (2)C, (2)B, (6)C, (1)B, (1)D, (2)C

Row 82 (L): (1)C, (1)B, (3)C, (2)B, (4)C, (1)B, (2)C

Row 83 (R): (3)C, (1)D, (4)C, (1)B, (1)C, (1)B, (3)C

Row 84 (L): (1)D, (5)C, (1)B, (3)C, (1)B, (1)D, (2)C

Row 85 (R): (1)C, (1)B, (2)C, (1)B, (3)C, (1)D, (2)C, (1)B, (2)C

Row 86 (L): (1)B, (3)C, (1)B, (9)C

Row 87 (R): (5)C, (1)B, (1)D, (1)C, (1)D, (1)C, (2)B, (1)C, (1)B

Row 88 (L): (4)C, (1)B, (3)C, (1)D, (1)B, (4)C

Row 89 (R): (6)C, (3)D, (1)C, (1)B, (3)D

Row 90 (L): (3)D, (2)B, (6)C, (1)B, (2)C

Row 91 (R): (2)B, (5)C, (1)D, (1)C, (5)D

Row 92 (L): (2)E, (2)D, (1)C, (1)B, (1)C, (1)B, (4)C, (1)B, (1)D

Row 93 (R): (2)C, (2)B, (3)C, (2)B, (2)D, (3)E

Row 94 (L): (6)E, (2)B, (1)C, (1)B, (1)C, (1)B, (1)D, (1)C

Row 95 (R): (2)B, (1)C, (1)D, (4)C, (2)D, (4)E

Row 96 (L): (6)E, (1)B, (3)C, (2)D, (2)B

Row 97 (R): (2)C, (2)B, (2)D, (1)B, (1)D, (4)E, (1)D, (1)E

Row 98 (L): (8)E, (2)D, (2)B, (2)C

Row 99 (R): (1)D, (1)B, (2)C, (1)B, (2)D, (7)E

Row 100 (L): (1)D, (3)E, (1)D, (3)E, (1)C, (2)B, (1)C, (1)D, (1)B

Row 101 (R): (2)C, (1)B, (1)D, (1)C, (3)D, (6)E

Row 102 (L): (6)E, (1)D, (1)E, (3)D, (1)B, (2)C

Row 103 (R): (4)C, (1)D, (1)B, (8)E

Row 104 (L): (2)E, (1)D, (5)E, (1)C, (1)D, (4)C

Row 105 (R): (2)B, (2)C, (2)B, (1)D, (7)E

Row 106 (L): (8)E, (2)B, (2)C, (1)B, (1)D

Row 107 (R): (3)C, (1)B, (2)C, (8)E

Row 108 (L): (8)E, (2)D, (1)C, (1)D, (2)C

Row 109 (R): (4)C, (1)D, (1)C, (3)E, (1)D, (1)E, (1)D, (2)E

Row 110 (L): (1)E, (1)D, (7)E, (1)B, (3)C, (1)B

Row 111 (R): (5)C, (1)B, (1)E, (1)D, (6)E

Row 112 (L): (8)E, (1)D, (1)B, (4)C

Row 113 (R): (6)C, (8)E

Row 114 (L): (5)E, (1)D, (2)E, (1)D, (1)C, (4)B

Row 115 (R): (4)B, (2)D, (6)E, (1)D, (1)E

Row 116 (L): (8)E, (1)D, (1)B, (3)D, (1)B

Row 117 (R): (3)B, (3)C, (1)D, (7)E

Row 118 (L): (6)E, (1)D, (1)E, (2)D, (4)C

Row 119 (R): (2)C, (2)B, (2)D, (8)E

Row 120 (L): (2)E, (1)D, (5)E, (1)C, (5)B

Row 121 (R): (1)B, (1)D, (1)C, (1)D, (1)B, (1)C, (2)D, (6)E

Row 122 (L): (5)E, (1)D, (2)E, (3)C, (3)B

Row 123 (R): (2)B, (6)C, (6)E

Row 124 (L): (7)E, (1)B, (6)C

Row 125 (R): (8)C, (6)E

Row 126 (L): (1)E, (1)D, (4)E, (1)D, (7)C

Row 127 (R): (5)C, (2)B, (3)D, (4)E

Row 128 (L): (5)E, (1)D, (1)B, (7)C

Row 129 (R): (6)C, (1)D, (3)C, (4)E

Row 130 (L): (4)E, (1)D, (3)C, (1)D, (4)C, (1)B

Row 131 (R): (10)C, (2)D, (2)E

Row 132 (L): (1)D, (1)E, (3)D, (3)C, (1)D, (1)B, (1)C, (1)B, (2)C

Row 133 (R): (12)C, (1)B, (1)D

Row 134 (L): (1)B, (3)C, (1)D, (4)C, (1)B, (4)C

Row 135 (R): (5)C, (1)B, (6)C, (1)D, (1)C

Row 136 (L): (5)C, (1)D, (8)C

Row 137 (R): (4)C, (1)D, (1)B, (7)C, (1)D

Row 138 (L): (5)C, (1)B, (4)C, (1)B, (3)C

Row 139 (R): (1)C, (1)B, (2)C, (1)B, (8)C, (1)B

Row 140 (L): (5)C, (1)B, (1)C, (1)B, (1)C, (1)B, (1)D, (1)B, (2)C

Row 141 (R): (3)C, (1)B, (9)C, (1)B

Row 142 (L): (1)C, (1)D, (1)B, (2)C, (1)B, (5)C, (1)D, (2)C

Row 143 (R): (2)C, (2)B, (10)C

Row 144 (L): (1)B, (1)D, (3)C, (1)B, (6)C, (1)B, (1)C

Row 145 (R): (2)C, (1)B, (6)C, (1)B, (4)C

Row 146 (L): (1)D, (4)C, (1)B, (8)C

Row 147 (R): (2)C, (1)D, (1)B, (4)C, (1)B, (1)D, (4)C

Row 148 (L): (1)B, (12)C, (1)A

Row 149 (R): (2)A, (1)B, (5)C, (1)D, (1)B, (4)C

Row 150 (L): (6)C, (1)B, (2)C, (1)B, (3)C, (1)A

Row 151 (R): (2)A, (6)C, (1)D, (2)B, (3)C

Row 152 (L): (5)C, (3)B, (6)C

Row 153 (R): (2)A, (1)D, (4)C, (3)B, (4)C

Row 154 (L): (5)C, (2)B, (7)C

Row 155 (R): (2)A, (2)B, (2)C, (1)D, (2)C, (1)B, (4)C

Row 156 (L): (5)C, (2)D, (1)C, (1)B, (2)C, (1)D, (1)C, (1)A

Row 157 (R): (2)A, (1)D, (1)B, (1)C, (1)B, (2)C, (1)B, (5)C

Row 158 (L): (4)C, (2)B, (1)C, (1)D, (3)C, (1)B, (1)C, (1)A

Row 159 (R): (2)A, (3)B, (3)C, (1)B, (3)C, (1)B, (1)C

Row 160 (L): (4)C, (3)B, (2)D, (1)C, (2)B, (2)A

Row 161 (R): (3)A, (1)B, (5)C, (1)B, (4)C

Row 162 (L): (4)C, (1)B, (1)A, (2)B, (1)C, (1)D, (1)C, (3)A

Row 163 (R): (4)A, (2)D, (2)C, (1)B, (1)A, (4)C

Row 164 (L): (4)C, (2)A, (4)C, (4)A

Row 165 (R): (4)A, (1)D, (2)C, (1)D, (1)B, (2)A, (3)C

Row 166 (L): (4)C, (2)A, (2)B, (2)C, (4)A

Row 167 (R): (4)A, (1)B, (1)C, (1)D, (1)B, (3)A, (1)B, (2)C

Row 168 (L): (3)C, (1)B, (3)A, (1)C, (1)D, (1)C, (4)A

Row 169 (R): (5)A, (1)D, (1)C, (1)B, (4)A, (2)C

Row 170 (L): (1)A, (2)B, (5)A, (1)B, (1)D, (4)A

Row 171 (R): (12)A, (2)C

Rows 172–214: (14)A*

* Rows 197–214 not shown on pattern.

Coral Branches

note
I chose to use limited colors with my coral design for this bracelet because I wanted to focus on the bends and twists created by Mother Nature.

There's something about the graceful curves of the coral branches that appeals to me. It reminds me of my trip to Australia's Great Barrier Reef many years ago. The coral formations there were spectacular and so full of vivid color.

SUPPLIES

- 11º cylinder beads
  - 8g color A (Miyuki DB-795, opaque cinnabar)
  - 8g color B (Miyuki DB-1490, opaque bisque white)
- Beading needle, size 10, 11, or 12
- Fireline, crystal, 6-lb. test
- 4-loop tube clasp
- Scissors, thread snips, or thread burner

A B

The bracelet measures 1½ in. (3.8cm) wide and up to 7½ in. (19.1cm) long, not including the clasp. You don't need to bead the entire piece (220 rows); stop when you've reached your desired length.

MAKE THE BRACELET

1. Follow the pattern or word chart below to complete the piece (see two-drop peyote stitch, p. 9), leaving an 8–10-in. (20–25cm) tail for adding the clasp. Add and end thread as needed.

2. Attach a 4-loop tube clasp to each end of the bracelet (see p. 7).

Rows 1 and 2 (L): (4)A, (8)B, (3)A, (9)B, (4)A
Row 3 (R): (2)A, (5)B, (2)A, (5)B
Row 4 (L): (2)A, (4)B, (2)A, (4)B, (2)A
Row 5 (R): (2)A, (5)B, (3)A, (4)B
Row 6 (L): (1)A, (5)B, (2)A, (5)B, (1)A
Row 7 (R): (2)A, (5)B, (3)A, (4)B
Row 8 (L): (4)B, (4)A, (6)B
Row 9 (R): (2)A, (5)B, (5)A, (2)B
Row 10 (L): (2)B, (6)A, (6)B
Row 11 (R): (2)A, (4)B, (7)A, (1)B

Row 12 (L): (2)B, (6)A, (6)B
Row 13 (R): (2)A, (4)B, (2)A, (1)B, (5)A
Row 14 (L): (6)A, (1)B, (1)A, (6)B
Row 15 (R): (2)A, (4)B, (2)A, (2)B, (4)A
Row 16 (L): (6)A, (1)B, (2)A, (5)B
Row 17 (R): (2)A, (4)B, (2)A, (2)B, (4)A
Row 18 (L): (6)A, (1)B, (2)A, (5)B
Row 19 (R): (2)A, (4)B, (2)A, (2)B, (4)A
Row 20 (L): (6)A, (7)B, (1)A
Row 21 (R): (2)A, (8)B, (4)A
Row 22 (L): (6)A, (7)B, (1)A
Row 23 (R): (2)A, (7)B, (5)A
Row 24 (L): (1)B, (5)A, (6)B, (2)A
Row 25 (R): (3)A, (6)B, (4)A, (1)B
Row 26 (L): (2)B, (4)A, (6)B, (2)A
Row 27 (R): (4)A, (4)B, (4)A, (2)B
Row 28 (L): (3)B, (3)A, (5)B, (3)A
Row 29 (R): (4)A, (4)B, (4)A, (2)B
Row 30 (L): (4)B, (3)A, (3)B, (4)A
Row 31 (R): (2)B, (3)A, (3)B, (3)A, (3)B
Row 32 (L): (2)B, (6)A, (2)B, (2)A, (2)B
Row 33 (R): (3)B, (3)A, (2)B, (2)A, (2)B, (1)A, (1)B
Row 34 (L): (2)B, (6)A, (2)B, (2)A, (2)B
Row 35 (R): (4)B, (2)A, (2)B, (2)A, (1)B, (3)A
Row 36 (L): (4)A, (1)B, (3)A, (6)B
Row 37 (R): (7)B, (3)A, (2)B, (2)A
Row 38 (L): (3)A, (2)B, (3)A, (4)B, (2)A
Row 39 (R): (2)B, (2)A, (3)B, (3)A, (2)B, (2)A
Row 40 (L): (2)A, (4)B, (2)A, (2)B, (3)A, (1)B
Row 41 (R): (2)B, (3)A, (2)B, (3)A, (2)B, (2)A
Row 42 (L): (2)A, (4)B, (2)A, (2)B, (2)A, (2)B
Row 43 (R): (4)B, (2)A, (1)B, (3)A, (3)B, (1)A
Row 44 (L): (2)A, (3)B, (3)A, (2)B, (2)A, (2)B
Row 45 (R): (2)B, (4)A, (1)B, (3)A, (3)B, (1)A
Row 46 (L): (2)A, (3)B, (3)A, (2)B, (3)A, (1)B
Row 47 (R): (2)B, (2)A, (3)B, (3)A, (4)B
Row 48 (L): (2)A, (3)B, (3)A, (3)B, (3)A
Row 49 (R): (1)B, (3)A, (3)B, (3)A, (4)B
Row 50 (L): (2)A, (3)B, (3)A, (4)B, (2)A
Row 51 (R): (2)A, (6)B, (2)A, (4)B
Row 52 (L): (1)A, (4)B, (3)A, (5)B, (1)A
Row 53 (R): (2)A, (6)B, (2)A, (4)B
Row 54 (L): (1)A, (3)B, (4)A, (6)B
Row 55 (R): (1)A, (7)B, (2)A, (4)B
Row 56 (L): (4)B, (4)A, (6)B
Row 57 (R): (1)A, (7)B, (2)A, (4)B
Row 58 (L): (4)B, (4)A, (2)B, (2)A, (2)B
Row 59 (R): (1)A, (1)B, (4)A, (2)B, (2)A, (4)B
Row 60 (L): (5)B, (3)A, (2)B, (3)A, (1)B
Row 61 (R): (2)B, (3)A, (2)B, (3)A, (4)B
Row 62 (L): (5)B, (3)A, (2)B, (4)A
Row 63 (R): (2)B, (2)A, (3)B, (3)A, (4)B
Row 64 (L): (6)B, (2)A, (3)B, (3)A
Row 65 (R): (2)B, (2)A, (2)B, (4)A, (4)B
Row 66 (L): (6)B, (2)A, (4)B, (2)A
Row 67 (R): (1)B, (3)A, (2)B, (3)A, (5)B
Row 68 (L): (6)B, (3)A, (3)B, (2)A
Row 69 (R): (1)B, (3)A, (2)B, (2)A, (6)B

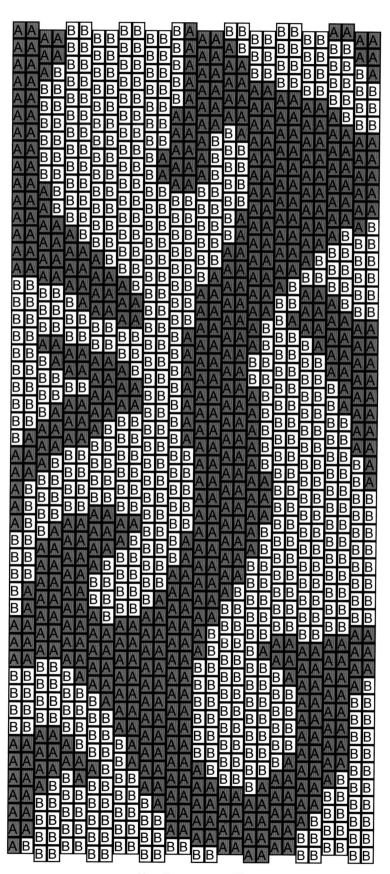

(Continues on p. 46)

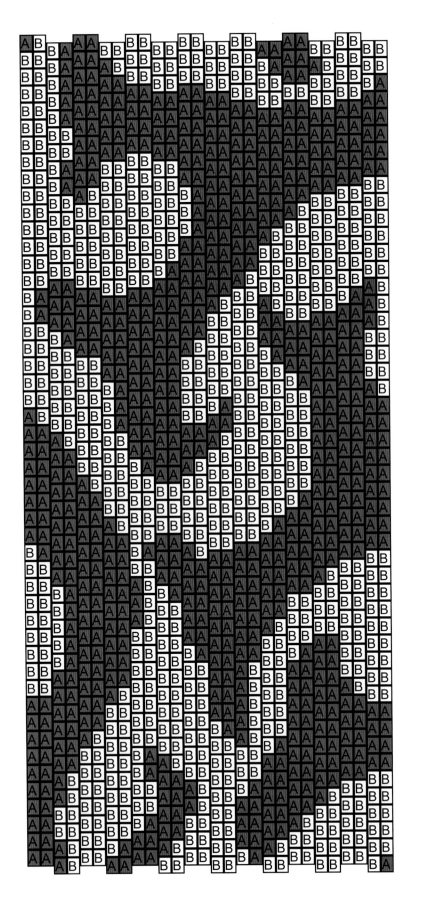

(Continues on p. 47)

Row 70 (L): (6)B, (4)A, (1)B, (3)A
Row 71 (R): (8)A, (6)B
Row 72 (L): (2)A, (5)B, (7)A
Row 73 (R): (8)A, (2)B, (4)A
Row 74 (L): (5)A, (2)B, (7)A
Row 75 (R): (8)A, (2)B, (4)A
Row 76 (L): (4)A, (4)B, (4)A, (2)B
Row 77 (R): (3)B, (5)A, (3)B, (3)A
Row 78 (L): (1)B, (3)A, (4)B, (4)A, (2)B
Row 79 (R): (4)B, (4)A, (4)B, (2)A
Row 80 (L): (2)B, (2)A, (4)B, (3)A, (3)B
Row 81 (R): (4)B, (4)A, (4)B, (2)A
Row 82 (L): (2)B, (2)A, (4)B, (2)A, (4)B
Row 83 (R): (4)B, (4)A, (4)B, (2)A
Row 84 (L): (2)B, (2)A, (4)B, (2)A, (2)B, (2)A
Row 85 (R): (3)A, (2)B, (3)A, (4)B, (2)A
Row 86 (L): (2)B, (2)A, (4)B, (2)A, (2)B, (2)A
Row 87 (R): (4)A, (1)B, (3)A, (3)B, (3)A
Row 88 (L): (2)B, (2)A, (3)B, (3)A, (1)B, (3)A
Row 89 (R): (2)A, (1)B, (1)A, (2)B, (2)A, (2)B, (3)A, (1)B
Row 90 (L): (2)B, (3)A, (1)B, (4)B, (3)B, (1)A
Row 91 (R): (2)A, (4)B, (6)A, (2)B
Row 92 (L): (2)B, (7)A, (5)B
Row 93 (R): (2)A, (4)B, (6)A, (2)B
Row 94 (L): (3)B, (5)A, (6)B
Row 95 (R): (2)A, (4)B, (6)A, (2)B
Row 96 (L): (4)B, (4)A, (6)B
Row 97 (R): (1)A, (7)B, (4)A, (2)B
Row 98 (L): (4)B, (2)A, (8)B
Row 99 (R): (1)A, (1)B, (2)A, (6)B, (2)A, (2)B
Row 100 (L): (4)B, (2)A, (6)B, (1)A, (1)B
Row 101 (R): (2)B, (2)A, (6)B, (2)A, (2)B
Row 102 (L): (3)B, (2)A, (6)B, (2)A, (1)B
Row 103 (R): (2)B, (2)A, (6)B, (2)A, (2)B
Row 104 (L): (1)A, (9)B, (3)A, (1)B
Row 105 (R): (2)B, (6)A, (6)B
Row 106 (L): (2)A, (4)B, (7)A, (1)B
Row 107 (R): (2)B, (12)A
Row 108 (L): (13)A, (1)B
Row 109 (R): (2)B, (12)A
Row 110 (L): (12)A, (2)B
Row 111 (R): (2)B, (12)A
Row 112 (L): (12)A, (2)B
Row 113 (R): (2)B, (2)A, (2)B, (8)A
Row 114 (L): (8)A, (4)B, (1)A, (1)B
Row 115 (R): (2)B, (2)A, (2)B, (8)A
Row 116 (L): (2)B, (6)A, (4)B, (1)A, (1)B
Row 117 (R): (2)B, (1)A, (4)B, (5)A, (2)B
Row 118 (L): (4)B, (4)A, (6)B
Row 119 (R): (7)B, (4)A, (3)B
Row 120 (L): (4)B, (4)A, (6)B
Row 121 (R): (7)B, (3)A, (4)B
Row 122 (L): (5)B, (3)A, (6)B
Row 123 (R): (6)B, (4)A, (4)B
Row 124 (L): (6)B, (2)A, (6)B
Row 125 (R): (6)B, (4)A, (4)B
Row 126 (L): (6)B, (3)A, (5)B

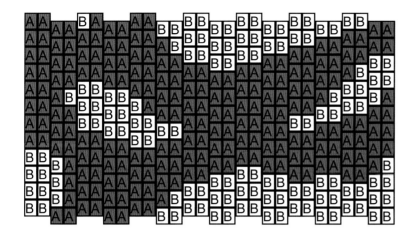

Row 127 (R): (6)B, (3)A, (5)B
Row 128 (L): (1)B, (1)A, (4)B, (4)A, (2)B, (2)A
Row 129 (R): (1)B, (7)A, (5)B, (1)A
Row 130 (L): (1)B, (1)A, (3)B, (1)A, (1)B, (7)A
Row 131 (R): (1)B, (7)A, (4)B, (2)A
Row 132 (L): (1)B, (5)A, (2)B, (6)A
Row 133 (R): (2)B, (6)A, (2)B, (4)A
Row 134 (L): (2)B, (4)A, (2)B, (5)A, (1)B
Row 135 (R): (2)B, (5)A, (3)B, (4)A
Row 136 (L): (2)B, (3)A, (3)B, (4)A, (2)B
Row 137 (R): (4)B, (2)A, (4)B, (4)A
Row 138 (L): (2)B, (2)A, (4)B, (4)A, (2)B
Row 139 (R): (4)B, (2)A, (5)B, (3)A
Row 140 (L): (1)B, (3)A, (4)B, (3)A, (3)B
Row 141 (R): (4)B, (2)A, (6)B, (2)A
Row 142 (L): (4)A, (2)B, (1)A, (1)B, (3)A, (3)B
Row 143 (R): (1)A, (3)B, (2)A, (6)B, (2)A
Row 144 (L): (4)A, (2)B, (5)A, (3)B
Row 145 (R): (2)A, (2)B, (4)A, (4)B, (2)A
Row 146 (L): (4)A, (3)B, (3)A, (3)B, (1)A
Row 147 (R): (2)A, (2)B, (4)A, (4)B, (2)A
Row 148 (L): (4)A, (4)B, (2)A, (2)B, (2)A
Row 149 (R): (2)A, (3)B, (2)A, (5)B, (2)A
Row 150 (L): (4)A, (4)B, (2)A, (2)B, (2)A
Row 151 (R): (3)A, (9)B, (2)A
Row 152 (L): (4)A, (8)B, (2)A
Row 153 (R): (4)A, (7)B, (3)A
Row 154 (L): (4)A, (8)B, (2)A
Row 155 (R): (4)A, (6)B, (4)A
Row 156 (L): (5)A, (6)B, (3)A
Row 157 (R): (4)A, (6)B, (4)A
Row 158 (L): (6)A, (2)B, (6)A
Row 159 (R): (1)B, (3)A, (1)B, (2)A, (1)B, (6)A
Row 160 (L): (2)B, (12)A
Row 161 (R): (2)B, (2)A, (2)B, (6)A, (2)B
Row 162 (L): (3)B, (11)A
Row 163 (R): (2)B, (3)A, (1)B, (6)A, (2)B
Row 164 (L): (4)B, (5)A, (1)B, (3)A, (1)B
Row 165 (R): (2)B, (3)A, (1)B, (4)A, (4)B
Row 166 (L): (4)B, (4)A, (2)B, (3)A, (1)B

Row 167 (R): (2)B, (3)A, (1)B, (4)A, (4)B
Row 168 (L): (5)B, (3)A, (2)B, (3)A, (1)B
Row 169 (R): (2)B, (2)A, (2)B, (4)A, (4)B
Row 170 (L): (2)B, (2)A, (2)B, (2)A, (2)B, (3)A, (1)B
Row 171 (R): (2)B, (2)A, (3)B, (3)A, (1)B, (1)A, (2)B
Row 172 (L): (2)B, (2)A, (2)B, (2)A, (2)B, (3)A, (1)B
Row 173 (R): (2)B, (2)A, (4)B, (1)A, (1)B, (2)A, (2)B
Row 174 (L): (2)B, (2)A, (2)B, (2)A, (2)B, (4)A
Row 175 (R): (2)B, (2)A, (4)B, (1)A, (1)B, (3)A, (1)B
Row 176 (L): (2)B, (2)A, (2)B, (2)A, (3)B, (3)A
Row 177 (R): (4)A, (4)B, (1)A, (1)B, (4)A
Row 178 (L): (4)A, (2)B, (2)A, (4)B, (2)A
Row 179 (R): (4)A, (4)B, (1)A, (1)B, (4)A
Row 180 (L): (4)A, (2)B, (1)A, (5)B, (2)A
Row 181 (R): (3)A, (5)B, (1)A, (1)B, (4)A
Row 182 (L): (5)A, (7)B, (2)A
Row 183 (R): (2)A, (3)B, (1)A, (4)B, (4)A
Row 184 (L): (6)A, (3)B, (1)A, (2)B, (2)A
Row 185 (R): (2)A, (3)B, (1)A, (4)B, (4)A
Row 186 (L): (2)B, (4)A, (2)B, (2)A, (3)B, (1)A
Row 187 (R): (2)A, (4)B, (1)A, (2)B, (3)A, (2)B
Row 188 (L): (3)B, (3)A, (2)B, (2)A, (3)B, (1)A
Row 189 (R): (2)A, (4)B, (1)A, (1)B, (4)A, (2)B
Row 190 (L): (4)B, (2)A, (2)B, (2)A, (4)B
Row 191 (R): (2)A, (3)B, (1)A, (2)B, (3)A, (3)B
Row 192 (L): (4)B, (2)A, (2)B, (2)A, (4)B
Row 193 (R): (2)A, (2)B, (2)A, (2)B, (2)A, (4)B
Row 194 (L): (5)B, (1)A, (3)B, (2)A, (2)B, (1)A

Row 195 (R): (2)A, (2)B, (2)A, (3)B, (1)A, (4)B
Row 196 (L): (1)A, (9)B, (2)A, (1)B, (1)A
Row 197 (R): (2)A, (1)B, (3)A, (8)B
Row 198 (L): (2)A, (8)B, (4)A
Row 199 (R): (6)A, (6)B, (2)A
Row 200 (L): (4)A, (5)B, (5)A
Row 201 (R): (6)A, (4)B, (4)A
Row 202 (L): (2)B, (4)A, (2)B, (6)A
Row 203 (R): (13)A, (1)B
Row 204 (L): (2)B, (12)A
Row 205 (R): (2)A, (2)B, (8)A, (2)B
Row 206 (L): (1)A, (2)B, (7)A, (3)B, (1)A
Row 207 (R): (2)A, (3)B, (7)A, (2)B
Row 208 (L): (2)A, (2)B, (6)A, (2)B, (2)A
Row 209 (R): (2)A, (4)B, (4)A, (2)B, (2)A
Row 210 (L): (8)A, (4)B, (2)A
Row 211 (R): (4)A, (2)B, (8)A
Row 212 (L): (14)A
Row 213 (R): (2)B, (12)A
Row 214 (L): (1)B, (12)A, (1)B
Row 215 (R): (2)B, (6)A, (2)B, (4)A
Row 216 (L): (8)B, (5)A, (1)B
Row 217 (R): (2)B, (4)A, (8)B
Row 218 (L): (9)B, (4)A, (1)B
Row 219 (R): (2)B, (4)A, (8)B
Row 220 (L): (10)B, (4)A

Bright Flames

This pattern was the result of pushing myself outside my color comfort zone. I wanted something bold, bright, and sizzling hot. Wear this flame without worrying about getting burned.

note

The bead counts are for the entire 216 rows; if you make a shorter bracelet, your actual bead counts will be lower.

SUPPLIES

- 11º cylinder beads
  - 4g color A (Miyuki DB-161, opaque orange AB)
  - 2g color B (Miyuki DB-1582, matte opaque canary)
  - 2g color C (Miyuki DB-683, semi-matte silver-lined dark ruby)
  - 9g color D (Miyuki DB-310, jet black matte)
- Beading needle, size 10, 11, or 12
- Fireline, smoke, 6-lb. test
- 3- or 4-loop tube clasp
- Scissors, thread snips, or thread burner

A   B   C   D

The bracelet measures 1½ in. (3.8cm) wide and up to 7½ in. (19.1cm) long, not including the clasp.

MAKE THE BRACELET

1. Follow the pattern or word chart below to complete the piece (see two-drop peyote stitch, p. 9), leaving an 8–10-in. (20–25cm) tail for adding the clasp. Add and end thread as needed.

2. Attach a 4-loop tube clasp to each end of the bracelet (see p. 7).

Rows 1 and 2 (L): (7)D, (3)C, (6)A, (8)D, (1)C, (3)A
Row 3 (R): (2)A, (5)D, (1)C, (1)A, (1)C, (4)D
Row 4 (L): (6)D, (1)C, (5)D, (1)C, (1)A
Row 5 (R): (2)A, (12)D
Row 6 (L): (1)A, (1)C, (10)D, (1)C, (1)A
Row 7 (R): (2)A, (10)D, (1)C, (1)A
Row 8 (L): (2)A, (10)D, (2)A
Row 9 (R): (2)A, (1)C, (9)D, (2)A
Row 10 (L): (2)A, (2)C, (8)D, (2)A

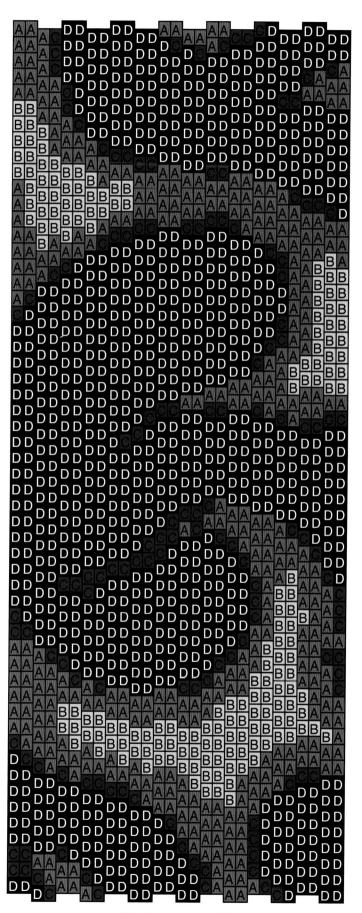

(Continues on p. 50)

Row 11 (R): (2)B, (1)C, (11)D
Row 12 (L): (12)D, (2)A
Row 13 (R): (2)B, (1)A, (1)C, (10)D
Row 14 (L): (12)D, (1)A, (1)B
Row 15 (R): (2)B, (2)A, (10)D
Row 16 (L): (10)D, (1)C, (2)A, (1)B
Row 17 (R): (2)B, (2)A, (2)C, (8)D
Row 18 (L): (8)D, (2)C, (2)A, (2)B
Row 19 (R): (4)B, (4)A, (2)C, (4)D
Row 20 (L): (4)D, (7)A, (3)B
Row 21 (R): (1)A, (5)B, (6)A, (2)D
Row 22 (L): (2)D, (1)C, (7)A, (4)B
Row 23 (R): (1)A, (5)B, (6)A, (2)C
Row 24 (L): (1)D, (1)C, (8)A, (4)B
Row 25 (R): (1)A, (3)B, (4)A, (2)C, (4)A
Row 26 (L): (5)A, (5)C, (1)A, (3)B
Row 27 (R): (2)A, (1)B, (1)A, (2)C, (4)D, (4)A
Row 28 (L): (4)A, (6)D, (1)C, (2)A, (1)B
Row 29 (R): (4)A, (7)D, (1)C, (2)A
Row 30 (L): (1)A, (1)B, (1)A, (1)C, (8)D, (2)A
Row 31 (R): (2)A, (1)C, (9)D, (1)A, (1)B
Row 32 (L): (2)B, (1)A, (1)C, (8)D, (1)C, (1)A
Row 33 (R): (2)A, (10)D, (1)A, (1)B
Row 34 (L): (2)B, (1)A, (11)D
Row 35 (R): (1)A, (1)C, (10)D, (1)A, (1)B
Row 36 (L): (2)B, (1)A, (11)D
Row 37 (R): (1)C, (11)D, (1)A, (1)B
Row 38 (L): (2)B, (1)A, (1)C, (10)D
Row 39 (R): (12)D, (1)A, (1)B
Row 40 (L): (2)B, (1)A, (1)C, (10)D
Row 41 (R): (11)D, (1)C, (1)A, (1)B
Row 42 (L): (2)B, (2)A, (10)D
Row 43 (R): (10)D, (1)C, (1)A, (2)B
Row 44 (L): (3)B, (1)A, (10)D
Row 45 (R): (10)D, (2)A, (2)B
Row 46 (L): (3)B, (3)A, (8)D
Row 47 (R): (8)D, (6)A
Row 48 (L): (8)A, (6)D
Row 49 (R): (6)D, (5)C, (3)A
Row 50 (L): (2)C, (1)A, (1)C, (4)D, (1)C, (5)D
Row 51 (R): (12)D, (2)C
Row 52 (L): (9)D, (1)C, (4)D
Row 53 (R): (5)D, (1)C, (8)D
Row 54 (L): (14)D
Row 55 (R): (14)D
Row 56 (L): (14)D
Row 57 (R): (14)D
Row 58 (L): (14)D
Row 59 (R): (14)D
Row 60 (L): (14)D
Row 61 (R): (8)D, (1)C, (1)A, (4)D
Row 62 (L): (4)D, (2)A, (2)C, (6)D
Row 63 (R): (7)D, (1)C, (4)A, (2)D
Row 64 (L): (2)D, (1)C, (3)A, (1)C, (1)A, (6)D
Row 65 (R): (6)D, (2)C, (1)D, (1)C, (2)A, (1)C, (1)D
Row 66 (L): (2)D, (3)A, (1)C, (2)D, (1)C, (5)D
Row 67 (R): (6)D, (1)C, (3)D, (3)A, (1)C

Row 68 (L): (2)D, (2)A, (1)C, (3)D, (2)C, (4)D
Row 69 (R): (4)D, (2)C, (4)D, (4)A
Row 70 (L): (1)D, (1)C, (1)B, (1)A, (6)D, (2)C, (2)D
Row 71 (R): (2)D, (2)C, (6)D, (1)C, (3)A
Row 72 (L): (1)C, (1)A, (2)B, (7)D, (1)C, (2)D
Row 73 (R): (10)D, (1)C, (3)A
Row 74 (L): (1)C, (1)A, (2)B, (10)D
Row 75 (R): (1)C, (9)D, (1)C, (1)A, (1)B, (1)A
Row 76 (L): (1)C, (1)A, (2)B, (10)D
Row 77 (R): (2)C, (8)D, (4)A
Row 78 (L): (2)A, (2)B, (1)C, (9)D
Row 79 (R): (2)A, (8)D, (1)A, (1)B, (2)A
Row 80 (L): (2)C, (2)B, (1)A, (1)C, (6)D, (1)C, (1)A
Row 81 (R): (2)A, (1)C, (6)D, (1)C, (1)A, (1)B, (2)A
Row 82 (L): (1)C, (1)A, (2)B, (2)A, (6)D, (2)A
Row 83 (R): (3)A, (1)C, (4)D, (1)C, (1)A, (2)B, (2)A
Row 84 (L): (1)C, (1)A, (2)B, (2)A, (2)C, (2)D, (1)C, (3)A
Row 85 (R): (10)A, (3)B, (1)A
Row 86 (L): (2)A, (4)B, (8)A
Row 87 (R): (2)A, (2)B, (5)A, (4)B, (1)A
Row 88 (L): (2)A, (4)B, (4)A, (2)B, (2)A
Row 89 (R): (2)A, (12)B
Row 90 (L): (1)A, (11)B, (2)A
Row 91 (R): (1)C, (2)A, (9)B, (2)A
Row 92 (L): (4)A, (7)B, (3)A
Row 93 (R): (1)D, (1)C, (3)A, (6)B, (3)A
Row 94 (L): (4)A, (5)B, (4)A, (1)C
Row 95 (R): (2)D, (1)C, (5)A, (2)B, (2)A, (2)C
Row 96 (L): (2)D, (1)C, (2)A, (2)B, (3)A, (2)C, (2)D
Row 97 (R): (4)D, (2)C, (2)A, (2)B, (2)A, (2)D
Row 98 (L): (4)D, (1)A, (1)B, (3)A, (1)C, (4)D
Row 99 (R): (6)D, (5)A, (3)D
Row 100 (L): (4)D, (4)A, (6)D
Row 101 (R): (7)D, (1)C, (2)A, (1)C, (3)D
Row 102 (L): (4)D, (4)A, (6)D
Row 103 (R): (8)D, (2)A, (1)C, (3)D
Row 104 (L): (4)D, (3)A, (1)C, (6)D
Row 105 (R): (3)C, (5)D, (2)A, (1)C, (3)D
Row 106 (L): (4)D, (2)A, (1)C, (5)D, (2)A
Row 107 (R): (2)C, (2)A, (4)D, (1)C, (1)A, (1)C, (3)D
Row 108 (L): (4)D, (2)A, (5)D, (1)C, (1)A, (1)C
Row 109 (R): (2)D, (2)A, (4)D, (1)C, (2)A, (1)C, (2)D
Row 110 (L): (3)D, (1)C, (2)A, (4)D, (1)C, (1)A, (1)C, (1)D
Row 111 (R): (2)D, (2)A, (5)D, (1)C, (2)A, (2)D
Row 112 (L): (2)D, (1)C, (3)A, (4)D, (2)A, (2)D
Row 113 (R): (2)D, (1)C, (1)A, (5)D, (1)C, (2)A, (2)D
Row 114 (L): (2)D, (4)A, (4)D, (2)A, (2)D
Row 115 (R): (2)D, (1)C, (1)A, (6)D, (3)A, (1)C
Row 116 (L): (2)D, (3)A, (1)C, (4)D, (2)A, (2)D
Row 117 (R): (3)D, (1)A, (6)D, (2)B, (2)A
Row 118 (L): (1)D, (1)C, (1)A, (1)B, (1)A, (1)C, (4)D, (2)A, (2)D
Row 119 (R): (3)D, (1)A, (6)D, (2)B, (2)A
Row 120 (L): (1)D, (1)C, (2)B, (1)A, (1)C, (4)D, (1)C, (1)A, (2)D
Row 121 (R): (3)D, (1)A, (6)D, (2)B, (2)A
Row 122 (L): (1)D, (1)A, (2)B, (1)A, (1)C, (5)D, (1)A, (2)D
Row 123 (R): (2)D, (1)C, (1)A, (6)D, (2)B, (2)A
Row 124 (L): (1)D, (1)A, (2)B, (2)A, (5)D, (1)A, (2)D

Row 125 (R): (2)D, (2)A, (6)D, (2)B, (2)A
Row 126 (L): (1)D, (1)C, (2)B, (2)A, (5)D, (1)A, (2)D
Row 127 (R): (2)D, (2)A, (5)D, (1)C, (2)B, (2)A
Row 128 (L): (1)D, (1)C, (1)A, (2)B, (1)A, (4)D, (1)C, (1)A, (1)C, (1)D
Row 129 (R): (2)D, (2)A, (4)D, (1)C, (1)A, (2)B, (2)A
Row 130 (L): (2)D, (1)A, (2)B, (1)A, (4)D, (1)C, (2)A, (1)C
Row 131 (R): (2)D, (1)A, (1)B, (1)C, (3)D, (2)A, (2)B, (1)A, (1)C
Row 132 (L): (2)D, (2)A, (2)B, (1)C, (3)D, (1)A, (1)D, (1)A, (1)C
Row 133 (R): (2)D, (1)A, (1)B, (1)A, (1)C, (2)D, (1)A, (2)B, (1)A, (2)D
Row 134 (L): (3)D, (1)C, (2)B, (2)A, (2)C, (2)B, (2)C
Row 135 (R): (2)D, (1)A, (2)B, (3)A, (2)B, (2)A, (2)D
Row 136 (L): (4)D, (3)B, (3)A, (2)B, (1)C, (1)D
Row 137 (R): (2)D, (2)C, (1)B, (3)A, (2)B, (1)A, (3)D
Row 138 (L): (4)D, (1)A, (1)B, (6)A, (2)D
Row 139 (R): (4)D, (5)A, (1)B, (1)A, (3)D
Row 140 (L): (4)D, (6)A, (1)C, (3)D
Row 141 (R): (4)D, (7)A, (3)D
Row 142 (L): (4)D, (2)A, (1)C, (3)A, (4)D
Row 143 (R): (4)D, (1)C, (1)A, (4)C, (1)A, (1)C, (2)D
Row 144 (L): (4)D, (1)A, (1)C, (2)D, (1)C, (1)A, (4)D
Row 145 (R): (1)C, (3)D, (1)C, (1)A, (4)D, (1)A, (1)C, (2)D
Row 146 (L): (4)D, (1)C, (4)D, (1)C, (4)D
Row 147 (R): (1)C, (1)A, (2)D, (2)A, (4)D, (1)A, (1)C, (2)D
Row 148 (L): (4)D, (1)C, (5)D, (1)C, (2)D, (1)C
Row 149 (R): (1)B, (1)A, (2)D, (1)A, (1)C, (4)D, (1)A, (1)C, (2)D
Row 150 (L): (1)A, (1)C, (8)D, (1)A, (1)C, (1)D, (1)C
Row 151 (R): (1)C, (1)A, (2)D, (1)A, (1)C, (4)D, (1)A, (1)C, (1)D, (1)C
Row 152 (L): (2)A, (2)D, (1)C, (5)D, (1)A, (1)C, (2)D
Row 153 (R): (1)C, (2)D, (1)C, (1)A, (1)C, (4)D, (1)C, (1)D, (1)C, (1)A
Row 154 (L): (1)B, (1)A, (2)D, (2)C, (4)D, (2)A, (2)D
Row 155 (R): (3)D, (1)C, (1)A, (1)C, (6)D, (2)A
Row 156 (L): (2)B, (1)C, (2)D, (1)C, (4)D, (2)A, (2)D
Row 157 (R): (3)D, (1)C, (1)B, (1)C, (3)D, (1)C, (2)D, (1)A, (1)B
Row 158 (L): (2)B, (1)A, (7)D, (1)B, (1)A, (2)D
Row 159 (R): (4)D, (1)B, (1)A, (6)D, (2)B
Row 160 (L): (1)A, (1)B, (1)A, (1)C, (5)D, (1)C, (1)A, (1)C, (2)D
Row 161 (R): (4)D, (2)B, (6)D, (2)B
Row 162 (L): (3)A, (1)C, (4)D, (1)C, (1)A, (1)C, (3)D
Row 163 (R): (4)D, (2)A, (6)D, (2)B
Row 164 (L): (1)A, (1)B, (1)A, (1)C, (4)D, (2)A, (4)D
Row 165 (R): (4)D, (1)C, (2)A, (1)C, (4)D, (2)B
Row 166 (L): (2)B, (1)A, (5)D, (2)A, (4)D
Row 167 (R): (5)D, (1)C, (2)A, (4)D, (1)A, (1)B
Row 168 (L): (2)B, (1)C, (3)D, (4)C, (4)D
Row 169 (R): (6)D, (4)C, (2)D, (2)A
Row 170 (L): (2)B, (3)D, (3)C, (4)D, (1)C, (1)D
Row 171 (R): (12)D, (1)C, (1)A
Row 172 (L): (1)B, (1)A, (10)D, (2)C
Row 173 (R): (1)D, (2)C, (9)D, (1)C, (1)A
Row 174 (L): (2)A, (10)D, (2)A

Row 175 (R): (1)D, (2)A, (1)C, (9)D, (1)C
Row 176 (L): (1)A, (1)C, (9)D, (1)C, (1)A, (1)C
Row 177 (R): (2)D, (2)A, (10)D
Row 178 (L): (1)C, (9)D, (1)C, (2)A, (1)C
Row 179 (R): (2)D, (3)A, (1)C, (8)D
Row 180 (L): (1)C, (7)D, (2)C, (2)A, (1)C, (1)D
Row 181 (R): (2)D, (1)C, (3)A, (1)C, (7)D
Row 182 (L): (8)D, (4)A, (2)D
Row 183 (R): (4)D, (3)A, (1)C, (6)D
Row 184 (L): (7)D, (1)C, (2)A, (1)C, (3)D
Row 185 (R): (4)D, (2)C, (2)A, (2)D, (2)C, (2)D
Row 186 (L): (4)D, (1)C, (1)D, (1)C, (1)A, (1)B, (1)A, (4)D
Row 187 (R): (6)D, (2)B, (2)D, (1)A, (1)C, (2)D
Row 188 (L): (3)D, (2)C, (1)D, (1)C, (2)A, (1)C, (4)D
Row 189 (R): (6)D, (2)B, (2)D, (1)A, (1)C, (2)D
Row 190 (L): (2)D, (1)A, (1)C, (2)D, (3)A, (5)D
Row 191 (R): (6)D, (1)A, (1)B, (1)C, (2)D, (2)C, (1)D
Row 192 (L): (2)D, (2)A, (2)D, (1)A, (1)B, (1)C, (5)D
Row 193 (R): (6)D, (2)B, (1)C, (1)D, (1)C, (1)A, (1)C, (1)D
Row 194 (L): (2)D, (2)A, (2)D, (1)A, (1)B, (1)C, (5)D
Row 195 (R): (6)D, (1)A, (1)B, (1)C, (1)D, (1)C, (1)A, (1)C, (1)D
Row 196 (L): (2)D, (1)C, (1)A, (1)C, (1)D, (1)A, (1)B, (1)A, (5)D
Row 197 (R): (6)D, (2)B, (2)D, (2)A, (2)D
Row 198 (L): (2)D, (2)C, (1)A, (1)C, (1)A, (1)B, (1)A, (5)D
Row 199 (R): (2)C, (4)D, (2)B, (2)C, (2)A, (2)D
Row 200 (L): (3)D, (1)C, (3)A, (2)B, (1)A, (4)D
Row 201 (R): (1)C, (1)A, (3)D, (1)C, (2)B, (3)A, (1)C, (2)D
Row 202 (L): (4)D, (4)A, (2)B, (1)C, (1)D, (1)C, (1)A
Row 203 (R): (1)C, (1)A, (2)C, (2)A, (2)B, (2)A, (1)C, (3)D
Row 204 (L): (4)D, (2)C, (2)A, (2)B, (4)A
Row 205 (R): (1)C, (3)A, (4)B, (1)A, (1)C, (4)D
Row 206 (L): (6)D, (2)A, (3)B, (3)A
Row 207 (R): (1)D, (1)C, (2)A, (4)B, (6)D
Row 208 (L): (6)D, (1)C, (1)A, (3)B, (2)A, (1)C
Row 209 (R): (2)D, (2)C, (1)A, (3)B, (6)D
Row 210 (L): (6)D, (1)C, (1)A, (2)B, (2)C, (2)D
Row 211 (R): (4)D, (1)C, (1)A, (2)B, (6)D
Row 212 (L): (6)D, (2)A, (2)B, (4)D
Row 213 (R): (2)C, (3)D, (1)C, (2)B, (1)C, (3)D, (2)C
Row 214 (L): (1)D, (5)C, (1)A, (2)B, (1)A, (3)D, (1)C
Row 215 (R): (2)A, (4)D, (2)B, (6)A
Row 216 (L): (4)C, (3)A, (1)B, (1)A, (1)C, (2)D, (2)C

Giraffe Print

These wonderful animals are among
my favorites, not only for their tall,
graceful shape, but for the patterns
on their hides. If you want your
giraffe bracelet to be unique, feel
free to let your imagination run wild!

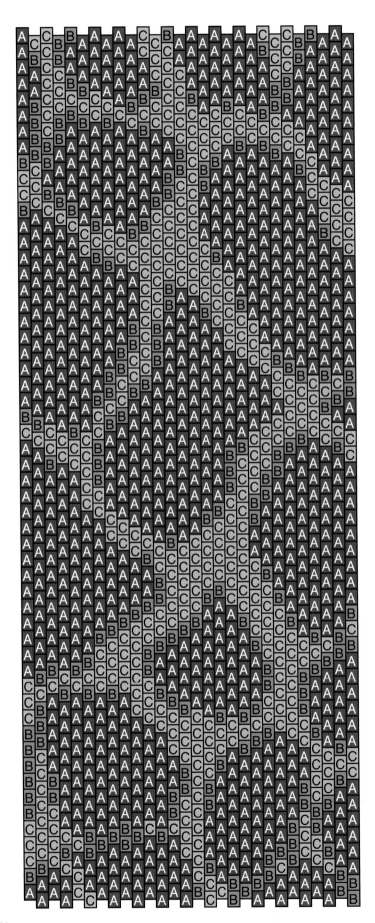

SUPPLIES

- 11º cylinder beads
  - 8–9g color A (Miyuki DB-794, matte opaque sienna)
  - 2–3g color B (Miyuki DB-272, lined topaz/yellow AB)
  - 4g color C (Miyuki DB208, opaque tan)
- 3- or 4-loop tube clasp
- Beading needle, size 10, 11, or 12
- Fireline, smoke, 6-lb. test
- Scissors, thread snips, or thread burner

A   B   C

The pattern is 1½ in. (3.8cm) wide and up to 7¼ in. (18.4cm) long. Adjust as needed.

MAKE THE BRACELET

1. Follow the pattern or word chart below to complete the piece (see two-drop peyote stitch, p. 9), leaving an 8–10-in. (20–25cm) tail for adding the clasp. Add and end thread as needed.

2. Attach a 4-loop tube clasp to each end of the bracelet (see p. 7).

Rows 1 and 2 (L): (3)A, (2)B, (3)C, (7)A, (1)B, (2)C, (5)A, (2)B, (2)C, (1)A

Row 3 (R): (1)A, (1)C, (3)A, (2)C, (3)A, (1)B, (1)C, (2)A

Row 4 (L): (2)A, (1)B, (1)C, (4)A, (1)C, (3)A, (2)B

Row 5 (R): (1)A, (1)C, (4)A, (1)C, (4)A, (1)C, (2)A

Row 6 (L): (3)A, (1)C, (3)A, (2)C, (3)A, (1)C, (1)A

Row 7 (R): (1)A, (1)C, (1)B, (3)A, (1)C, (4)A, (1)B, (2)A

Row 8 (L): (3)A, (1)B, (3)A, (1)C, (1)B, (2)A, (1)B, (1)C, (1)A

Row 9 (R): (1)A, (3)C, (1)A, (1)B, (1)C, (1)B, (3)A, (1)B, (2)A

Row 10 (L): (3)A, (1)B, (1)A, (1)B, (1)A, (2)C, (1)B, (3)C, (1)B

Row 11 (R): (1)A, (1)C, (1)B, (7)C, (1)B, (3)A

Row 12 (L): (3)A, (7)C, (4)B

Row 13 (R): (1)A, (1)C, (3)A, (1)B, (6)C, (2)A

Row 14 (L): (2)A, (6)C, (4)A, (2)B

Row 15 (R): (1)A, (1)B, (5)A, (2)C, (2)B, (1)C, (2)A

Row 16 (L): (2)A, (1)C, (1)B, (2)A, (1)C, (1)B, (5)A, (1)B

Row 17 (R): (2)B, (5)A, (1)C, (1)B, (3)A, (1)C, (1)A

Row 18 (L): (2)A, (1)B, (3)A, (2)B, (5)A, (1)C
Row 19 (R): (1)C, (5)A, (1)B, (1)C, (4)A, (1)C, (1)A
Row 20 (L): (1)A, (1)C, (4)A, (1)B, (1)C, (5)A, (1)C
Row 21 (R): (1)C, (1)B, (4)A, (1)B, (1)C, (4)A, (2)C
Row 22 (L): (2)C, (5)A, (1)C, (1)B, (3)A, (1)B, (1)C
Row 23 (R): (1)B, (1)C, (1)B, (3)A, (2)C, (5)A, (1)C
Row 24 (L): (2)C, (5)A, (2)C, (3)A, (1)C, (1)A
Row 25 (R): (2)A, (1)C, (1)B, (1)A, (1)B, (2)C, (5)A, (1)C
Row 26 (L): (1)C, (1)B, (5)A, (2)C, (1)B, (2)C, (2)A
Row 27 (R): (3)A, (5)C, (5)A, (1)C
Row 28 (L): (1)C, (5)A, (6)C, (2)A
Row 29 (R): (3)A, (1)B, (4)C, (1)B, (5)A
Row 30 (L): (6)A, (4)C, (1)B, (3)A
Row 31 (R): (5)A, (4)C, (5)A
Row 32 (L): (5)A, (4)C, (5)A
Row 33 (R): (5)A, (1)C, (1)B, (2)C, (5)A
Row 34 (L): (5)A, (2)C, (1)A, (1)C, (5)A
Row 35 (R): (5)A, (1)C, (1)B, (1)A, (1)C, (1)B, (4)A
Row 36 (L): (5)A, (1)C, (1)B, (1)A, (1)C, (5)A
Row 37 (R): (5)A, (1)C, (2)A, (2)C, (4)A
Row 38 (L): (4)A, (2)C, (2)A, (2)B, (4)A
Row 39 (R): (5)A, (1)C, (3)A, (1)C, (4)A
Row 40 (L): (4)A, (2)C, (2)A, (2)B, (4)A
Row 41 (R): (4)A, (1)B, (1)C, (3)A, (2)C, (3)A
Row 42 (L): (3)A, (1)B, (1)C, (3)A, (1)B, (1)C, (4)A
Row 43 (R): (4)A, (1)B, (1)C, (4)A, (1)C, (1)B, (2)A
Row 44 (L): (3)B, (1)C, (5)A, (1)C, (1)B, (3)A
Row 45 (R): (4)A, (1)C, (1)B, (5)A, (3)C
Row 46 (L): (1)B, (3)C, (5)A, (2)B, (3)A
Row 47 (R): (3)A, (1)B, (1)C, (6)A, (2)C, (1)B
Row 48 (L): (1)A, (1)B, (1)C, (7)A, (1)C, (3)A
Row 49 (R): (1)B, (2)A, (1)C, (1)B, (6)A, (2)C, (1)A
Row 50 (L): (1)A, (3)C, (6)A, (1)B, (2)A, (1)B
Row 51 (R): (2)C, (1)B, (1)C, (6)A, (4)C
Row 52 (L): (2)C, (1)B, (2)C, (6)A, (3)C
Row 53 (R): (1)A, (2)C, (1)B, (5)A, (1)B, (1)C, (1)B, (1)A, (1)B
Row 54 (L): (1)C, (2)A, (1)B, (1)C, (1)B, (5)A, (2)C, (1)A
Row 55 (R): (1)A, (1)B, (1)C, (1)B, (5)A, (2)C, (3)A
Row 56 (L): (3)A, (1)B, (1)C, (1)B, (5)A, (1)C, (2)A
Row 57 (R): (3)A, (1)B, (5)A, (1)C, (1)B, (3)A
Row 58 (L): (4)A, (1)C, (1)B, (5)A, (1)C, (2)A
Row 59 (R): (3)A, (1)C, (5)A, (1)C, (1)B, (3)A
Row 60 (L): (4)A, (1)B, (1)C, (5)A, (1)C, (2)A
Row 61 (R): (3)A, (1)C, (4)A, (1)B, (1)C, (4)A
Row 62 (L): (4)A, (1)B, (1)C, (1)B, (3)A, (1)C, (3)A
Row 63 (R): (4)A, (1)C, (3)A, (2)C, (4)A
Row 64 (L): (5)A, (2)C, (2)A, (2)C, (3)A
Row 65 (R): (4)A, (2)C, (1)B, (3)C, (4)A
Row 66 (L): (5)A, (5)C, (4)A
Row 67 (R): (5)A, (1)B, (4)C, (4)A
Row 68 (L): (4)A, (5)C, (5)A
Row 69 (R): (6)A, (4)C, (1)B, (3)A
Row 70 (L): (4)A, (4)C, (1)B, (5)A
Row 71 (R): (6)A, (2)C, (1)B, (2)C, (3)A
Row 72 (L): (3)A, (1)B, (2)C, (1)B, (1)C, (1)B, (5)A
Row 73 (R): (5)A, (1)B, (2)C, (1)A, (2)C, (3)A
Row 74 (L): (1)B, (2)A, (2)C, (2)A, (2)C, (1)B, (4)A

Row 75 (R): (4)A, (1)B, (2)C, (1)B, (1)A, (1)B, (1)C, (1)B, (2)A
Row 76 (L): (1)C, (2)A, (2)C, (2)A, (1)B, (2)C, (1)B, (3)A
Row 77 (R): (3)A, (1)B, (2)C, (1)B, (3)A, (2)C, (2)B
Row 78 (L): (1)B, (3)C, (1)B, (3)A, (1)B, (2)C, (3)A
Row 79 (R): (3)A, (2)C, (1)B, (4)A, (3)C, (1)B
Row 80 (L): (1)A, (1)B, (2)C, (5)A, (2)C, (1)B, (2)A
Row 81 (R): (1)A, (2)B, (2)C, (1)B, (4)A, (1)B, (1)C, (1)B, (1)A
Row 82 (L): (2)A, (1)B, (1)C, (5)A, (4)C, (1)B
Row 83 (R): (6)C, (4)A, (1)B, (1)C, (2)A
Row 84 (L): (2)A, (1)B, (1)C, (4)A, (1)B, (1)C, (3)B, (1)C
Row 85 (R): (1)C, (4)A, (1)C, (1)B, (3)A, (2)C, (2)A
Row 86 (L): (2)A, (1)B, (1)C, (1)B, (2)A, (1)B, (2)C, (3)A, (1)B
Row 87 (R): (1)C, (4)A, (3)C, (2)B, (2)C, (2)A
Row 88 (L): (2)A, (7)C, (4)A, (1)B
Row 89 (R): (1)B, (5)A, (4)C, (1)B, (1)C, (1)B, (1)A
Row 90 (L): (2)A, (1)C, (1)A, (1)B, (3)C, (5)A, (1)B
Row 91 (R): (1)B, (5)A, (3)C, (1)B, (2)A, (1)C, (1)B
Row 92 (L): (2)C, (4)A, (2)C, (5)A, (1)C
Row 93 (R): (1)B, (6)A, (1)C, (1)B, (3)A, (2)C
Row 94 (L): (2)C, (4)A, (1)C, (1)B, (5)A, (1)C
Row 95 (R): (2)B, (5)A, (1)C, (4)A, (1)C, (1)B
Row 96 (L): (1)A, (1)C, (1)B, (3)A, (2)B, (5)A, (1)C
Row 97 (R): (2)B, (4)A, (1)B, (1)C, (4)A, (1)C, (1)A
Row 98 (L): (1)A, (2)B, (3)A, (1)B, (1)C, (5)A, (1)C
Row 99 (R): (1)B, (1)C, (4)A, (1)B, (1)C, (4)A, (1)B, (1)A
Row 100 (L): (2)A, (1)C, (4)A, (1)C, (5)A, (1)C
Row 101 (R): (2)C, (2)A, (1)B, (3)C, (3)A, (2)B, (1)A
Row 102 (L): (2)A, (1)C, (4)A, (1)C, (4)B, (2)C
Row 103 (R): (3)C, (2)B, (2)A, (1)C, (3)A, (1)B, (1)C, (1)A
Row 104 (L): (1)A, (1)B, (1)C, (1)B, (3)A, (1)C, (3)A, (2)B, (1)C
Row 105 (R): (2)C, (5)A, (1)C, (2)A, (2)B, (1)C, (1)A
Row 106 (L): (1)A, (1)C, (1)A, (1)C, (2)A, (1)B, (5)A, (1)C, (1)B
Row 107 (R): (1)B, (1)A, (1)C, (4)A, (1)C, (2)A, (1)B, (2)A, (1)B
Row 108 (L): (1)B, (3)A, (2)B, (1)C, (7)A
Row 109 (R): (2)A, (1)C, (4)A, (1)B, (1)C, (1)B, (3)A, (1)B
Row 110 (L): (1)B, (4)A, (1)B, (1)C, (4)A, (1)C, (2)A
Row 111 (R): (3)A, (1)C, (3)A, (1)B, (1)C, (5)A
Row 112 (L): (1)B, (4)A, (1)B, (1)C, (3)A, (2)C, (2)A
Row 113 (R): (3)A, (1)C, (3)A, (1)B, (1)C, (5)A
Row 114 (L): (5)A, (2)C, (1)B, (2)A, (1)C, (1)B, (2)A
Row 115 (R): (3)A, (2)C, (1)A, (1)B, (2)C, (5)A
Row 116 (L): (5)A, (3)C, (1)B, (2)C, (3)A
Row 117 (R): (4)A, (3)C, (2)B, (1)C, (4)A
Row 118 (L): (4)A, (1)C, (2)A, (3)C, (1)B, (3)A
Row 119 (R): (4)A, (3)C, (2)A, (2)C, (3)A
Row 120 (L): (1)B, (2)A, (2)C, (2)A, (1)B, (2)C, (4)A
Row 121 (R): (5)A, (1)C, (1)B, (3)A, (2)C, (1)A, (1)B
Row 122 (L): (1)C, (1)B, (2)C, (4)A, (1)B, (1)C, (4)A
Row 123 (R): (5)A, (1)C, (4)A, (1)B, (3)C
Row 124 (L): (4)C, (5)A, (1)B, (4)A
Row 125 (R): (5)A, (1)C, (4)A, (1)B, (3)C
Row 126 (L): (1)B, (3)C, (5)A, (1)B, (4)A
Row 127 (R): (5)A, (1)C, (4)A, (1)B, (1)C, (1)B, (1)A
Row 128 (L): (2)A, (2)C, (4)A, (2)B, (4)A

Row 129 (R): (5)A, (1)C, (4)A, (1)B, (1)C, (1)B, (1)A
Row 130 (L): (2)A, (1)C, (2)B, (3)A, (1)C, (1)B, (4)A
Row 131 (R): (1)A, (1)B, (2)A, (1)B, (2)C, (1)A, (2)B, (1)A, (2)B, (1)A
Row 132 (L): (2)A, (1)C, (2)A, (1)C, (2)B, (2)C, (1)B, (2)A, (1)C
Row 133 (R): (1)A, (1)C, (2)B, (5)C, (2)A, (1)B, (2)A
Row 134 (L): (2)A, (1)B, (2)A, (1)B, (8)C
Row 135 (R): (1)B, (1)C, (3)B, (4)C, (2)A, (1)B, (2)A
Row 136 (L): (2)A, (1)B, (3)A, (3)C, (1)B, (2)A, (1)B, (1)C
Row 137 (R): (1)C, (1)B, (3)A, (1)C, (1)B, (1)C, (1)B, (2)A, (1)B, (2)A
Row 138 (L): (2)A, (1)B, (3)A, (1)C, (1)A, (1)C, (4)A, (1)B
Row 139 (R): (1)C, (4)A, (1)C, (2)A, (1)C, (2)A, (1)C, (2)A
Row 140 (L): (2)A, (2)B, (1)A, (1)C, (1)B, (1)A, (1)B, (5)A
Row 141 (R): (1)B, (4)A, (1)C, (2)A, (2)C, (1)B, (1)C, (2)A
Row 142 (L): (3)A, (3)C, (2)A, (2)B, (4)A
Row 143 (R): (1)B, (4)A, (1)C, (3)A, (3)C, (2)A
Row 144 (L): (3)A, (2)C, (3)A, (2)B, (4)A
Row 145 (R): (1)B, (4)A, (1)C, (4)A, (1)C, (1)B, (2)A
Row 146 (L): (3)A, (1)C, (1)B, (3)A, (1)C, (1)B, (4)A
Row 147 (R): (1)B, (4)A, (1)C, (4)A, (1)C, (3)A
Row 148 (L): (3)A, (1)C, (4)A, (1)C, (1)B, (4)A
Row 149 (R): (1)B, (3)A, (1)B, (1)C, (1)B, (3)A, (1)B, (3)A
Row 150 (L): (3)A, (1)C, (4)A, (2)C, (4)A
Row 151 (R): (1)C, (3)A, (1)B, (2)C, (3)A, (1)B, (3)A
Row 152 (L): (3)A, (1)C, (2)A, (1)B, (1)C, (1)B, (1)C, (3)A, (1)B
Row 153 (R): (1)C, (3)A, (2)B, (1)A, (2)C, (1)B, (1)C, (3)B
Row 154 (L): (7)C, (2)A, (1)C, (1)B, (2)A, (1)C
Row 155 (R): (2)C, (2)A, (1)C, (3)A, (1)B, (5)C
Row 156 (L): (3)B, (1)C, (2)B, (3)A, (2)B, (2)A, (1)C
Row 157 (R): (1)A, (1)C, (3)B, (5)A, (1)C, (1)B, (2)A
Row 158 (L): (3)A, (1)C, (6)A, (1)B, (2)C, (1)A
Row 159 (R): (1)A, (1)B, (2)C, (6)A, (1)C, (3)A
Row 160 (L): (3)A, (1)C, (1)B, (5)A, (1)B, (2)C, (1)A
Row 161 (R): (1)A, (1)B, (2)C, (6)A, (1)C, (3)A
Row 162 (L): (3)A, (1)C, (1)B, (5)A, (3)C, (1)A
Row 163 (R): (1)A, (1)B, (3)C, (4)A, (3)B, (2)A
Row 164 (L): (3)A, (1)C, (1)B, (4)A, (4)C, (1)A
Row 165 (R): (1)A, (1)B, (1)C, (1)B, (2)C, (3)A, (1)C, (1)A, (1)C, (2)A
Row 166 (L): (5)A, (1)B, (2)A, (2)C, (1)A, (1)B, (1)C, (1)B
Row 167 (R): (1)C, (2)B, (1)A, (1)B, (2)C, (1)A, (2)B, (1)A, (1)C, (2)A
Row 168 (L): (2)A, (1)C, (2)A, (2)B, (3)C, (3)A, (1)B
Row 169 (R): (1)C, (4)A, (4)C, (2)A, (1)B, (2)A
Row 170 (L): (2)A, (1)C, (2)A, (1)B, (3)C, (4)A, (1)B
Row 171 (R): (1)B, (5)A, (2)C, (1)B, (3)A, (1)C, (1)A
Row 172 (L): (1)B, (2)C, (3)A, (2)C, (6)A
Row 173 (R): (7)A, (2)C, (2)A, (1)B, (2)C
Row 174 (L): (3)C, (3)A, (1)C, (7)A
Row 175 (R): (8)A, (1)C, (2)A, (1)B, (2)C
Row 176 (L): (1)B, (2)C, (2)B, (1)C, (1)B, (7)A
Row 177 (R): (8)A, (3)C, (1)B, (1)C, (1)B
Row 178 (L): (1)A, (1)C, (2)B, (2)C, (1)B, (7)A
Row 179 (R): (8)A, (2)C, (1)B, (1)A, (1)C, (1)A
Row 180 (L): (1)A, (1)C, (2)A, (1)B, (1)C, (1)B, (7)A
Row 181 (R): (1)B, (7)A, (1)C, (1)B, (3)A, (1)B

Row 182 (L): (1)A, (1)C, (3)A, (1)B, (1)C, (6)A, (1)B
Row 183 (R): (1)C, (1)B, (5)A, (2)B, (4)A, (1)B
Row 184 (L): (1)A, (1)B, (4)A, (1)C, (4)A, (1)B, (2)C
Row 185 (R): (3)C, (1)B, (3)A, (1)C, (1)B, (4)A, (1)C
Row 186 (L): (1)A, (2)B, (3)A, (1)C, (1)B, (2)A, (4)C
Row 187 (R): (1)A, (1)B, (3)C, (2)A, (1)C, (3)A, (1)B, (2)C
Row 188 (L): (1)B, (2)C, (3)A, (3)B, (3)C, (1)B, (1)A
Row 189 (R): (3)A, (5)C, (4)A, (2)C
Row 190 (L): (3)C, (3)A, (1)B, (4)C, (3)A
Row 191 (R): (4)A, (3)C, (1)B, (4)A, (2)C
Row 192 (L): (2)C, (5)A, (2)C, (1)B, (4)A
Row 193 (R): (6)A, (2)C, (4)A, (1)B, (1)C
Row 194 (L): (2)C, (4)A, (2)C, (1)B, (5)A
Row 195 (R): (6)A, (3)C, (3)A, (1)B, (1)C
Row 196 (L): (1)B, (1)C, (1)B, (2)A, (1)B, (3)C, (5)A
Row 197 (R): (5)A, (1)B, (1)C, (1)B, (1)C, (3)A, (2)C
Row 198 (L): (1)A, (2)C, (2)A, (4)C, (5)A
Row 199 (R): (5)A, (2)C, (1)B, (2)C, (1)A, (1)B, (1)C, (1)B
Row 200 (L): (1)A, (1)B, (1)C, (1)A, (1)B, (1)C, (1)A, (1)B, (1)C,
(1)B, (4)A
Row 201 (R): (4)A, (1)B, (1)C, (1)B, (2)A, (1)C, (1)A, (1)B, (1)C, (1)A
Row 202 (L): (1)A, (1)B, (1)C, (1)A, (1)C, (1)B, (2)A, (2)C, (4)A
Row 203 (R): (4)A, (1)B, (1)C, (1)B, (2)A, (1)C, (1)B, (1)C, (1)B, (1)A
Row 204 (L): (2)A, (3)C, (3)A, (1)B, (1)C, (1)B, (3)A
Row 205 (R): (3)A, (1)B, (1)C, (1)B, (3)A, (3)C, (2)A
Row 206 (L): (2)A, (3)C, (4)A, (2)C, (1)B, (2)A
Row 207 (R): (1)A, (2)B, (2)C, (1)B, (4)A, (2)C, (2)A
Row 208 (L): (2)A, (2)C, (5)A, (1)B, (3)C, (1)B
Row 209 (R): (1)B, (1)C, (1)B, (2)C, (6)A, (2)C, (1)B
Row 210 (L): (3)C, (1)B, (5)A, (2)C, (1)A, (1)B, (1)C
Row 211 (R): (1)C, (1)B, (1)A, (2)C, (6)A, (3)C
Row 212 (L): (3)C, (1)B, (5)A, (2)C, (2)A, (1)B

Batik Paisley

Several years ago, I watched a batik artist create amazing fabrics, and I was captivated with both the process and the finished fabrics. Not a fabric artist? No worries—you can wear your beaded batik on your wrist.

note
I chose a color palette similar to the dyes traditionally used in batik, but why not use your favorite colors instead?

SUPPLIES

- 11º cylinder beads
  - 4g color A (Miyuki DB-165, opaque royal blue AB)
  - 4g color B (Miyuki DB-325, matte metallic blue AB)
  - 2g color C (Miyuki DB-881, matte opaque light blue AB)
  - 4g color D (Miyuki DB-202, white pearl AB)
  - 2g color E (Miyuki DB-306, dark grey matte metallic)
  - 2g color F (Miyuki DB-1497, opaque light sky blue)
- Beading needle, size 10, 11, or 12
- Fireline, crystal, 6-lb. test
- 3- or 4-loop tube clasp
- Scissors, thread snips, or thread burner

A B C D E F

This pattern measures 1½ in. (3.8cm) wide and approximately 6½ in. (16.5cm) long, not including the clasp.

MAKE THE BRACELET

1. Follow the pattern or word chart below to complete the piece (see two-drop peyote stitch, p. 9), leaving an 8–10-in. (20–25cm) tail for adding the clasp. Add and end thread as needed.

2. Attach a 4-loop tube clasp to each end of the bracelet (see p. 7).

Rows 1 and 2 (L): (2)D, (1)C, (3)A, (1)E, (1)D, (1)F, (1)C, (1)E, (1)D, (1)A, (1)B, (1)C, (1)E, (1)A, (1)E, (1)C, (4)A, (1)C, (1)E, (3)A
Row 3 (R): (2)A, (1)D, (2)C, (1)E, (1)C, (1)E, (4)D, (2)B
Row 4 (L): (1)D, (1)F, (1)A, (2)E, (1)C, (1)A, (1)B, (2)A, (1)C, (1)F, (1)C, (1)B

(Continues on p. 60)

Row 5 (R): (1)A, (1)B, (2)D, (2)A, (1)F, (1)E, (1)D, (1)E, (1)A, (1)D, (2)B

Row 6 (L): (1)F, (1)E, (1)A, (1)F, (3)A, (1)B, (1)E, (2)A, (1)C, (1)F, (1)A

Row 7 (R): (2)B, (1)F, (1)E, (2)A, (1)D, (1)E, (1)D, (1)E, (1)B, (1)F, (2)A

Row 8 (L): (1)D, (2)A, (1)D, (2)B, (1)E, (1)A, (1)F, (3)A, (2)F

Row 9 (R): (1)C, (1)F, (1)B, (3)A, (1)F, (1)A, (2)D, (1)C, (1)D, (2)A

Row 10 (L): (1)F, (1)B, (1)C, (1)D, (3)C, (1)A, (2)C, (2)A, (1)E, (1)D

Row 11 (R): (2)D, (2)B, (1)A, (1)E, (1)C, (1)A, (1)D, (1)C, (1)E, (1)D, (2)A

Row 12 (L): (1)F, (1)B, (1)C, (1)D, (1)B, (1)A, (1)C, (2)A, (1)C, (2)A, (1)C, (1)D

Row 13 (R): (2)D, (1)E, (1)B, (1)C, (1)E, (1)C, (1)A, (1)F, (2)A, (1)E, (2)A

Row 14 (L): (1)C, (1)B, (1)C, (1)D, (1)A, (1)B, (1)C, (1)B, (1)E, (1)A, (2)C, (2)D

Row 15 (R): (4)D, (1)E, (3)A, (1)F, (1)B, (1)A, (1)E, (2)A

Row 16 (L): (1)C, (1)B, (1)A, (1)D, (2)B, (1)C, (1)B, (1)E, (1)B, (1)A, (1)C, (2)D

Row 17 (R): (3)D, (1)C, (1)B, (2)A, (1)B, (1)D, (1)F, (1)E, (1)F, (2)A

Row 18 (L): (1)F, (1)A, (1)B, (1)E, (1)C, (1)F, (1)A, (1)B, (1)F, (1)A, (1)B, (1)A, (2)D

Row 19 (R): (3)D, (1)E, (1)B, (2)A, (1)B, (1)C, (1)D, (1)F, (1)C, (2)B

Row 20 (L): (1)D, (1)A, (2)B, (1)F, (1)D, (1)A, (1)B, (1)F, (1)C, (1)B, (1)A, (2)D

Row 21 (R): (3)D, (2)B, (2)A, (1)B, (1)A, (1)B, (1)A, (3)B

Row 22 (L): (1)D, (1)C, (4)B, (1)A, (1)B, (1)D, (1)F, (2)B, (2)D

Row 23 (R): (1)B, (1)E, (2)D, (1)E, (1)F, (2)A, (2)B, (2)A, (1)B, (1)A

Row 24 (L): (1)F, (1)D, (6)B, (1)D, (1)F, (1)C, (1)D, (1)C, (1)E

Row 25 (R): (1)D, (1)F, (2)D, (1)C, (1)E, (1)C, (1)A, (2)B, (3)A, (1)C

Row 26 (L): (1)C, (1)D, (2)B, (1)A, (1)B, (2)A, (1)D, (1)C, (1)E, (1)F, (2)D

Row 27 (R): (4)E, (1)A, (1)E, (1)D, (1)E, (4)A, (1)E, (1)D

Row 28 (L): (1)A, (1)F, (1)E, (5)A, (1)C, (1)D, (1)A, (3)B

Row 29 (R): (4)B, (1)A, (2)C, (1)D, (4)A, (2)D

Row 30 (L): (1)B, (1)C, (1)D, (1)F, (1)B, (1)A, (1)C, (1)D, (1)F, (1)D, (4)A

Row 31 (R): (2)B, (1)A, (1)B, (1)E, (1)F, (1)E, (1)D, (1)F, (2)C, (1)F, (2)D

Row 32 (L): (1)B, (1)E, (2)D, (2)F, (4)D, (3)A, (1)B

Row 33 (R): (1)A, (1)E, (2)A, (2)F, (2)E, (4)D, (2)F

Row 34 (L): (2)B, (7)D, (1)E, (1)C, (1)A, (1)E, (1)F

Row 35 (R): (2)D, (2)B, (1)F, (1)E, (1)C, (1)B, (5)D, (1)F

Row 36 (L): (2)B, (4)D, (2)B, (1)C, (1)A, (1)C, (2)A, (1)E

Row 37 (R): (1)D, (1)C, (2)B, (1)E, (1)A, (1)D, (1)A, (1)B, (1)E, (1)C, (2)D, (1)E

Row 38 (L): (1)B, (1)A, (2)D, (4)B, (1)E, (1)A, (2)C, (1)A, (1)B

Row 39 (R): (1)C, (1)A, (1)B, (1)E, (1)C, (1)E, (2)D, (4)B, (1)D, (1)E

Row 40 (L): (2)A, (1)D, (2)B, (1)A, (1)B, (1)A, (1)B, (2)A, (1)C, (1)B, (1)A

Row 41 (R): (1)A, (1)B, (1)E, (1)F, (1)C, (1)A, (1)C, (1)D, (4)B, (1)F, (1)A

Row 42 (L): (2)A, (1)F, (3)B, (1)E, (1)D, (5)A, (1)B

Row 43 (R): (1)A, (1)B, (1)F, (1)E, (2)A, (1)B, (1)F, (1)A, (1)B, (2)A, (1)F, (1)A

Row 44 (L): (2)A, (1)D, (1)F, (2)A, (2)D, (4)A, (1)F, (1)E

Row 45 (R): (1)A, (1)E, (1)C, (3)A, (2)B, (2)D, (1)C, (2)F, (1)B

Row 46 (L): (2)A, (5)D, (4)C, (1)E, (1)F, (1)D

Row 47 (R): (1)C, (1)F, (5)A, (1)B, (5)D, (1)B

Row 48 (L): (1)A, (1)B, (1)D, (2)F, (1)C, (1)F, (1)B, (1)D, (1)A, (1)F, (1)D, (1)C, (1)D

Row 49 (R): (2)D, (1)A, (1)D, (2)A, (1)D, (1)A, (1)D, (1)C, (2)A, (1)D, (1)A

Row 50 (L): (1)A, (3)B, (1)A, (5)B, (1)C, (1)F, (1)A, (1)F

Row 51 (R): (2)D, (1)C, (1)F, (1)A, (2)B, (2)A, (1)D, (2)A, (1)F, (1)C

Row 52 (L): (2)B, (1)E, (1)A, (1)C, (1)D, (1)B, (1)A, (2)B, (1)A, (1)E, (1)A, (1)E

Row 53 (R): (2)F, (4)A, (1)B, (2)A, (1)B, (1)F, (1)E, (2)D

Row 54 (L): (1)B, (1)C, (1)D, (1)F, (1)D, (1)E, (2)B, (2)F, (1)B, (3)A

Row 55 (R): (1)C, (1)F, (2)A, (2)B, (2)D, (1)B, (1)A, (4)D

Row 56 (L): (1)C, (3)D, (1)A, (1)B, (1)A, (2)D, (1)C, (1)B, (1)F, (2)A

Row 57 (R): (1)F, (1)C, (1)A, (1)F, (2)B, (1)F, (1)D, (2)B, (1)F, (3)D

Row 58 (L): (4)D, (2)B, (2)D, (1)E, (2)A, (1)D, (2)A

Row 59 (R): (1)D, (1)E, (1)C, (1)D, (1)B, (1)A, (1)E, (1)D, (1)F, (2)B, (1)C, (2)D

Row 60 (L): (4)D, (2)B, (2)F, (1)B, (2)A, (1)F, (2)A

Row 61 (R): (1)F, (1)E, (2)D, (1)A, (3)B, (4)A, (2)D

Row 62 (L): (3)D, (3)A, (2)B, (1)A, (1)C, (1)B, (2)C, (1)A

Row 63 (R): (1)F, (1)A, (1)D, (1)F, (1)A, (1)F, (1)C, (3)B, (2)A, (2)D

Row 64 (L): (1)C, (1)D, (1)E, (1)B, (2)A, (2)B, (2)D, (2)A, (1)C, (1)A

Row 65 (R): (1)D, (1)A, (1)C, (1)A, (1)C, (2)D, (1)E, (1)C, (1)E, (2)A, (2)D

Row 66 (L): (1)B, (1)C, (2)B, (1)A, (1)E, (1)F, (1)A, (2)D, (1)B, (3)A

Row 67 (R): (1)D, (2)A, (1)B, (1)A, (2)D, (1)C, (2)D, (1)A, (1)B, (1)E, (1)D

Row 68 (L): (1)B, (4)A, (2)D, (1)F, (2)D, (2)B, (2)A

Row 69 (R): (1)D, (3)A, (1)B, (1)E, (1)C, (1)F, (2)D, (2)A, (1)B, (1)D

Row 70 (L): (2)B, (1)A, (1)B, (1)A, (1)F, (2)D, (1)A, (1)C, (2)A, (1)B, (1)A

Row 71 (R): (1)D, (1)A, (2)B, (1)D, (1)C, (2)B, (2)D, (2)A, (1)B, (1)F

Row 72 (L): (1)B, (1)A, (3)B, (1)C, (1)D, (2)B, (1)A, (1)D, (1)C, (2)B

Row 73 (R): (1)D, (1)E, (1)B, (1)A, (1)D, (1)F, (2)A, (1)C, (1)E, (1)B, (1)A, (1)B, (1)E

Row 74 (L): (1)A, (1)E, (4)A, (1)F, (2)A, (1)B, (2)D, (2)B

Row 75 (R): (2)F, (1)B, (1)A, (2)D, (2)A, (1)D, (1)C, (3)A, (1)C

Row 76 (L): (1)E, (1)F, (4)A, (1)D, (1)C, (1)B, (1)C, (2)D, (2)B

Row 77 (R): (2)D, (2)B, (1)F, (3)C, (2)D, (3)A, (1)F

Row 78 (L): (1)D, (1)C, (1)A, (1)B, (1)A, (1)F, (3)D, (1)F, (1)E, (2)B, (1)C

Row 79 (R): (1)F, (1)D, (1)A, (1)B, (1)A, (1)C, (1)D, (1)F, (2)D, (2)A, (1)E, (1)F

Row 80 (L): (1)B, (1)A, (2)B, (1)A, (1)C, (1)D, (1)C, (2)D, (3)A, (1)D

Row 81 (R): (1)D, (1)F, (1)B, (2)A, (2)F, (1)C, (1)D, (1)F, (2)A, (2)C

Row 82 (L): (6)A, (1)C, (1)B, (2)D, (1)B, (1)A, (2)F

Row 83 (R): (1)C, (1)A, (1)C, (1)B, (1)A, (1)B, (1)C, (5)A, (1)E, (1)B

Row 84 (L): (2)A, (1)C, (5)A, (1)C, (3)A, (1)F, (1)A

Row 85 (R): (2)B, (1)D, (1)E, (9)A, (1)B

Row 86 (L): (2)A, (2)E, (8)A, (1)F, (1)E

Row 87 (R): (1)D, (2)C, (1)F, (6)A, (2)E, (2)A

Row 88 (L): (1)C, (7)A, (1)B, (1)A, (1)E, (1)D, (1)C, (1)D

Row 89 (R): (1)F, (1)D, (2)B, (1)E, (1)A, (2)B, (2)A, (1)F, (1)D, (2)A

Row 90 (L): (1)D, (1)F, (1)C, (1)D, (2)C, (1)A, (2)B, (1)A, (1)D, (2)A, (1)F

Row 91 (R): (1)A, (3)B, (2)D, (2)E, (2)C, (1)A, (1)C, (2)D

Row 92 (L): (3)E, (1)F, (2)A, (2)F, (3)D, (2)E, (1)D

Row 93 (R): (2)A, (2)C, (4)D, (1)E, (2)A, (1)F, (1)E, (1)D

Row 94 (L): (1)A, (1)E, (4)A, (1)C, (7)D

Row 95 (R): (1)C, (1)F, (2)D, (1)F, (1)C, (2)D, (2)A, (2)E, (1)A, (1)F

Row 96 (L): (1)A, (1)E, (5)A, (1)C, (2)D, (1)F, (1)E, (2)D

Row 97 (R): (2)D, (1)C, (1)E, (1)D, (1)B, (2)D, (2)A, (1)C, (1)A, (1)B, (1)C

Row 98 (L): (7)A, (1)E, (1)D, (1)C, (1)F, (1)B, (1)C, (1)D

Row 99 (R): (2)D, (2)B, (1)D, (1)A, (2)D, (2)A, (1)C, (2)A, (1)C

Row 100 (L): (4)A, (1)C, (1)A, (1)B, (2)F, (1)B, (1)D, (1)C, (1)A, (1)F

Row 101 (R): (2)D, (1)A, (1)C, (1)F, (1)B, (2)D, (2)A, (1)C, (1)B, (1)A, (1)F

Row 102 (L): (1)A, (1)F, (2)B, (1)D, (2)F, (1)D, (1)A, (1)B, (2)D, (1)F, (1)D

Row 103 (R): (2)C, (2)D, (1)C, (1)B, (3)D, (1)F, (1)C, (1)A, (1)E, (1)D

Row 104 (L): (1)F, (1)D, (2)A, (1)D, (1)F, (2)D, (1)B, (1)A, (2)D, (1)C, (1)A

Row 105 (R): (2)B, (1)F, (1)D, (2)A, (1)F, (1)D, (1)F, (1)C, (1)D, (1)F, (2)D

Row 106 (L): (8)D, (2)A, (1)F, (1)D, (2)B

Row 107 (R): (3)B, (1)D, (2)B, (1)C, (1)D, (1)E, (2)F, (1)C, (2)D

Row 108 (L): (1)C, (2)D, (1)E, (2)D, (1)F, (1)D, (2)A, (1)C, (1)D, (2)B

Row 109 (R): (2)A, (1)B, (1)C, (2)A, (1)E, (1)D, (1)E, (1)D, (2)A, (2)D

Row 110 (L): (1)A, (1)F, (2)A, (1)C, (1)D, (1)F, (1)D, (1)B, (1)A, (1)E, (1)D, (2)A

Row 111 (R): (2)A, (1)B, (1)E, (2)B, (1)A, (1)D, (1)E, (1)D, (2)A, (1)F, (1)D

Row 112 (L): (1)C, (1)D, (1)E, (1)A, (1)E, (1)D, (1)C, (1)D, (2)B, (1)A, (1)F, (1)A, (1)F

Row 113 (R): (1)B, (1)E, (1)B, (1)C, (2)B, (1)A, (1)D, (1)A, (1)D, (2)A, (1)F, (1)D

Row 114 (L): (2)D, (1)C, (1)E, (2)D, (1)E, (1)D, (3)A, (1)F, (1)A, (1)F

Row 115 (R): (1)F, (1)D, (1)B, (1)C, (2)A, (1)C, (1)D, (1)B, (2)D, (1)C, (1)D, (1)F

Row 116 (L): (2)A, (1)F, (3)D, (1)E, (1)D, (2)A, (1)B, (1)D, (1)B, (1)C

Row 117 (R): (1)D, (1)F, (1)E, (1)D, (1)B, (1)A, (1)F, (1)D, (1)B, (1)C, (2)D, (2)A

Row 118 (L): (1)B, (2)A, (1)F, (2)D, (1)C, (1)D, (2)A, (1)E, (1)D, (1)B, (1)A

Row 119 (R): (1)C, (1)E, (2)D, (1)B, (1)A, (2)D, (1)A, (1)B, (2)D, (2)A

Row 120 (L): (3)B, (1)E, (2)D, (1)F, (1)D, (1)F, (1)E, (2)D, (1)F, (1)E

Row 121 (R): (1)B, (1)E, (3)D, (1)C, (2)D, (2)A, (1)D, (1)F, (1)B, (1)A

Row 122 (L): (2)B, (1)A, (1)B, (1)D, (1)A, (8)D

Row 123 (R): (1)F, (1)D, (1)F, (1)D, (1)F, (3)D, (1)E, (1)A, (1)D, (1)F, (2)A
Row 124 (L): (6)B, (1)F, (7)D
Row 125 (R): (2)D, (1)C, (1)F, (2)D, (1)C, (1)D, (1)F, (1)A, (1)B, (1)F, (2)A
Row 126 (L): (1)B, (5)A, (2)D, (1)C, (1)F, (2)D, (1)F, (1)D
Row 127 (R): (2)D, (2)B, (1)D, (1)F, (1)A, (1)F, (1)D, (1)C, (1)A, (1)B, (2)A
Row 128 (L): (6)A, (2)D, (2)A, (2)D, (1)A, (1)E
Row 129 (R): (1)D, (1)F, (2)B, (1)F, (2)A, (1)F, (2)D, (2)B, (2)A
Row 130 (L): (4)A, (1)C, (3)D, (2)A, (1)D, (1)F, (2)B
Row 131 (R): (1)D, (1)E, (2)B, (1)E, (1)B, (1)E, (2)D, (1)F, (1)C, (3)A
Row 132 (L): (4)A, (1)F, (1)A, (1)C, (1)D, (2)B, (1)F, (1)D, (2)B
Row 133 (R): (1)F, (1)A, (1)B, (1)A, (2)B, (1)C, (1)D, (2)B, (2)D, (1)C, (1)E
Row 134 (L): (1)D, (1)F, (2)D, (1)F, (2)A, (1)E, (1)A, (1)B, (1)C, (1)D, (2)B
Row 135 (R): (1)C, (2)B, (1)C, (2)B, (1)F, (1)E, (1)A, (1)B, (4)D
Row 136 (L): (5)D, (1)F, (1)A, (1)B, (1)F, (2)E, (1)D, (2)B
Row 137 (R): (1)C, (2)B, (1)F, (1)B, (2)A, (1)B, (1)A, (1)C, (4)D
Row 138 (L): (6)D, (2)B, (1)E, (1)F, (1)B, (1)E, (2)B
Row 139 (R): (1)E, (1)B, (1)C, (1)F, (1)C, (1)D, (2)B, (1)F, (5)D
Row 140 (L): (4)D, (2)E, (2)C, (1)E, (1)D, (2)C, (1)E, (1)B
Row 141 (R): (1)A, (1)B, (1)F, (3)C, (2)F, (1)E, (2)A, (1)B, (2)D
Row 142 (L): (1)B, (1)E, (1)D, (1)F, (1)A, (1)B, (2)E, (1)C, (1)A, (2)B, (2)C
Row 143 (R): (2)E, (1)A, (3)B, (1)A, (1)D, (2)B, (1)A, (1)C, (2)D
Row 144 (L): (1)B, (1)E, (1)D, (1)F, (1)E, (1)A, (1)E, (1)F, (5)B, (1)A
Row 145 (R): (1)E, (7)B, (2)F, (4)D
Row 146 (L): (1)F, (4)D, (1)F, (1)D, (7)B
Row 147 (R): (8)B, (1)C, (1)B, (1)F, (2)D, (1)F
Row 148 (L): (1)C, (1)A, (2)D, (1)A, (6)B, (1)A, (2)B
Row 149 (R): (2)B, (1)E, (1)C, (4)B, (1)F, (1)E, (2)A, (1)C, (1)A
Row 150 (L): (2)A, (1)D, (1)E, (1)B, (1)A, (4)B, (1)A, (2)C, (1)E
Row 151 (R): (1)E, (1)C, (1)D, (1)F, (4)B, (1)E, (1)F, (2)E, (1)F, (1)A
Row 152 (L): (1)E, (1)A, (3)D, (1)F, (6)B, (1)D, (1)F
Row 153 (R): (1)C, (1)A, (1)D, (1)C, (5)B, (1)E, (3)D, (1)C
Row 154 (L): (2)F, (2)D, (1)A, (9)B
Row 155 (R): (2)B, (1)A, (1)E, (4)B, (1)A, (1)F, (1)C, (1)F, (1)C, (1)F
Row 156 (L): (1)D, (1)F, (1)C, (1)D, (10)B
Row 157 (R): (3)B, (1)C, (4)B, (1)C, (1)D, (1)B, (1)C, (2)B
Row 158 (L): (1)D, (1)A, (1)B, (1)D, (1)C, (1)D, (1)A, (7)B
Row 159 (R): (2)B, (1)E, (1)D, (4)B, (2)D, (1)F, (1)C, (2)B
Row 160 (L): (1)F, (1)E, (1)A, (3)D, (1)C, (4)B, (1)F, (2)B
Row 161 (R): (2)B, (1)F, (1)D, (3)B, (1)A, (4)D, (1)A, (1)E
Row 162 (L): (1)E, (1)F, (1)D, (1)C, (3)D, (1)F, (1)A, (1)B, (2)D, (1)F, (1)E
Row 163 (R): (2)C, (1)A, (1)B, (2)D, (2)F, (1)D, (1)C, (1)E, (1)B, (2)D
Row 164 (L): (1)B, (1)E, (1)F, (1)B, (1)D, (1)C, (2)D, (1)F, (2)D, (1)B, (2)A
Row 165 (R): (2)A, (2)B, (4)D, (1)F, (1)B, (1)C, (1)B, (1)D, (1)C
Row 166 (L): (2)B, (1)F, (1)E, (1)D, (1)E, (4)D, (1)F, (3)B
Row 167 (R): (1)E, (2)B, (1)A, (5)D, (1)F, (1)D, (2)F, (1)A
Row 168 (L): (2)A, (2)D, (2)F, (5)D, (1)F, (2)C
Row 169 (R): (2)D, (4)C, (3)D, (2)E, (1)B, (2)D
Row 170 (L): (2)D, (3)B, (1)C, (2)D, (1)E, (1)A, (1)B, (1)A, (1)E, (1)F
Row 171 (R): (2)D, (2)C, (2)B, (1)E, (2)D, (1)F, (1)B, (1)C, (1)B, (1)C
Row 172 (L): (1)D, (1)F, (1)B, (1)F, (1)D, (1)C, (2)D, (2)B, (1)C, (1)F, (2)E
Row 173 (R): (4)B, (1)F, (3)B, (1)D, (1)E, (1)D, (3)B
Row 174 (L): (1)E, (1)B, (1)D, (3)B, (1)D, (1)F, (2)B, (1)A, (3)B
Row 175 (R): (1)C, (3)B, (1)F, (1)C, (2)B, (1)F, (1)A, (1)E, (1)F, (1)D, (1)B
Row 176 (L): (6)B, (1)D, (1)E, (6)B
Row 177 (R): (1)D, (1)F, (2)B, (1)C, (1)F, (2)B, (1)F, (2)B, (1)F, (1)E, (1)F
Row 178 (L): (3)B, (1)F, (2)B, (1)D, (3)B, (1)A, (2)B, (1)E

Row 179 (R): (1)B, (1)C, (1)A, (1)B, (1)F, (1)C, (2)B, (1)D, (2)B, (1)C, (1)B, (1)F
Row 180 (L): (1)B, (1)F, (1)A, (1)D, (2)B, (1)D, (1)E, (2)B, (2)C, (2)D
Row 181 (R): (2)B, (1)F, (1)C, (1)A, (3)B, (1)D, (1)F, (1)E, (1)F, (2)B
Row 182 (L): (1)A, (1)D, (1)E, (1)D, (1)E, (1)C, (1)D, (1)F, (2)B, (2)A, (1)F, (1)B
Row 183 (R): (2)B, (1)D, (3)B, (1)E, (1)F, (4)D, (2)B
Row 184 (L): (1)F, (2)C, (5)D, (3)C, (1)B, (1)A, (1)B
Row 185 (R): (2)B, (1)D, (1)A, (4)D, (1)E, (1)A, (2)D, (2)B
Row 186 (L): (1)D, (1)E, (1)C, (1)D, (2)B, (1)A, (1)C, (1)D, (1)F, (4)B
Row 187 (R): (2)B, (1)D, (1)E, (1)F, (2)D, (1)F, (3)B, (1)F, (2)B
Row 188 (L): (1)D, (1)E, (1)A, (1)D, (4)B, (2)D, (2)B, (1)E, (1)B
Row 189 (R): (1)C, (1)A, (1)C, (1)A, (1)C, (1)D, (1)F, (1)E, (6)B
Row 190 (L): (1)D, (1)C, (1)B, (1)E, (4)B, (2)D, (2)B, (2)F
Row 191 (R): (1)B, (1)E, (2)B, (1)E, (1)D, (1)C, (6)B, (1)A
Row 192 (L): (1)D, (1)F, (1)B, (1)A, (4)B, (2)D, (4)B
Row 193 (R): (4)B, (1)C, (1)D, (1)F, (6)B, (1)E
Row 194 (L): (1)E, (1)F, (6)B, (2)D, (1)A, (3)B
Row 195 (R): (1)D, (3)B, (3)D, (5)B, (1)A, (1)F
Row 196 (L): (1)A, (1)C, (2)B, (2)A, (2)B, (2)D, (1)C, (1)A, (2)B

Pucci

This bracelet was inspired by the graceful swirl prints of the fabrics designed by Emilio Pucci. He frequently used shades of blue and aqua, but I decided to change it up a bit and opted for red with grays, black, and cream.

The pattern is 1½ in. (3.8cm) wide and up to 7½ in. (19.1cm) long.

note

For a traditional Pucci look, use the following colors:

A: DB-361, matte opaque cobalt
B: DB-1783, white lined capri blue AB
C: DB-352, matte cream
D: DB-2122, duracoat opaque catalina
E: DB-310, jet black matte

SUPPLIES

- 11° cylinder beads
  - 7–8g color A (Miyuki DB-1564, opaque cadillac red luster)
  - 2g color B (Miyuki DB-306, matte metallic slate)
  - 2–3g color C (Miyuki DB-352, matte cream)
  - 3g color D (Miyuki DB-1498, opaque light smoke)
  - 2g color E (Miyuki DB-310, jet black matte)
- Beading needle, size 10, 11, or 12
- Fireline, crystal, 6-lb. test
- 4-loop tube clasp
- Scissors, thread snips, or thread burner

A   B   C   D   E

The pattern is 1½ in. (3.8cm) wide and up to 7½ in. (19.1cm) long.

MAKE THE BRACELET

1. Follow the pattern or word chart below to complete the piece (see two-drop peyote stitch, p. 9), leaving an 8–10-in. (20–25cm) tail for adding the clasp. Add and end thread as needed.

2. Attach a 4-loop tube clasp to each end of the bracelet (see p. 7).

Rows 1 and 2 (L): (28)A
Row 3 (R): (10)A, (2)B, (2)A
Row 4 (L): (3)A, (2)B, (9)A
Row 5 (R): (10)A, (2)B, (2)A
Row 6 (L): (2)A, (4)B, (8)A
Row 7 (R): (8)A, (4)B, (2)A
Row 8 (L): (2)A, (5)B, (7)A
Row 9 (R): (8)A, (5)B, (1)A
Row 10 (L): (2)A, (6)B, (6)A
Row 11 (R): (6)A, (8)B
Row 12 (L): (2)A, (7)B, (5)A
Row 13 (R): (6)A, (8)B
Row 14 (L): (1)A, (9)B, (4)A
Row 15 (R): (5)A, (9)B
Row 16 (L): (10)B, (4)A
Row 17 (R): (4)A, (10)B
Row 18 (L): (11)B, (3)A
Row 19 (R): (4)A, (10)B
Row 20 (L): (12)B, (2)A
Row 21 (R): (3)A, (11)B
Row 22 (L): (12)B, (2)A
Row 23 (R): (2)A, (8)B, (2)A, (2)B
Row 24 (L): (2)B, (4)A, (6)B, (2)A
Row 25 (R): (2)A, (6)B, (2)A, (2)C, (2)A
Row 26 (L): (2)A, (4)C, (2)A, (5)B, (1)A
Row 27 (R): (2)A, (4)B, (2)A, (6)C
Row 28 (L): (8)C, (2)A, (4)B
Row 29 (R): (2)A, (2)B, (2)A, (8)C
Row 30 (L): (10)C, (1)A, (3)B
Row 31 (R): (1)A, (3)B, (1)A, (3)C, (2)A, (4)C
Row 32 (L): (4)C, (4)A, (2)C, (2)A, (2)B
Row 33 (R): (1)A, (2)B, (1)A, (2)C, (6)A, (2)C
Row 34 (L): (2)C, (8)A, (1)C, (1)A, (2)B
Row 35 (R): (2)B, (2)A, (1)C, (9)A
Row 36 (L): (2)C, (8)A, (2)C, (1)A, (1)B
Row 37 (R): (2)B, (2)C, (10)A
Row 38 (L): (1)C, (11)A, (1)C, (1)A
Row 39 (R): (1)B, (1)A, (1)C, (11)A
Row 40 (L): (12)A, (2)C
Row 41 (R): (1)A, (1)C, (12)A
Row 42 (L): (14)A
Row 43 (R): (1)C, (13)A
Row 44 (L): (14)A

Row 45 (R): (14)A
Row 46 (L): (14)A
Row 47 (R): (14)A
Row 48 (L): (1)C, (13)A
Row 49 (R): (14)A
Row 50 (L): (2)C, (12)A
Row 51 (R): (12)A, (2)C
Row 52 (L): (4)C, (10)A
Row 53 (R): (1)A, (1)D, (8)A, (4)C
Row 54 (L): (6)C, (2)A, (6)D
Row 55 (R): (1)A, (5)D, (8)C
Row 56 (L): (10)C, (4)D
Row 57 (R): (2)A, (2)D, (10)C
Row 58 (L): (12)C, (1)D, (1)A
Row 59 (R): (2)A, (2)D, (10)C
Row 60 (L): (10)C, (2)D, (2)A
Row 61 (R): (3)A, (3)D, (8)C
Row 62 (L): (8)C, (4)D, (2)A
Row 63 (R): (4)A, (4)D, (6)C
Row 64 (L): (6)C, (5)D, (3)A
Row 65 (R): (4)A, (10)D
Row 66 (L): (10)D, (4)A
Row 67 (R): (6)A, (8)D
Row 68 (L): (8)D, (6)A
Row 69 (R): (8)A, (6)D
Row 70 (L): (6)D, (8)A
Row 71 (R): (12)A, (2)D
Row 72 (L): (2)D, (12)A
Row 73 (R): (6)A, (4)D, (3)A, (1)D
Row 74 (L): (2)D, (2)A, (6)D, (4)A
Row 75 (R): (4)A, (8)D, (1)A, (1)D
Row 76 (L): (2)D, (2)A, (8)D, (2)A
Row 77 (R): (2)A, (10)D, (1)A, (1)D
Row 78 (L): (2)D, (2)A, (9)D, (1)A
Row 79 (R): (2)A, (9)D, (2)A, (1)D
Row 80 (L): (2)D, (2)A, (10)D
Row 81 (R): (1)A, (9)D, (2)A, (2)D
Row 82 (L): (2)D, (3)A, (9)D
Row 83 (R): (10)D, (2)A, (2)D
Row 84 (L): (2)D, (4)A, (8)D
Row 85 (R): (9)D, (3)A, (2)D
Row 86 (L): (2)D, (4)A, (8)D
Row 87 (R): (8)D, (4)A, (2)D
Row 88 (L): (1)C, (2)D, (5)A, (6)D
Row 89 (R): (6)D, (6)A, (2)D
Row 90 (L): (1)C, (2)D, (7)A, (4)D
Row 91 (R): (2)A, (2)D, (8)A, (2)D
Row 92 (L): (2)C, (2)D, (10)A
Row 93 (R): (12)A, (2)D
Row 94 (L): (2)C, (2)D, (10)A
Row 95 (R): (11)A, (2)D, (1)C
Row 96 (L): (2)C, (2)D, (10)A
Row 97 (R): (11)A, (1)D, (2)C
Row 98 (L): (2)C, (2)D, (10)A
Row 99 (R): (10)A, (2)D, (2)C
Row 100 (L): (3)C, (1)D, (10)A

(Continues on p. 66)

(Continues on p. 67)

Row 101 (R): (10)A, (2)D, (2)C
Row 102 (L): (4)C, (1)D, (9)A
Row 103 (R): (10)A, (2)D, (2)C
Row 104 (L): (4)C, (2)D, (8)A
Row 105 (R): (9)A, (2)D, (3)C
Row 106 (L): (4)C, (2)D, (8)A
Row 107 (R): (8)A, (2)D, (4)C
Row 108 (L): (5)C, (2)D, (7)A
Row 109 (R): (8)A, (2)D, (4)C
Row 110 (L): (6)C, (2)D, (6)A
Row 111 (R): (7)A, (2)D, (5)C
Row 112 (L): (6)C, (2)D, (6)A
Row 113 (R): (6)A, (2)D, (6)C
Row 114 (L): (7)C, (2)D, (5)A
Row 115 (R): (6)A, (2)D, (6)C
Row 116 (L): (8)C, (2)D, (4)A
Row 117 (R): (4)A, (3)D, (7)C
Row 118 (L): (8)C, (3)D, (3)A
Row 119 (R): (4)A, (2)D, (8)C
Row 120 (L): (10)C, (2)D, (2)A
Row 121 (R): (2)A, (3)D, (9)C
Row 122 (L): (10)C, (4)D
Row 123 (R): (4)D, (10)C
Row 124 (L): (1)D, (10)C, (3)D
Row 125 (R): (4)D, (10)C
Row 126 (L): (2)D, (10)C, (2)D
Row 127 (R): (2)D, (12)C
Row 128 (L): (2)D, (10)C, (2)D
Row 129 (R): (2)D, (11)C, (1)D
Row 130 (L): (1)A, (1)D, (10)C, (2)D
Row 131 (R): (4)D, (9)C, (1)D
Row 132 (L): (2)A, (9)C, (3)D
Row 133 (R): (2)A, (2)D, (8)C, (2)D
Row 134 (L): (1)E, (1)A, (8)C, (3)D, (1)A
Row 135 (R): (2)A, (4)D, (6)C, (1)D, (1)A
Row 136 (L): (2)E, (2)D, (4)C, (4)D, (2)A
Row 137 (R): (4)A, (8)D, (2)A
Row 138 (L): (2)E, (8)D, (4)A
Row 139 (R): (6)A, (6)D, (1)A, (1)E
Row 140 (L): (2)E, (2)A, (4)D, (6)A
Row 141 (R): (12)A, (2)E
Row 142 (L): (3)E, (11)A
Row 143 (R): (12)A, (2)E
Row 144 (L): (4)E, (10)A
Row 145 (R): (11)A, (3)E
Row 146 (L): (4)E, (10)A
Row 147 (R): (11)A, (3)E
Row 148 (L): (4)E, (10)A
Row 149 (R): (8)A, (1)B, (1)A, (4)E
Row 150 (L): (5)E, (1)A, (1)B, (7)A
Row 151 (R): (8)A, (1)B, (1)A, (4)E
Row 152 (L): (6)E, (2)B, (6)A
Row 153 (R): (6)A, (2)B, (2)A, (4)E
Row 154 (L): (6)E, (4)B, (4)A
Row 155 (R): (4)A, (4)B, (1)A, (5)E
Row 156 (L): (6)E, (1)A, (5)B, (2)A
Row 157 (R): (2)A, (6)B, (6)E

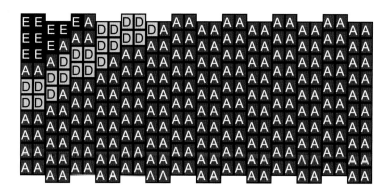

Row 158 (L): (7)E, (1)A, (6)B
Row 159 (R): (8)B, (6)E
Row 160 (L): (7)E, (1)A, (6)B
Row 161 (R): (6)B, (2)A, (6)E
Row 162 (L): (8)E, (2)C, (4)B
Row 163 (R): (4)B, (2)C, (1)A, (7)E
Row 164 (L): (1)A, (7)E, (1)A, (3)C, (2)B
Row 165 (R): (2)B, (4)C, (8)E
Row 166 (L): (1)A, (8)E, (1)A, (4)C
Row 167 (R): (5)C, (1)A, (8)E
Row 168 (L): (1)D, (1)A, (8)E, (4)C
Row 169 (R): (4)C, (1)A, (8)E, (1)A
Row 170 (L): (2)D, (8)E, (2)A, (2)C
Row 171 (R): (3)C, (1)A, (8)E, (1)A, (1)D
Row 172 (L): (2)D, (1)A, (8)E, (1)A, (2)C
Row 173 (R): (2)C, (2)A, (8)E, (2)D
Row 174 (L): (1)A, (2)D, (1)A, (8)E, (1)A, (1)C
Row 175 (R): (2)C, (1)A, (9)E, (2)D
Row 176 (L): (2)A, (2)D, (8)E, (2)A
Row 177 (R): (2)A, (8)E, (2)A, (1)D, (1)A
Row 178 (L): (2)A, (2)D, (9)E, (1)A
Row 179 (R): (2)A, (8)E, (2)D, (2)A
Row 180 (L): (2)E, (1)A, (1)D, (2)A, (8)E
Row 181 (R): (10)E, (2)D, (1)A, (1)E

Row 182 (L): (2)E, (2)A, (2)D, (8)E
Row 183 (R): (9)E, (1)A, (1)D, (2)A, (1)E
Row 184 (L): (2)E, (2)A, (2)D, (8)E
Row 185 (R): (8)E, (2)D, (2)A, (2)E
Row 186 (L): (2)E, (2)A, (2)D, (1)A, (7)E
Row 187 (R): (8)E, (2)D, (2)A, (2)E
Row 188 (L): (2)E, (4)A, (2)D, (6)E
Row 189 (R): (6)E, (2)A, (2)D, (2)A, (2)E
Row 190 (L): (2)E, (4)A, (2)D, (6)E
Row 191 (R): (6)E, (3)D, (3)A, (2)E
Row 192 (L): (2)E, (4)A, (2)D, (2)A, (4)E
Row 193 (R): (5)E, (1)A, (2)D, (5)A, (1)E
Row 194 (L): (2)E, (6)A, (2)D, (4)E
Row 195 (R): (4)E, (1)A, (2)D, (7)A
Row 196 (L): (2)E, (6)A, (2)D, (2)A, (2)E
Row 197 (R): (3)E, (1)A, (2)D, (8)A
Row 198 (L): (9)A, (3)D, (2)E
Row 199 (R): (2)E, (2)A, (2)D, (8)A
Row 200 (L): (10)A, (2)D, (1)A, (1)E
Row 201 (R): (2)E, (2)D, (10)A
Row 202 (L): (11)A, (2)D, (1)A
Row 203 (R): (2)A, (2)D, (10)A
Row 204 (L): (12)A, (2)D
Row 205 (R): (2)D, (12)A

Row 206 (L): (13)A, (1)D
Row 207 (R): (2)D, (12)A
Row 208 (L): (14)A
Row 209 (R): (14)A
Row 210 (L): (14)A
Row 211 (R): (14)A
Row 212 (L): (14)A
Row 213 (R): (14)A
Row 214 (L): (14)A
Row 215 (R): (14)A
Row 216 (L): (14)A

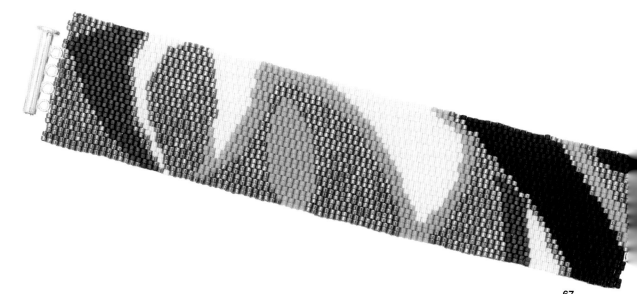

Floral Swirls

I came across a piece of vintage fabric with gracefully curved stylized flowers and immediately thought of the paper cutouts created by Henri Matisse later in his career.

note

I chose picasso finish turquoise beads because it gives the appearance of fabric with nubby texture. Choose a color combination with strong contrast, one that's monochromatic, or elegant, or fun—it's entirely up to you.

SUPPLIES

- 11º cylinder beads
  - 7–8g color A (Miyuki DB-2264, opaque turquoise blue picasso)
  - 7.5–8.25g color B (Miyuki DB-1490, opaque bisque white)
- Beading needle, size 10, 11, or 12
- Fireline, crystal, 6-lb. test
- 4-loop tube clasp
- Scissors, thread snips, or thread burner

A   B

The pattern measures 1½ in. (3.8cm) wide and up to 7½ in. (19.1cm) long, not including the clasp.

MAKE THE BRACELET

1. Follow the pattern or word chart below to complete the piece (see two-drop peyote stitch, p. 9), leaving an 8–10-in. (20–25cm) tail for adding the clasp. Add and end thread as needed.

2. Attach a 4-loop tube clasp to each end of the bracelet (see p. 7).

Rows 1 and 2 (L): (12)A, (14)B, (2)A
Row 3 (R): (1)A, (8)B, (5)A
Row 4 (L): (2)A, (2)B, (2)A, (8)B
Row 5 (R): (9)B, (2)A, (3)B
Row 6 (L): (1)A, (3)B, (2)A, (8)B
Row 7 (R): (2)B, (2)A, (3)B, (1)A, (6)B
Row 8 (L): (2)A, (5)B, (1)A, (3)B, (3)A
Row 9 (R): (4)A, (3)B, (1)A, (4)B, (2)A
Row 10 (L): (2)A, (4)B, (2)A, (1)B, (1)A, (2)B, (2)A
Row 11 (R): (4)A, (4)B, (1)A, (3)B, (2)A
Row 12 (L): (3)A, (3)B, (2)A, (1)B, (1)A, (2)B, (2)A
Row 13 (R): (3)A, (5)B, (2)A, (2)B, (2)A
Row 14 (L): (3)A, (3)B, (1)A, (1)B, (2)A, (2)B, (2)A
Row 15 (R): (3)A, (2)B, (1)A, (2)B, (2)A, (2)B, (2)A
Row 16 (L): (3)A, (3)B, (1)A, (1)B, (2)A, (2)B, (2)A
Row 17 (R): (1)B, (5)A, (2)B, (2)A, (2)B, (2)A
Row 18 (L): (2)A, (6)B, (6)A
Row 19 (R): (2)B, (4)A, (2)B, (2)A, (2)B, (2)A

Row 20 (L): (2)A, (3)B, (1)A, (2)B, (4)A, (2)B
Row 21 (R): (1)A, (3)B, (3)A, (1)B, (2)A, (3)B, (1)A
Row 22 (L): (2)A, (3)B, (1)A, (2)B, (2)A, (4)B
Row 23 (R): (2)A, (4)B, (4)A, (4)B
Row 24 (L): (6)B, (3)A, (3)B, (2)A
Row 25 (R): (4)A, (2)B, (4)A, (4)B
Row 26 (L): (6)B, (2)A, (2)B, (4)A
Row 27 (R): (5)A, (9)B
Row 28 (L): (10)B, (4)A
Row 29 (R): (5)A, (9)B
Row 30 (L): (2)A, (8)B, (4)A
Row 31 (R): (2)B, (2)A, (8)B, (2)A
Row 32 (L): (3)A, (11)B
Row 33 (R): (12)B, (2)A
Row 34 (L): (2)A, (4)B, (2)A, (6)B
Row 35 (R): (6)B, (4)A, (4)B
Row 36 (L): (4)B, (6)A, (4)B
Row 37 (R): (4)B, (8)A, (2)B
Row 38 (L): (2)B, (10)A, (2)B
Row 39 (R): (2)B, (11)A, (1)B
Row 40 (L): (2)B, (4)A, (2)B, (5)A, (1)B
Row 41 (R): (2)B, (5)A, (3)B, (4)A
Row 42 (L): (2)B, (4)A, (2)B, (6)A
Row 43 (R): (4)A, (2)B, (1)A, (3)B, (4)A
Row 44 (L): (1)B, (5)A, (2)B, (1)A, (2)B, (3)A
Row 45 (R): (4)A, (2)B, (2)A, (2)B, (4)A
Row 46 (L): (1)B, (5)A, (5)B, (3)A
Row 47 (R): (4)A, (8)B, (2)A
Row 48 (L): (1)B, (1)A, (3)B, (1)A, (4)B, (4)A
Row 49 (R): (5)A, (8)B, (1)A
Row 50 (L): (1)B, (1)A, (8)B, (4)A
Row 51 (R): (4)A, (9)B, (1)A
Row 52 (L): (12)B, (2)A
Row 53 (R): (3)A, (9)B, (2)A
Row 54 (L): (2)B, (2)A, (8)B, (2)A
Row 55 (R): (3)A, (8)B, (2)A, (1)B
Row 56 (L): (2)B, (2)A, (8)B, (2)A
Row 57 (R): (4)A, (7)B, (1)A, (2)B
Row 58 (L): (10)B, (4)A
Row 59 (R): (6)A, (8)B
Row 60 (L): (10)B, (4)A
Row 61 (R): (4)A, (10)B
Row 62 (L): (11)B, (3)A
Row 63 (R): (4)A, (6)B, (2)A, (2)B
Row 64 (L): (2)B, (3)A, (6)B, (3)A
Row 65 (R): (4)A, (2)B, (2)A, (2)B, (4)A
Row 66 (L): (4)A, (2)B, (4)A, (1)B, (3)A
Row 67 (R): (2)B, (2)A, (2)B, (2)A, (2)B, (4)A
Row 68 (L): (4)A, (2)B, (6)A, (2)B
Row 69 (R): (3)B, (11)A
Row 70 (L): (12)A, (2)B
Row 71 (R): (2)A, (2)B, (10)A
Row 72 (L): (10)A, (4)B
Row 73 (R): (2)A, (6)B, (4)A, (2)B
Row 74 (L): (1)A, (3)B, (2)A, (8)B
Row 75 (R): (14)B
Row 76 (L): (14)B

(Continues on p. 70)

(Continues on p. 71)

Row 77 (R): (2)B, (6)A, (6)B
Row 78 (L): (6)B, (7)A, (1)B
Row 79 (R): (2)B, (4)A, (1)B, (2)A, (5)B
Row 80 (L): (2)A, (4)B, (2)A, (2)B, (4)A
Row 81 (R): (6)A, (2)B, (2)A, (2)B, (2)A
Row 82 (L): (3)A, (2)B, (3)A, (2)B, (4)A
Row 83 (R): (2)A, (2)B, (2)A, (2)B, (2)A, (2)B, (2)A
Row 84 (L): (2)A, (2)B, (3)A, (2)B, (1)A, (2)B, (2)A
Row 85 (R): (2)A, (3)B, (1)A, (4)B, (1)A, (2)B, (1)A
Row 86 (L): (2)A, (6)B, (2)A, (2)B, (2)A
Row 87 (R): (3)A, (7)B, (2)A, (2)B
Row 88 (L): (3)B, (1)A, (8)B, (2)A
Row 89 (R): (4)A, (6)B, (2)A, (2)B
Row 90 (L): (2)B, (3)A, (5)B, (4)A
Row 91 (R): (5)A, (5)B, (2)A, (2)B
Row 92 (L): (2)B, (4)A, (4)B, (4)A
Row 93 (R): (3)A, (7)B, (2)A, (2)B
Row 94 (L): (2)B, (4)A, (6)B, (2)A
Row 95 (R): (3)A, (7)B, (2)A, (2)B
Row 96 (L): (1)A, (1)B, (3)A, (7)B, (2)A
Row 97 (R): (4)A, (6)B, (2)A, (2)B
Row 98 (L): (1)A, (1)B, (2)A, (7)B, (3)A
Row 99 (R): (4)A, (4)B, (2)A, (1)B, (1)A, (2)B
Row 100 (L): (1)A, (1)B, (2)A, (8)B, (2)A
Row 101 (R): (3)A, (5)B, (4)A, (2)B
Row 102 (L): (1)A, (1)B, (5)A, (5)B, (2)A
Row 103 (R): (2)A, (2)B, (1)A, (3)B, (4)A, (2)B
Row 104 (L): (1)A, (2)B, (3)A, (4)B, (1)A, (1)B, (2)A
Row 105 (R): (2)A, (2)B, (1)A, (3)B, (4)A, (2)B
Row 106 (L): (2)A, (1)B, (3)A, (4)B, (4)A
Row 107 (R): (2)A, (2)B, (1)A, (1)B, (2)A, (1)B, (3)A, (2)B
Row 108 (L): (2)A, (2)B, (2)A, (4)B, (4)A
Row 109 (R): (5)A, (1)B, (2)A, (5)B, (1)A
Row 110 (L): (2)A, (5)B, (1)A, (2)B, (4)A
Row 111 (R): (5)A, (1)B, (2)A, (5)B, (1)A
Row 112 (L): (2)A, (4)B, (2)A, (2)B, (4)A
Row 113 (R): (5)A, (2)B, (2)A, (3)B, (2)A
Row 114 (L): (3)A, (3)B, (2)A, (2)B, (4)A
Row 115 (R): (5)A, (2)B, (3)A, (2)B, (2)A
Row 116 (L): (4)A, (2)B, (2)A, (2)B, (4)A
Row 117 (R): (4)A, (4)B, (2)A, (2)B, (2)A
Row 118 (L): (4)A, (2)B, (2)A, (3)B, (3)A
Row 119 (R): (4)A, (4)B, (2)A, (1)B, (3)A
Row 120 (L): (4)A, (1)B, (2)A, (4)B, (3)A
Row 121 (R): (4)A, (4)B, (2)A, (1)B, (3)A
Row 122 (L): (4)A, (1)B, (2)A, (3)B, (2)A, (2)B
Row 123 (R): (3)B, (2)A, (3)B, (2)A, (1)B, (3)A
Row 124 (L): (4)A, (1)B, (3)A, (2)B, (2)A, (2)B
Row 125 (R): (3)B, (3)A, (2)B, (2)A, (2)B, (2)A
Row 126 (L): (4)A, (1)B, (3)A, (2)B, (2)A, (2)B
Row 127 (R): (4)B, (6)A, (4)B
Row 128 (L): (5)B, (6)A, (3)B
Row 129 (R): (2)A, (2)B, (6)A, (4)B
Row 130 (L): (6)B, (4)A, (3)B, (1)A
Row 131 (R): (2)A, (2)B, (6)A, (4)B
Row 132 (L): (1)A, (5)B, (4)A, (3)B, (1)A

Row 133 (R): (2)A, (3)B, (5)A, (4)B
Row 134 (L): (2)A, (4)B, (4)A, (2)B, (2)A
Row 135 (R): (6)B, (4)A, (2)B, (2)A
Row 136 (L): (2)A, (4)B, (3)A, (3)B, (1)A, (1)B
Row 137 (R): (2)B, (1)A, (3)B, (3)A, (3)B, (2)A
Row 138 (L): (3)A, (3)B, (2)A, (4)B, (1)A, (1)B
Row 139 (R): (2)B, (2)A, (2)B, (2)A, (4)B, (2)A
Row 140 (L): (4)A, (2)B, (2)A, (4)B, (1)A, (1)B
Row 141 (R): (2)B, (2)A, (2)B, (2)A, (3)B, (3)A
Row 142 (L): (1)B, (3)A, (3)B, (1)A, (3)B, (3)A
Row 143 (R): (2)B, (2)A, (2)B, (2)A, (2)B, (4)A
Row 144 (L): (2)B, (2)A, (3)B, (1)A, (2)B, (4)A
Row 145 (R): (4)B, (1)A, (1)B, (2)A, (2)B, (4)A
Row 146 (L): (2)B, (3)A, (2)B, (1)A, (2)B, (2)A, (1)B, (1)A
Row 147 (R): (4)B, (2)A, (1)B, (1)A, (2)B, (4)A
Row 148 (L): (2)B, (4)A, (1)B, (1)A, (2)B, (1)A, (3)B
Row 149 (R): (4)B, (2)A, (4)B, (1)A, (1)B, (2)A
Row 150 (L): (2)B, (1)A, (1)B, (2)A, (1)B, (1)A, (1)B, (3)A, (2)B
Row 151 (R): (2)B, (4)A, (6)B, (1)A, (1)B
Row 152 (L): (5)B, (1)A, (3)B, (3)A, (2)B
Row 153 (R): (2)B, (4)A, (3)B, (1)A, (4)B
Row 154 (L): (5)B, (1)A, (2)B, (4)A, (2)B
Row 155 (R): (3)B, (3)A, (3)B, (1)A, (4)B
Row 156 (L): (2)B, (4)A, (2)B, (4)A, (2)B
Row 157 (R): (4)B, (2)A, (3)B, (3)A, (2)B
Row 158 (L): (3)B, (3)A, (2)B, (3)A, (3)B
Row 159 (R): (4)B, (2)A, (4)B, (2)A, (2)B
Row 160 (L): (3)B, (3)A, (2)B, (2)A, (4)B
Row 161 (R): (4)B, (2)A, (4)B, (2)A, (2)B
Row 162 (L): (2)B, (3)A, (3)B, (3)A, (3)B
Row 163 (R): (2)B, (4)A, (4)B, (2)A, (2)B
Row 164 (L): (1)B, (4)A, (4)B, (4)A, (1)B
Row 165 (R): (2)B, (4)A, (4)B, (4)A
Row 166 (L): (2)B, (3)A, (5)B, (4)A
Row 167 (R): (2)B, (2)A, (6)B, (4)A
Row 168 (L): (2)B, (3)A, (5)B, (4)A
Row 169 (R): (2)B, (2)A, (6)B, (2)A, (2)B
Row 170 (L): (3)B, (3)A, (5)B, (3)A

Row 171 (R): (1)B, (3)A, (6)B, (2)A, (2)B
Row 172 (L): (4)B, (2)A, (6)B, (2)A
Row 173 (R): (3)A, (6)B, (3)A, (2)B
Row 174 (L): (4)B, (2)A, (6)B, (2)A
Row 175 (R): (2)A, (7)B, (3)A, (2)B
Row 176 (L): (1)B, (5)A, (7)B, (1)A
Row 177 (R): (2)A, (8)B, (4)A
Row 178 (L): (1)B, (5)A, (2)B, (2)A, (4)B
Row 179 (R): (2)A, (2)B, (4)A, (2)B, (4)A
Row 180 (L): (1)B, (4)A, (2)B, (3)A, (4)B
Row 181 (R): (1)A, (3)B, (4)A, (2)B, (4)A
Row 182 (L): (1)B, (4)A, (1)B, (5)A, (3)B
Row 183 (R): (4)B, (4)A, (2)B, (4)A
Row 184 (L): (2)B, (3)A, (1)B, (5)A, (3)B
Row 185 (R): (4)B, (4)A, (2)B, (3)A, (1)B
Row 186 (L): (2)B, (2)A, (2)B, (5)A, (3)B
Row 187 (R): (4)B, (4)A, (2)B, (3)A, (1)B
Row 188 (L): (2)B, (2)A, (2)B, (5)A, (3)B
Row 189 (R): (4)B, (4)A, (3)B, (3)A
Row 190 (L): (1)B, (3)A, (2)B, (5)A, (3)B
Row 191 (R): (6)B, (3)A, (3)B, (2)A
Row 192 (L): (1)B, (3)A, (2)B, (4)A, (4)B
Row 193 (R): (6)B, (3)A, (3)B, (2)A
Row 194 (L): (1)B, (3)A, (2)B, (4)A, (4)B
Row 195 (R): (5)B, (4)A, (3)B, (2)A
Row 196 (L): (1)B, (3)A, (2)B, (4)A, (4)B
Row 197 (R): (4)B, (4)A, (3)B, (3)A
Row 198 (L): (2)B, (2)A, (4)B, (2)A, (4)B
Row 199 (R): (1)A, (3)B, (2)A, (5)B, (3)A
Row 200 (L): (2)B, (2)A, (4)B, (3)A, (3)B
Row 201 (R): (1)A, (3)B, (2)A, (5)B, (2)A, (1)B
Row 202 (L): (2)B, (2)A, (4)B, (4)A, (2)B
Row 203 (R): (7)A, (7)B
Row 204 (L): (8)B, (6)A
Row 205 (R): (7)A, (7)B
Row 206 (L): (8)B, (6)A
Row 207 (R): (2)B, (6)A, (6)B
Row 208 (L): (6)B, (7)A, (1)B
Row 209 (R): (2)B, (7)A, (5)B
Row 210 (L): (6)B, (6)A, (2)B
Row 211 (R): (2)B, (8)A, (4)B
Row 212 (L): (2)A, (4)B, (7)A, (1)B

Row 213 (R): (2)B, (6)A, (4)B, (2)A
Row 214 (L): (4)A, (3)B, (7)A
Row 215 (R): (1)B, (7)A, (2)B, (4)A
Row 216 (L): (5)A, (2)B, (7)A
Row 217 (R): (8)A, (2)B, (4)A
Row 218 (L): (6)A, (2)B, (6)A

Ukranian Embroidery

In much of Eastern Europe, embroidery
is commonly used to decorate clothing,
tablecloths, and other textiles. While
traditionally done in red, black, and white,
other colors are also used.

SUPPLIES

- 11° cylinder beads
  - 4g color A (Miyuki DB-1588, matte opaque cyan blue)
  - 4g color B (Miyuki DB-2, metallic dark blue AB)
  - 4g color C (Miyuki DB-1490, opaque bisque white)
  - 4g color D (Miyuki DB-725, opaque turquoise blue)
- Beading needle, size 10, 11, or 12
- Fireline, crystal, 6-lb. test
- 4-loop tube clasp
- Scissors, thread snips, or thread burner

A B C D

This bracelet is 7 in. (18cm) long, not including the clasp.

MAKE THE BRACELET

1. Follow the pattern or word chart below to complete the piece (see two-drop peyote stitch, p. 9), leaving an 8–10-in. (20–25cm) tail for adding the clasp. Add and end thread as needed.

2. Attach a 4-loop tube clasp to each end of the bracelet (see p. 7).

Rows 1 and 2 (L): (1)A, (2)D, (2)A, (1)D, (1)C, (1)B, (3)C, (3)B, (3)A, (3)D, (1)B, (1)D, (1)C, (1)B, (1)A, (1)D, (1)B, (1)A

Row 3 (R): (1)B, (1)C, (2)D, (1)C, (1)D, (1)A, (1)B, (2)A, (1)D, (2)B, (1)C

Row 4 (L): (3)C, (1)B, (1)C, (1)D, (1)A, (1)B, (2)A, (1)D, (1)B, (2)C

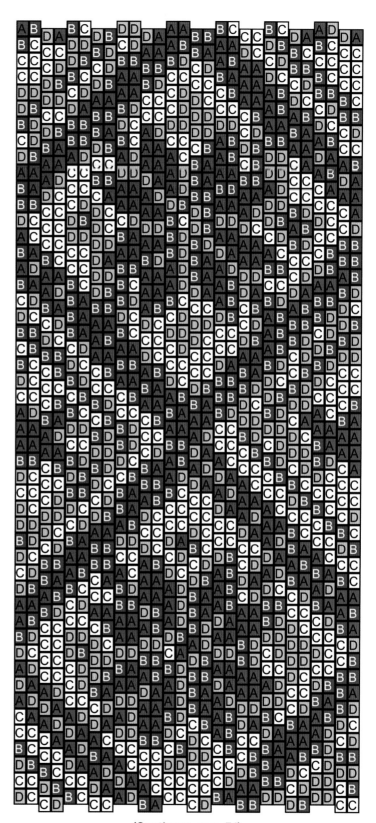

(Continues on p. 74)

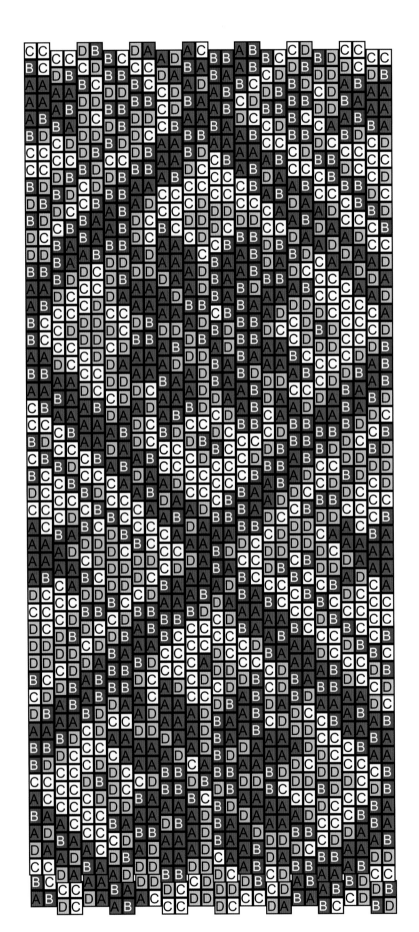

Row 5 (R): (2)C, (1)D, (4)B, (1)D, (1)A, (1)B, (1)C, (1)D, (2)C

Row 6 (L): (2)C, (2)B, (2)A, (1)D, (1)C, (2)B, (1)D, (1)C, (1)D, (1)C

Row 7 (R): (2)C, (1)B, (1)C, (2)A, (2)C, (1)B, (1)A, (1)D, (1)C, (1)B, (1)C

Row 8 (L): (2)C, (1)D, (1)C, (2)A, (2)C, (1)D, (2)B, (1)D, (1)B, (1)D

Row 9 (R): (2)D, (1)C, (1)D, (2)A, (1)C, (1)D, (1)C, (1)B, (1)A, (3)B

Row 10 (L): (1)C, (1)B, (1)C, (1)D, (2)A, (1)C, (1)D, (2)C, (2)A, (2)D

Row 11 (R): (1)D, (1)B, (1)D, (1)A, (1)B, (1)D, (1)C, (1)D, (2)C, (1)A, (1)B, (1)C, (1)D

Row 12 (L): (3)B, (1)A, (1)B, (1)C, (2)D, (2)C, (2)B, (2)C

Row 13 (R): (1)B, (1)D, (2)B, (1)D, (1)C, (4)D, (2)A, (1)D, (1)C

Row 14 (L): (1)D, (1)C, (1)A, (1)B, (1)D, (1)C, (3)D, (2)A, (2)B, (1)D

Row 15 (R): (1)C, (1)D, (3)B, (3)C, (1)A, (3)B, (1)A, (1)B

Row 16 (L): (2)C, (2)A, (1)B, (1)D, (1)B, (1)C, (2)A, (1)B, (1)D, (1)A, (1)B

Row 17 (R): (1)D, (1)B, (1)A, (1)D, (1)A, (1)D, (1)A, (1)C, (1)A, (1)B, (3)D, (1)A

Row 18 (L): (1)B, (2)A, (1)C, (1)B, (1)C, (1)A, (1)B, (2)A, (2)C, (2)A

Row 19 (R): (2)A, (2)C, (2)D, (1)A, (1)D, (2)A, (2)D, (1)A, (1)B

Row 20 (L): (1)A, (1)D, (2)C, (2)B, (1)A, (1)B, (1)A, (1)D, (2)B, (1)D, (1)A

Row 21 (R): (1)B, (1)A, (2)C, (3)A, (1)D, (2)B, (1)A, (1)D, (1)C, (1)A

Row 22 (L): (2)A, (2)C, (2)A, (2)B, (1)D, (2)A, (2)C, (1)D

Row 23 (R): (2)B, (1)C, (1)D, (2)A, (1)D, (1)B, (2)A, (2)D, (2)C

Row 24 (L): (1)A, (1)C, (1)D, (1)B, (1)D, (1)A, (1)B, (1)D, (2)A, (1)C, (1)D, (2)C

Row 25 (R): (1)D, (1)C, (1)D, (1)B, (1)C, (1)D, (1)B, (1)C, (3)D, (1)B, (1)D, (1)C

Row 26 (L): (1)D, (1)C, (1)B, (1)A, (1)C, (1)D, (1)B, (3)D, (1)C, (1)D, (2)C

Row 27 (R): (1)A, (1)C, (2)D, (1)B, (1)A, (1)B, (1)D, (2)A, (1)C, (1)D, (2)C

Row 28 (L): (2)B, (1)D, (1)B, (2)A, (1)D, (1)B, (2)A, (2)D, (2)C

Row 29 (R): (1)B, (1)A, (2)C, (2)A, (1)B, (2)D, (2)A, (2)C, (1)B

Row 30 (L): (2)B, (2)C, (3)A, (1)B, (1)D, (1)B, (1)A, (1)D, (1)C, (1)B

Row 31 (R): (1)A, (1)D, (2)C, (2)B, (1)A, (1)D, (1)A, (1)D, (2)B, (1)D, (1)B

Row 32 (L): (1)B, (1)A, (1)D, (1)C, (2)D, (1)A, (1)B, (2)A, (2)D, (2)A

Row 33 (R): (1)B, (1)A, (1)B, (1)C, (1)B, (1)C, (1)A, (1)D, (1)A, (1)B, (2)C, (2)A

Row 34 (L): (1)D, (1)B, (1)A, (1)D, (1)A, (1)D, (1)A, (1)D, (2)A, (1)B, (2)D, (1)A

Row 35 (R): (1)C, (1)D, (1)B, (1)A, (1)B, (1)D, (1)B, (1)C, (1)A, (2)B, (1)D, (2)B

Row 36 (L): (1)C, (1)D, (1)B, (1)A, (1)B, (3)C, (1)B, (1)A, (2)B, (1)A, (1)B

Row 37 (R): (1)D, (1)C, (1)B, (1)A, (1)D, (2)C, (2)D, (1)B, (1)A, (2)B, (1)D

Row 38 (L): (1)B, (1)D, (2)B, (1)D, (1)C, (2)D, (1)C, (1)D, (2)A, (1)D, (1)C

Row 39 (R): (3)B, (1)A, (1)B, (1)C, (2)D, (2)C, (1)A, (1)B, (1)C, (1)D

Row 40 (L): (1)D, (1)B, (1)D, (2)B, (1)D, (1)C, (1)D, (2)C, (1)B, (1)A, (1)C, (1)D

Row 41 (R): (1)C, (1)B, (1)C, (1)D, (2)A, (1)C, (1)D, (2)C, (1)A, (1)B, (1)D, (1)B

Row 42 (L): (3)D, (1)C, (2)A, (3)C, (1)D, (2)A, (2)B

Row 43 (R): (1)B, (1)C, (1)D, (1)C, (2)B, (2)C, (1)D, (1)A, (1)B, (1)D, (1)B, (1)D

Row 44 (L): (2)C, (1)B, (1)C, (1)A, (1)B, (2)C, (1)B, (1)A, (1)B, (1)C, (1)B, (1)C

Row 45 (R): (1)D, (1)C, (1)B, (1)D, (2)A, (1)D, (1)C, (2)B, (1)D, (1)C, (1)D, (1)C

Row 46 (L): (2)C, (1)D, (1)B, (1)D, (2)B, (1)D, (1)A, (1)B, (4)C

Row 47 (R): (3)C, (1)B, (1)C, (1)B, (1)A, (3)B, (1)D, (1)B, (2)C

Row 48 (L): (1)B, (1)C, (2)D, (1)C, (1)D, (1)A, (1)B, (2)A, (1)D, (2)B, (1)C

Row 49 (R): (1)A, (1)D, (1)B, (3)C, (1)B, (1)A, (1)B, (1)D, (1)B, (1)D, (1)A, (1)C

Row 50 (L): (1)A, (1)B, (1)A, (1)C, (2)D, (2)A, (1)B, (1)C, (1)B, (1)C, (1)A, (1)B

Row 51 (R): (2)A, (2)D, (1)B, (1)D, (2)A, (2)C, (2)D, (2)A

Row 52 (L): (2)A, (1)C, (2)D, (1)B, (1)D, (1)A, (2)C, (1)D, (1)B, (1)D, (1)A

Row 53 (R): (2)A, (2)C, (1)B, (1)D, (2)B, (3)C, (1)D, (1)B, (1)A

Row 54 (L): (2)A, (2)D, (1)B, (1)C, (1)A, (2)D, (1)C, (2)D, (2)A

Row 55 (R): (3)B, (2)D, (1)C, (1)A, (1)B, (1)A, (1)C, (1)B, (1)D, (1)B, (1)D

Row 56 (L): (1)A, (1)C, (1)D, (3)C, (1)D, (2)A, (1)B, (1)D, (2)B, (1)C

Row 57 (R): (1)D, (1)C, (1)D, (1)B, (1)C, (1)B, (1)A, (2)D, (1)A, (1)C, (1)B, (1)D, (1)C

Row 58 (L): (3)C, (1)B, (1)C, (2)A, (1)D, (2)B, (1)C, (1)D, (2)C

Row 59 (R): (2)C, (3)B, (1)A, (1)B, (1)C, (1)A, (1)D, (4)C

Row 60 (L): (2)C, (1)B, (1)D, (2)A, (2)C, (1)B, (1)A, (1)D, (1)C, (1)D, (1)C

Row 61 (R): (1)D, (1)C, (1)D, (1)C, (1)B, (1)A, (2)C, (1)D, (2)A, (1)C, (1)B, (1)C

Row 62 (L): (1)D, (3)C, (1)D, (1)A, (3)C, (1)D, (1)B, (3)D

Row 63 (R): (2)D, (1)C, (1)D, (1)A, (1)B, (4)C, (2)A, (1)C, (1)B

Row 64 (L): (1)C, (1)B, (1)C, (1)B, (1)A, (1)D, (1)C, (1)D, (2)C, (2)A, (1)C, (1)D

Row 65 (R): (1)B, (1)D, (1)B, (1)A, (3)D, (1)A, (2)C, (1)A, (1)D, (2)C

Row 66 (L): (1)B, (1)D, (1)A, (1)B, (3)C, (1)B, (1)C, (1)D, (2)B, (1)D, (1)C

Row 67 (R): (1)D, (1)C, (2)A, (3)C, (2)D, (1)B, (1)D, (2)A, (1)C

Row 68 (L): (2)C, (1)B, (1)A, (1)D, (1)C, (1)D, (1)C, (1)B, (1)A, (4)B

Row 69 (R): (1)C, (1)D, (1)A, (1)B, (1)A, (1)C, (1)D, (1)C, (1)A, (1)B, (1)A, (1)D, (1)B, (1)A

Row 70 (L): (1)C, (1)B, (1)A, (1)B, (1)A, (1)D, (1)B, (1)D, (3)A, (1)C, (1)A, (1)B

Row 71 (R): (1)D, (2)B, (1)C, (1)B, (1)D, (1)A, (1)D, (1)A, (1)B, (1)D, (1)C, (1)A, (1)D

Row 72 (L): (2)A, (1)D, (1)C, (1)D, (1)C, (1)A, (1)B, (2)A, (2)C, (1)B, (1)A

Row 73 (R): (2)A, (1)C, (1)D, (2)B, (1)A, (1)D, (1)A, (4)B, (1)A

Row 74 (L): (1)B, (1)A, (2)C, (3)A, (2)B, (1)D, (2)A, (1)D, (1)B

Row 75 (R): (1)A, (1)B, (2)C, (3)A, (2)D, (1)A, (1)B, (1)D, (1)C, (1)D

Row 76 (L): (1)A, (1)B, (1)C, (1)D, (2)A, (1)D, (2)B, (1)A, (1)B, (3)C

Row 77 (R): (1)B, (3)D, (2)A, (1)D, (1)B, (2)A, (2)D, (2)C

Row 78 (L): (1)D, (1)C, (3)D, (1)B, (1)D, (1)A, (2)D, (1)C, (1)D, (2)C

Row 79 (R): (1)D, (1)C, (1)D, (1)B, (2)D, (1)C, (1)A, (2)D, (1)C, (2)D, (1)C

Row 80 (L): (1)B, (1)C, (3)D, (2)B, (1)D, (2)B, (2)D, (2)C

Row 81 (R): (1)A, (1)D, (1)C, (1)D, (1)B, (1)A, (1)B, (1)D, (2)A, (4)C

Row 82 (L): (2)B, (1)C, (1)D, (2)A, (3)B, (1)A, (1)B, (1)D, (2)C

Row 83 (R): (1)D, (1)A, (1)C, (1)D, (3)A, (2)D, (2)A, (2)D, (1)B

Row 84 (L): (1)A, (1)B, (2)C, (3)A, (1)B, (1)A, (1)D, (1)A, (1)B, (1)D, (1)A

Row 85 (R): (1)A, (1)D, (2)C, (2)D, (1)A, (1)D, (1)A, (3)D, (1)B, (1)A

Row 86 (L): (1)D, (1)B, (1)D, (1)C, (2)D, (1)A, (1)B, (2)A, (1)D, (1)C, (1)A, (1)D

Row 87 (R): (1)C, (2)A, (1)D, (1)A, (1)D, (1)B, (1)D, (1)A, (2)B, (1)C, (1)A, (1)B

Row 88 (L): (1)C, (1)D, (1)A, (1)B, (1)A, (1)D, (1)B, (1)C, (3)A, (2)D, (1)A

Row 89 (R): (2)C, (1)D, (1)A, (3)D, (1)C, (1)A, (1)B, (1)D, (2)A, (1)D

Row 90 (L): (1)D, (1)C, (2)A, (3)C, (1)D, (2)B, (1)C, (2)A, (1)C

Row 91 (R): (1)B, (1)C, (1)A, (1)D, (3)C, (1)B, (1)C, (2)B, (1)A, (1)B, (1)D

Row 92 (L): (3)B, (1)A, (1)B, (1)C, (2)D, (2)C, (1)A, (1)B, (2)C

Row 93 (R): (1)D, (1)B, (1)D, (2)A, (1)C, (2)D, (2)C, (1)B, (1)A, (1)C, (1)D

Row 94 (L): (2)D, (1)C, (1)D, (1)B, (1)D, (4)C, (1)D, (1)A, (1)C, (1)B

Row 95 (R): (4)C, (1)D, (1)A, (3)C, (1)D, (2)B, (2)D

Row 96 (L): (1)B, (1)C, (1)D, (1)C, (2)A, (3)C, (2)A, (1)D, (1)B, (1)D
Row 97 (R): (1)D, (1)C, (1)B, (1)C, (1)A, (1)D, (2)C, (1)B, (1)A, (4)D
Row 98 (L): (2)C, (1)B, (1)D, (2)B, (1)D, (1)C, (1)A, (1)B, (2)C, (1)D, (1)C
Row 99 (R): (2)C, (1)D, (1)B, (1)D, (2)A, (1)C, (1)A, (1)B, (1)C, (1)D, (2)C
Row 100 (L): (2)C, (1)D, (1)B, (1)C, (3)B, (1)D, (1)A, (1)C, (1)B, (2)C
Row 101 (R): (1)B, (2)C, (1)D, (2)C, (1)B, (2)A, (1)B, (1)D, (1)B, (1)D, (1)C
Row 102 (L): (1)B, (4)D, (1)C, (1)A, (1)B, (1)A, (1)D, (3)B, (1)D
Row 103 (R): (2)A, (1)B, (1)C, (1)B, (1)C, (1)A, (1)D, (1)B, (1)C, (1)B, (1)D, (1)A, (1)B
Row 104 (L): (2)A, (1)D, (1)C, (1)B, (1)D, (1)B, (1)A, (1)D, (1)C, (2)D, (2)A
Row 105 (R): (2)A, (2)D, (3)B, (1)A, (1)C, (1)D, (3)B, (1)A
Row 106 (L): (2)A, (2)D, (3)B, (1)A, (1)D, (1)C, (3)B, (1)A
Row 107 (R): (1)A, (1)B, (1)D, (1)C, (2)D, (2)A, (1)D, (1)C, (1)B, (1)C, (1)A, (1)B
Row 108 (L): (1)A, (1)B, (1)A, (1)C, (1)D, (1)C, (1)A, (2)B, (1)C, (1)B, (1)D, (1)A, (1)B
Row 109 (R): (1)B, (4)D, (1)C, (2)B, (1)A, (4)B, (1)D
Row 110 (L): (1)D, (2)C, (1)D, (2)C, (4)A, (1)D, (1)B, (1)D, (1)C
Row 111 (R): (2)C, (1)D, (1)B, (1)D, (2)B, (1)D, (2)A, (1)C, (1)D, (2)C
Row 112 (L): (2)C, (3)B, (1)A, (1)B, (1)C, (2)A, (4)C
Row 113 (R): (2)C, (1)B, (1)D, (2)B, (1)D, (1)C, (1)A, (1)B, (2)C, (1)D, (1)C
Row 114 (L): (1)D, (1)C, (1)B, (1)C, (1)A, (1)D, (2)C, (1)B, (1)A, (1)B, (1)D, (1)B, (1)D
Row 115 (R): (1)B, (1)D, (1)C, (1)D, (2)A, (3)C, (1)B, (1)A, (3)B
Row 116 (L): (1)C, (1)D, (2)C, (1)B, (1)A, (4)C, (2)B, (1)D, (1)B
Row 117 (R): (1)D, (1)B, (1)C, (1)B, (1)A, (1)D, (1)C, (1)D, (2)C, (1)D, (1)A, (1)C, (1)B
Row 118 (L): (1)D, (1)B, (1)D, (2)A, (1)C, (2)D, (2)C, (1)B, (1)A, (1)C, (1)D
Row 119 (R): (1)B, (1)D, (1)B, (1)A, (1)D, (1)C, (4)D, (1)A, (1)B, (2)C
Row 120 (L): (1)B, (1)C, (1)A, (1)D, (3)C, (1)D, (1)C, (2)B, (1)A, (1)B, (1)C
Row 121 (R): (1)D, (1)C, (1)B, (1)A, (1)D, (2)C, (1)D, (2)B, (1)D, (2)A, (1)D
Row 122 (L): (2)C, (1)D, (1)A, (1)B, (1)D, (1)B, (1)C, (2)A, (2)B, (1)A, (1)B
Row 123 (R): (2)D, (1)A, (1)B, (1)A, (1)D, (1)A, (1)C, (1)A, (2)B, (2)D, (1)A
Row 124 (L): (1)D, (2)A, (1)C, (1)A, (1)D, (1)A, (1)B, (2)A, (2)D, (1)A, (1)B
Row 125 (R): (2)B, (1)D, (1)C, (2)D, (1)A, (1)D, (1)A, (1)B, (1)D, (1)C, (1)A, (1)D
Row 126 (L): (1)A, (1)D, (2)C, (2)B, (1)A, (1)B, (1)A, (1)D, (1)B, (2)D, (1)B
Row 127 (R): (2)A, (2)C, (3)A, (1)D, (1)B, (1)D, (1)A, (1)B, (1)C, (1)A
Row 128 (L): (1)D, (1)A, (2)C, (3)A, (1)B, (1)D, (2)A, (1)D, (1)C, (1)D
Row 129 (R): (1)A, (1)B, (1)C, (1)D, (2)A, (3)B, (1)A, (2)D, (2)C
Row 130 (L): (1)A, (2)C, (2)D, (1)A, (1)B, (1)C, (2)A, (4)C
Row 131 (R): (1)B, (1)C, (3)D, (1)B, (1)A, (1)D, (2)B, (1)C, (1)D, (2)C
Row 132 (L): (1)D, (1)C, (1)D, (1)B, (1)C, (2)D, (1)B, (2)D, (1)C, (2)D, (1)C

Row 133 (R): (1)B, (1)C, (2)D, (2)B, (1)D, (3)B, (1)C, (1)D, (2)C
Row 134 (L): (1)B, (3)D, (2)A, (1)D, (1)A, (1)B, (1)A, (1)D, (3)C
Row 135 (R): (2)A, (1)C, (1)D, (2)A, (2)D, (1)B, (1)A, (1)B, (2)C, (1)D
Row 136 (L): (1)B, (1)A, (2)C, (3)A, (1)B, (1)D, (2)A, (1)D, (1)C, (1)D
Row 137 (R): (2)B, (2)C, (3)A, (1)D, (1)B, (1)D, (1)A, (1)B, (1)D, (1)B
Row 138 (L): (1)B, (1)A, (1)D, (1)C, (2)D, (1)A, (1)B, (1)A, (1)B, (2)D, (2)A
Row 139 (R): (2)A, (1)D, (1)C, (1)D, (1)C, (1)A, (1)D, (1)A, (1)B, (2)C, (1)B, (1)A
Row 140 (L): (1)D, (1)B, (1)A, (1)D, (1)A, (1)D, (1)A, (1)D, (2)A, (1)D, (1)C, (1)A, (1)B
Row 141 (R): (1)C, (1)B, (1)A, (1)B, (1)A, (1)D, (1)B, (1)D, (1)A, (1)B, (1)A, (1)D, (1)B, (1)A
Row 142 (L): (1)C, (1)D, (3)A, (1)C, (1)D, (1)C, (1)B, (2)A, (1)D, (2)A
Row 143 (R): (2)C, (2)A, (1)D, (3)C, (5)B, (1)D
Row 144 (L): (1)B, (1)C, (2)B, (1)D, (2)C, (2)D, (2)B, (1)A, (1)B, (1)C
Row 145 (R): (1)B, (1)D, (2)A, (1)D, (1)C, (1)D, (1)B, (2)C, (2)B, (1)D, (1)C
Row 146 (L): (1)D, (1)B, (1)D, (2)B, (1)D, (1)C, (1)B, (2)C, (1)A, (1)D, (2)C
Row 147 (R): (1)C, (1)B, (1)C, (1)B, (1)A, (1)B, (1)C, (1)D, (1)C, (1)D, (1)A, (1)B, (2)D
Row 148 (L): (2)D, (2)C, (2)B, (4)C, (1)B, (1)A, (1)D, (1)B
Row 149 (R): (1)B, (3)C, (1)D, (1)A, (3)C, (1)B, (1)A, (1)D, (1)B, (1)D
Row 150 (L): (1)D, (1)C, (1)D, (1)C, (1)B, (1)A, (2)C, (1)D, (2)A, (1)C, (1)B, (1)C
Row 151 (R): (1)D, (1)C, (1)B, (1)D, (1)A, (1)B, (2)C, (1)B, (1)A, (1)D, (1)C, (1)D, (1)C
Row 152 (L): (2)C, (2)B, (1)D, (1)A, (1)B, (1)C, (1)A, (1)D, (4)C
Row 153 (R): (3)C, (1)B, (1)C, (2)A, (1)D, (1)B, (1)A, (1)C, (1)B, (2)C
Row 154 (L): (1)B, (1)C, (2)D, (1)C, (1)D, (3)B, (1)A, (1)C, (1)B, (1)D, (1)C
Row 155 (R): (1)A, (1)C, (1)B, (3)C, (1)D, (1)A, (2)B, (2)D, (1)A, (1)C
Row 156 (L): (1)A, (1)B, (1)A, (1)C, (1)D, (1)C, (3)A, (1)C, (1)B, (1)D, (1)A, (1)B
Row 157 (R): (2)A, (2)D, (1)B, (1)C, (2)A, (1)D, (1)C, (2)D, (2)A
Row 158 (L): (2)A, (1)C, (4)D, (1)B, (3)C, (2)D, (1)A
Row 159 (R): (2)A, (1)C, (4)D, (1)A, (3)C, (1)B, (1)D, (1)A
Row 160 (L): (2)A, (2)D, (1)B, (1)D, (1)A, (1)B, (1)D, (1)C, (2)D, (2)A
Row 161 (R): (1)A, (2)B, (1)C, (1)D, (1)C, (2)A, (1)B, (1)C, (1)B, (1)C, (1)A, (1)D
Row 162 (L): (1)A, (1)C, (1)B, (3)C, (1)D, (2)A, (1)B, (2)D, (1)A, (1)C
Row 163 (R): (1)D, (1)C, (2)D, (1)C, (1)D, (1)A, (2)B, (1)A, (1)C, (1)B, (1)D, (1)C
Row 164 (L): (3)C, (1)B, (1)C, (1)B, (1)A, (1)D, (2)A, (1)C, (1)B, (2)C
Row 165 (R): (2)C, (5)B, (1)D, (2)A, (4)C
Row 166 (L): (2)C, (1)B, (1)D, (2)A, (1)D, (1)C, (2)B, (1)D, (1)C, (1)D, (1)C
Row 167 (R): (1)D, (1)C, (1)D, (1)C, (1)A, (1)B, (2)C, (1)B, (1)A, (1)B, (1)C, (1)B, (1)C
Row 168 (L): (1)B, (3)C, (1)B, (1)A, (3)C, (2)B, (1)D, (1)B, (1)D
Row 169 (R): (2)D, (1)C, (1)D, (2)A, (3)C, (1)D, (2)A, (1)D, (1)B
Row 170 (L): (1)C, (1)B, (1)C, (1)D, (1)A, (1)B, (1)C, (1)D, (2)C, (1)A, (1)B, (2)D
Row 171 (R): (3)D, (1)A, (1)B, (1)D, (1)C, (1)A, (2)C, (2)A, (2)C
Row 172 (L): (1)B, (1)D, (1)B, (1)A, (1)D, (1)C, (2)D, (2)C, (2)B, (1)D, (1)C

Row 173 (R): (1)B, (1)C, (1)A, (1)B, (1)D, (2)C, (2)D, (2)B, (1)A, (1)D, (1)C

Row 174 (L): (1)D, (1)C, (2)B, (1)D, (1)C, (1)D, (1)C, (1)D, (1)A, (3)B, (1)D

Row 175 (R): (1)C, (1)D, (1)A, (1)B, (1)A, (3)C, (1)A, (2)B, (1)D, (2)A

Row 176 (L): (1)C, (1)D, (3)A, (1)D, (1)B, (1)D, (3)A, (1)D, (1)B, (1)A

Row 177 (R): (1)D, (2)B, (1)D, (1)A, (1)D, (1)A, (1)D, (1)A, (1)B, (1)D, (1)C, (1)A, (1)B

Row 178 (L): (1)B, (1)A, (1)B, (1)C, (1)D, (1)C, (1)A, (1)B, (2)A, (2)C, (2)A

Row 179 (R): (2)A, (1)C, (3)D, (1)A, (1)D, (1)A, (1)B, (2)D, (2)A

Row 180 (L): (1)A, (1)B, (2)C, (3)A, (1)B, (1)A, (1)D, (2)A, (1)D, (1)B

Row 181 (R): (2)B, (2)C, (3)A, (2)D, (2)A, (1)D, (1)C, (1)B

Row 182 (L): (2)A, (1)C, (1)D, (2)A, (1)D, (1)B, (1)D, (2)A, (2)C, (1)D

Row 183 (R): (1)B, (1)D, (1)C, (1)D, (2)A, (1)C, (3)A, (1)D, (3)C

Row 184 (L): (1)B, (1)C, (3)D, (5)B, (1)C, (1)D, (2)C

Row 185 (R): (2)C, (1)D, (1)B, (1)C, (2)D, (1)B, (5)D, (1)C

Row 186 (L): (1)B, (2)D, (1)B, (1)C, (2)B, (1)D, (2)B, (1)C, (1)D, (2)C

Row 187 (R): (1)A, (2)C, (1)D, (1)B, (1)A, (1)B, (1)C, (2)A, (4)C

Row 188 (L): (1)A, (1)B, (1)C, (1)D, (2)A, (1)D, (1)B, (2)A, (2)D, (2)C

Row 189 (R): (1)B, (1)A, (2)C, (3)A, (2)D, (2)A, (1)D, (1)C, (1)B

Row 190 (L): (1)A, (1)B, (2)C, (3)A, (2)B, (1)D, (1)A, (1)B, (1)C, (1)A

Row 191 (R): (1)A, (1)D, (2)C, (2)B, (1)A, (1)D, (1)A, (1)D, (2)B, (1)D, (1)A

Row 192 (L): (1)B, (1)A, (1)D, (1)C, (2)D, (1)A, (1)B, (2)A, (1)D, (1)C, (1)A, (1)B

Row 193 (R): (1)D, (2)A, (1)C, (1)A, (1)D, (1)A, (1)D, (1)A, (1)B, (1)D, (1)C, (2)A

Row 194 (L): (2)D, (2)B, (1)A, (1)D, (1)A, (1)C, (2)A, (1)B, (2)D, (1)A

Row 195 (R): (2)C, (1)B, (1)A, (4)D, (1)A, (3)B, (1)A, (1)B

Row 196 (L): (2)C, (2)A, (1)D, (2)C, (1)D, (2)B, (1)D, (2)A, (1)D

Row 197 (R): (1)B, (1)C, (2)A, (2)D, (1)C, (2)D, (1)B, (1)A, (2)B, (1)D

Row 198 (L): (1)B, (1)D, (1)B, (1)A, (1)D, (1)C, (2)D, (1)C, (1)D, (1)A, (1)B, (2)C

Row 199 (R): (1)A, (1)B, (1)D, (2)A, (1)C, (2)D, (2)C, (1)B, (1)A, (1)C, (1)D

Row 200 (L): (1)D, (1)B, (1)C, (1)B, (1)A, (1)D, (1)C, (1)D, (2)C, (1)B, (1)A, (1)C, (1)D

To make a pendant, use thicker thread (Fireline 0.17mm or 0.20mm). Follow the pattern or word chart, stopping after row 103, and end the thread. Sew a 5mm closed jump ring to each upper corner of your beadwork, re-inforcing several times. Finish the necklace as desired (I attached a simple chain to each end). You can stiffen the beadwork with floor finish.

Delft Flowers

The Dutch city of Delft is known for its beautiful ceramics, traditionally in shades of blue on a white background. This bracelet captures a slice of the pattern on a large platter with a floral motif.

SUPPLIES

- 11° cylinder beads
  - 8g color A (Miyuki DB-1490, opaque bisque white)
  - 3g color B (Miyuki DB-240, lined crystal/sapphire)
  - 1–2g color C (Miyuki DB-1498, opaque light smoke)
  - 2g color D (Miyuki DB-880, matte opaque dark blue AB)
  - 3g color E (Miyuki DB-756, matte opaque cobalt)
- Beading needle, size 10, 11, or 12
- Fireline, crystal, 6-lb. test
- 4-loop tube clasp
- Scissors, thread snips, or thread burner

A B C D E

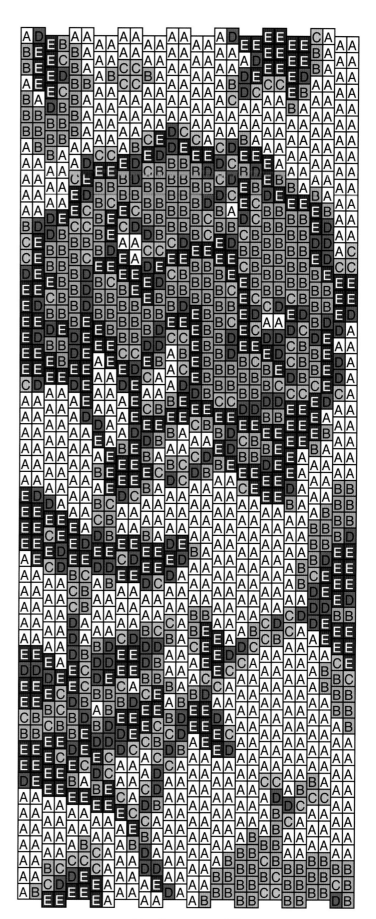

The pattern measures 1½ in. (3.8cm) wide and up to 7½ in. (19.1cm) long, not including the clasp.

MAKE THE BRACELET

1. Follow the pattern or word chart below to complete the piece (see two-drop peyote stitch, p. 9), leaving an 8–10-in. (20–25cm) tail for adding the clasp. Add and end thread as needed.

2. Attach a 4-loop tube clasp to each end of the bracelet (see p. 7).

Rows 1 and 2 (L): (3)A, (1)C, (6)E, (1)D, (13)A, (1)B, (1)E, (1)D, (1)A
Row 3 (R): (1)B, (1)E, (1)B, (7)A, (2)E, (1)B, (1)A
Row 4 (L): (2)A, (2)E, (1)D, (7)A, (1)C, (1)E
Row 5 (R): (1)B, (1)E, (1)B, (1)A, (2)C, (4)A, (2)E, (1)B, (1)A
Row 6 (L): (2)A, (1)D, (2)E, (1)D, (3)A, (2)B, (1)A, (1)D, (1)E

(Continues on p. 80)

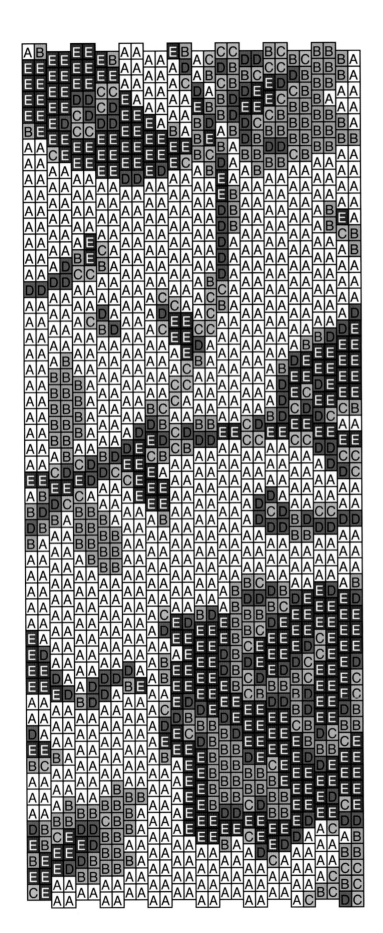

Row 7 (R): (1)A, (1)E, (2)B, (2)C, (3)A, (1)B, (2)C, (2)A

Row 8 (L): (2)A, (1)B, (1)E, (1)C, (1)D, (6)A, (1)C, (1)E

Row 9 (R): (1)B, (1)A, (1)B, (6)A, (1)C, (4)A

Row 10 (L): (3)A, (1)B, (8)A, (1)B, (1)D

Row 11 (R): (3)B, (11)A

Row 12 (L): (12)A, (2)B

Row 13 (R): (3)B, (3)A, (1)D, (1)C, (6)A

Row 14 (L): (5)A, (1)B, (1)A, (1)C, (1)E, (1)C, (2)A, (2)B

Row 15 (R): (1)A, (1)B, (3)A, (1)B, (1)D, (1)E, (1)C, (1)D, (4)A

Row 16 (L): (4)A, (4)E, (1)D, (1)E, (2)C, (1)A, (1)B

Row 17 (R): (3)A, (1)D, (1)E, (1)D, (2)B, (1)D, (1)C, (1)E, (3)A

Row 18 (L): (4)A, (1)D, (1)B, (1)D, (2)B, (1)C, (2)E, (2)A

Row 19 (R): (2)A, (1)C, (1)E, (1)B, (1)D, (2)B, (1)C, (1)D, (1)E, (1)B, (2)A

Row 20 (L): (3)A, (2)B, (1)E, (6)B, (2)A

Row 21 (R): (2)A, (1)E, (1)D, (4)B, (1)D, (1)C, (1)D, (1)E, (1)B, (1)A

Row 22 (L): (2)A, (2)E, (1)C, (1)E, (1)D, (3)B, (1)C, (1)B, (2)A

Row 23 (R): (2)A, (1)E, (1)C, (1)E, (1)C, (3)B, (1)A, (2)B, (1)E, (1)B

Row 24 (L): (2)A, (2)B, (1)C, (1)D, (1)C, (3)B, (1)E, (1)B, (1)E, (1)D

Row 25 (R): (1)B, (1)D, (3)C, (1)D, (6)B, (1)E, (1)D

Row 26 (L): (2)A, (3)B, (2)C, (2)B, (1)D, (1)E, (2)B, (1)D

Row 27 (R): (1)C, (1)E, (2)B, (2)A, (1)C, (1)D, (1)E, (1)D, (2)B, (2)D

Row 28 (L): (1)C, (1)A, (4)B, (2)E, (2)C, (1)D, (3)B

Row 29 (R): (1)C, (1)E, (1)B, (1)C, (1)E, (1)A, (4)E, (2)B, (1)E, (1)D

Row 30 (L): (2)C, (3)B, (1)C, (2)B, (1)E, (1)D, (2)E, (2)B

Row 31 (R): (1)D, (1)E, (1)B, (1)D, (2)E, (1)C, (2)B, (1)E, (3)B, (1)E

Row 32 (L): (2)E, (3)B, (1)E, (2)B, (1)D, (1)E, (1)C, (2)B, (1)E

Row 33 (R): (2)E, (1)B, (1)D, (1)B, (1)E, (3)B, (1)C, (4)B

Row 34 (L): (2)E, (1)B, (2)C, (1)E, (3)B, (1)E, (3)B, (1)C

Row 35 (R): (1)E, (1)D, (1)B, (1)D, (3)B, (1)D, (2)B, (1)C, (1)D, (2)B

Row 36 (L): (1)D, (1)E, (1)D, (1)E, (1)D, (1)E, (1)B, (1)E, (6)B

Row 37 (R): (2)E, (1)B, (1)E, (2)B, (2)E, (1)B, (1)C, (2)A, (1)B, (1)D

Row 38 (L): (1)A, (1)D, (1)C, (1)D, (1)C, (1)E, (1)B, (1)E, (1)D, (2)B, (2)E, (1)D

Row 39 (R): (1)E, (2)D, (1)E, (2)B, (2)C, (1)B, (4)D, (1)E

Row 40 (L): (2)A, (1)B, (1)C, (2)E, (1)B, (1)E, (2)D, (2)E, (2)B

Row 41 (R): (2)E, (1)D, (1)E, (2)C, (1)A, (2)B, (1)D, (1)E, (1)D, (1)B, (1)E

Row 42 (L): (1)A, (1)D, (1)B, (2)C, (2)B, (1)E, (1)B, (2)E, (1)A, (1)B, (1)E

Row 43 (R): (5)E, (1)D, (1)A, (1)C, (3)B, (1)E, (1)B, (1)E

Row 44 (L): (1)A, (1)D, (1)B, (1)D, (3)B, (1)E, (1)A, (1)C, (2)A, (2)E

Row 45 (R): (1)C, (2)D, (1)E, (1)D, (1)E, (1)A, (1)D, (3)B, (2)C, (1)E

Row 46 (L): (1)A, (3)C, (3)B, (1)D, (6)A

Row 47 (R): (3)A, (1)E, (1)A, (1)E, (1)B, (1)E, (2)C, (2)D, (1)E, (1)D

Row 48 (L): (2)A, (2)E, (2)D, (2)E, (1)B, (1)C, (4)A

Row 49 (R): (3)A, (1)D, (1)A, (5)E, (2)B, (1)E, (1)A

Row 50 (L): (2)A, (4)E, (1)B, (1)C, (2)E, (1)A, (1)D, (2)A

Row 51 (R): (5)A, (1)D, (1)B, (1)A, (1)B, (1)D, (3)E, (1)B

Row 52 (L): (2)A, (2)E, (1)B, (1)C, (2)A, (1)B, (1)D, (1)A, (1)E, (2)A

Row 53 (R): (4)A, (1)B, (1)E, (2)A, (1)E, (1)D, (1)B, (1)E, (1)B, (1)A

Row 54 (L): (3)A, (1)E, (2)B, (1)D, (1)C, (1)A, (1)B, (1)E, (3)A

Row 55 (R): (4)A, (2)E, (1)B, (1)C, (1)B, (1)E, (1)D, (1)E, (2)A

Row 56 (L): (3)A, (3)E, (1)B, (1)D, (1)C, (2)E, (1)B, (2)A

Row 57 (R): (4)A, (2)E, (1)D, (1)C, (2)A, (2)E, (2)A

Row 58 (L): (2)B, (1)A, (1)D, (1)E, (1)C, (3)A, (1)B, (1)E, (3)A

Row 59 (R): (1)E, (1)D, (2)A, (1)D, (1)C, (4)A, (2)E, (2)A

Row 60 (L): (2)B, (1)A, (1)B, (6)A, (1)C, (1)B, (1)A, (1)D

Row 61 (R): (2)E, (11)A, (1)B

Row 62 (L): (2)B, (8)A, (1)B, (1)C, (2)E

Row 63 (R): (3)E, (9)A, (2)B

Row 64 (L): (1)D, (1)B, (7)A, (2)B, (1)D, (1)E, (1)C

Row 65 (R): (3)E, (1)D, (2)E, (1)D, (1)E, (4)A, (2)B

Row 66 (L): (2)E, (5)A, (1)B, (4)E, (1)D, (1)E

Row 67 (R): (1)A, (3)E, (1)C, (1)D, (1)E, (1)D, (4)A, (1)B, (1)D

Row 68 (L): (2)E, (1)B, (5)A, (2)E, (3)D, (1)C

Row 69 (R): (2)A, (1)B, (1)C, (2)E, (1)D, (5)A, (1)C, (1)E

Row 70 (L): (2)E, (1)B, (5)A, (1)C, (1)D, (1)B, (3)A

Row 71 (R): (2)A, (1)C, (1)B, (8)A, (1)D, (1)E

Row 72 (L): (1)D, (1)E, (12)A

Row 73 (R): (2)A, (1)C, (1)B, (8)A, (2)D

Row 74 (L): (2)B, (1)D, (1)C, (2)A, (2)B, (6)A

Row 75 (R): (2)A, (1)D, (3)A, (1)C, (3)A, (1)C, (2)D, (1)E

Row 76 (L): (2)E, (1)A, (1)C, (1)B, (1)A, (1)E, (1)B, (1)C, (1)B, (4)A

Row 77 (R): (2)A, (1)D, (1)A, (1)C, (1)D, (1)B, (1)A, (1)E, (1)A, (1)C, (1)B, (1)A, (1)E

Row 78 (L): (2)E, (2)A, (1)C, (1)D, (1)E, (1)C, (3)D, (1)B, (2)A

Row 79 (R): (2)E, (1)D, (1)B, (2)E, (2)A, (1)E, (1)D, (4)A

Row 80 (L): (1)E, (1)C, (3)A, (1)C, (1)E, (1)A, (1)B, (3)D, (1)A, (1)E

Row 81 (R): (2)D, (1)E, (1)C, (2)E, (2)A, (1)E, (1)C, (3)A, (1)B

Row 82 (L): (1)C, (1)B, (4)A, (1)C, (1)A, (2)B, (1)E, (1)D, (1)E, (1)D

Row 83 (R): (3)E, (2)C, (1)A, (1)B, (1)A, (1)C, (4)A, (1)B

Row 84 (L): (2)B, (4)A, (1)D, (1)B, (1)E, (1)C, (2)B, (1)C, (1)E

Row 85 (R): (2)E, (1)D, (2)B, (1)D, (1)A, (1)B, (6)A

Row 86 (L): (2)B, (4)A, (4)E, (1)B, (1)A, (1)C, (1)B

Row 87 (R): (1)C, (2)B, (1)D, (2)E, (1)B, (2)D, (5)A

Row 88 (L): (1)B, (5)A, (2)E, (1)C, (1)E, (1)D, (2)B, (1)C

Row 89 (R): (3)B, (1)E, (1)D, (1)E, (1)C, (1)D, (1)E, (1)C, (4)A

Row 90 (L): (6)A, (1)E, (1)A, (1)B, (1)C, (2)D, (2)E

Row 91 (R): (2)E, (1)D, (1)E, (1)D, (1)C, (1)D, (1)B, (1)E, (1)D, (4)A

Row 92 (L): (8)A, (1)C, (1)A, (1)C, (1)E, (1)C, (1)E

Row 93 (R): (3)E, (1)C, (2)A, (1)C, (7)A

Row 94 (L): (8)A, (1)D, (1)A, (1)C, (1)D, (2)E

Row 95 (R): (1)D, (1)E, (1)B, (7)A, (2)C, (1)B, (1)A

Row 96 (L): (2)A, (1)B, (5)A, (1)D, (1)C, (1)E, (1)B, (2)E

Row 97 (R): (2)A, (2)E, (1)C, (6)A, (1)D, (2)C

Row 98 (L): (2)A, (1)C, (1)D, (4)A, (1)B, (1)D, (2)E, (2)A

Row 99 (R): (4)A, (1)E, (1)C, (5)A, (1)B, (2)A

Row 100 (L): (3)A, (1)C, (5)A, (1)C, (4)A

Row 101 (R): (5)A, (1)E, (5)A, (1)B, (2)A

Row 102 (L): (4)A, (1)B, (4)A, (1)B, (4)A

Row 103 (R): (3)A, (1)B, (1)A, (1)B, (4)A, (2)B, (2)A

Row 104 (L): (4)A, (2)B, (3)A, (1)D, (1)A, (1)C, (2)A

Row 105 (R): (2)A, (2)C, (5)A, (1)B, (1)C, (3)B

Row 106 (L): (6)B, (2)A, (2)D, (1)A, (2)C, (1)B

Row 107 (R): (2)A, (1)D, (1)E, (4)A, (3)B, (1)C, (2)B

Row 108 (L): (1)B, (1)C, (4)B, (2)A, (1)E, (2)A, (1)E, (1)D, (1)C

Row 109 (R): (1)A, (1)B, (2)E, (2)A, (1)D, (1)A, (2)B, (2)C, (2)B

Row 110 (L): (1)B, (1)D, (5)B, (4)A, (3)E

Row 111 (R): (1)A, (1)B, (2)E, (2)A, (1)E, (1)B, (2)C, (1)B, (1)C, (2)B

Row 112 (L): (1)A, (1)B, (1)C, (1)B, (2)D, (1)C, (3)A, (1)B, (3)E

Row 113 (R): (4)E, (3)A, (2)D, (1)B, (2)C, (2)B

Row 114 (L): (1)A, (2)B, (1)D, (1)C, (2)B, (3)A, (4)E

Row 115 (R): (4)E, (3)A, (2)C, (1)B, (1)E, (1)D, (2)B

Row 116 (L): (2)A, (1)B, (1)C, (1)E, (1)D, (1)A, (1)D, (2)A, (2)C, (2)E

Row 117 (R): (2)E, (2)D, (1)E, (3)A, (1)B, (1)D, (1)E, (1)C, (1)B, (1)A

Row 118 (L): (2)A, (2)B, (2)E, (1)B, (1)E, (2)A, (1)D, (1)C, (2)E

Row 119 (R): (2)E, (1)C, (1)D, (2)E, (2)A, (1)B, (1)D, (1)C, (3)B

Row 120 (L): (1)A, (3)B, (1)C, (2)D, (1)B, (1)A, (1)E, (3)D, (1)E

Row 121 (R): (1)B, (1)E, (2)C, (2)E, (1)B, (2)A, (5)B

Row 122 (L): (5)B, (1)D, (1)E, (1)B, (6)E

Row 123 (R): (2)A, (6)E, (1)B, (1)A, (2)D, (2)B

Row 124 (L): (2)A, (1)B, (1)C, (2)B, (1)C, (1)B, (5)E, (1)C

Row 125 (R): (2)A, (5)E, (1)C, (1)D, (1)A, (2)B, (2)A

Row 126 (L): (4)A, (1)B, (1)A, (1)B, (1)A, (1)D, (3)E, (2)A

Row 127 (R): (4)A, (2)D, (2)A, (1)E, (5)A

Row 128 (L): (14)A

Row 129 (R): (8)A, (1)E, (1)B, (4)A

Row 130 (L): (14)A

Row 131 (R): (8)A, (1)D, (1)B, (3)A, (1)B

Row 132 (L): (1)A, (1)E, (12)A

Row 133 (R): (8)A, (1)D, (1)B, (3)A, (1)B
Row 134 (L): (1)B, (1)C, (12)A
Row 135 (R): (3)A, (1)E, (4)A, (1)D, (5)A
Row 136 (L): (1)B, (10)A, (1)C, (2)A
Row 137 (R): (2)A, (1)B, (1)E, (4)A, (1)D, (5)A
Row 138 (L): (11)A, (1)B, (1)D, (1)A
Row 139 (R): (2)A, (2)C, (4)A, (1)D, (5)A
Row 140 (L): (6)A, (1)B, (5)A, (2)D
Row 141 (R): (2)D, (6)A, (1)C, (5)A
Row 142 (L): (6)A, (1)C, (1)A, (1)C, (5)A
Row 143 (R): (6)A, (1)C, (1)A, (1)B, (5)A
Row 144 (L): (1)D, (5)A, (1)C, (1)A, (1)D, (2)A, (1)D, (2)A
Row 145 (R): (3)A, (1)C, (2)A, (2)E, (6)A
Row 146 (L): (1)E, (1)D, (4)A, (3)C, (1)A, (1)D, (1)B, (2)A
Row 147 (R): (6)A, (2)E, (4)A, (1)B, (1)D
Row 148 (L): (2)E, (1)B, (4)A, (1)D, (6)A
Row 149 (R): (7)A, (1)E, (4)A, (2)E
Row 150 (L): (3)E, (1)D, (3)A, (1)B, (4)A, (1)B, (1)A
Row 151 (R): (7)A, (1)C, (3)A, (1)B, (2)E
Row 152 (L): (4)E, (8)A, (2)B
Row 153 (R): (2)A, (1)B, (3)A, (2)C, (3)A, (2)D, (1)E
Row 154 (L): (2)E, (1)C, (1)E, (8)A, (2)B
Row 155 (R): (2)A, (1)B, (3)A, (1)C, (4)A, (1)D, (2)E
Row 156 (L): (1)B, (1)C, (1)D, (1)C, (4)A, (1)C, (1)B, (2)A, (2)B
Row 157 (R): (2)A, (1)B, (7)A, (1)B, (2)D, (1)C
Row 158 (L): (2)A, (2)E, (1)D, (1)C, (3)B, (1)D, (2)A, (2)B
Row 159 (R): (2)A, (1)B, (2)A, (1)D, (1)C, (1)D, (6)E
Row 160 (L): (2)E, (4)C, (3)D, (1)E, (2)A, (2)B
Row 161 (R): (4)A, (1)D, (1)E, (1)C, (1)B, (4)A, (2)D
Row 162 (L): (2)C, (6)A, (1)B, (1)C, (1)D, (2)B, (1)A
Row 163 (R): (2)A, (1)C, (1)D, (2)E, (7)A, (1)D
Row 164 (L): (1)C, (1)D, (7)A, (1)E, (1)C, (2)D, (1)C
Row 165 (R): (3)E, (1)D, (1)C, (1)E, (8)A
Row 166 (L): (8)A, (2)E, (2)A, (2)E
Row 167 (R): (1)A, (1)B, (1)C, (2)A, (1)E, (4)A, (1)D, (3)A
Row 168 (L): (4)A, (1)D, (3)A, (2)E, (2)A, (1)C, (1)D
Row 169 (R): (1)B, (1)D, (2)B, (6)A, (1)C, (1)D, (2)C
Row 170 (L): (3)D, (1)B, (1)D, (3)A, (1)B, (2)A, (1)B, (1)A, (1)B
Row 171 (R): (1)D, (3)B, (6)A, (4)D
Row 172 (L): (2)A, (2)B, (6)A, (2)B, (2)A
Row 173 (R): (1)B, (1)A, (2)B, (10)A
Row 174 (L): (10)A, (2)B, (2)A
Row 175 (R): (3)A, (1)B, (10)A
Row 176 (L): (10)A, (2)B, (2)A
Row 177 (R): (14)A
Row 178 (L): (1)B, (3)A, (1)C, (1)B, (8)A
Row 179 (R): (9)A, (1)B, (1)D, (1)B, (1)E, (1)D
Row 180 (L): (1)D, (2)E, (3)D, (8)A
Row 181 (R): (9)A, (2)B, (1)C, (2)E
Row 182 (L): (4)E, (2)B, (1)D, (1)B, (1)C, (5)A
Row 183 (R): (6)A, (1)E, (1)D, (1)E, (1)B, (1)D, (3)E
Row 184 (L): (4)E, (1)C, (1)B, (2)E, (1)D, (5)A
Row 185 (R): (1)E, (5)A, (3)E, (1)B, (2)E, (1)C, (1)E
Row 186 (L): (2)E, (1)D, (2)E, (1)C, (2)E, (6)A
Row 187 (R): (1)E, (1)D, (5)A, (1)E, (1)D, (1)B, (2)E, (1)C, (1)E
Row 188 (L): (1)D, (1)E, (1)C, (1)D, (1)E, (1)D, (2)E, (1)B, (5)A
Row 189 (R): (2)E, (2)A, (1)D, (1)A, (2)E, (1)D, (1)B, (1)E, (1)D, (2)E

Row 190 (L): (1)C, (1)E, (1)C, (1)B, (1)D, (1)C, (2)E, (1)B, (1)A, (2)D, (1)A, (1)D
Row 191 (R): (2)E, (1)A, (1)D, (1)B, (4)E, (3)B, (2)E
Row 192 (L): (1)C, (1)E, (1)D, (2)B, (1)C, (2)E, (3)A, (2)D, (1)E
Row 193 (R): (2)A, (1)B, (1)D, (2)A, (1)E, (1)D, (2)E, (2)D, (2)E
Row 194 (L): (1)B, (2)D, (1)B, (3)E, (1)D, (1)C, (5)A
Row 195 (R): (6)A, (1)D, (1)B, (1)D, (5)E
Row 196 (L): (3)B, (1)C, (2)E, (2)B, (1)D, (5)A
Row 197 (R): (1)D, (5)A, (1)E, (1)C, (1)B, (1)D, (2)E, (1)D, (1)C
Row 198 (L): (1)E, (1)C, (1)B, (3)E, (1)B, (1)D, (1)E, (5)A
Row 199 (R): (2)E, (4)A, (2)E, (2)B, (2)E, (2)B
Row 200 (L): (2)E, (1)D, (2)E, (1)D, (1)B, (1)E, (1)B, (4)A, (1)B
Row 201 (R): (1)B, (1)C, (5)A, (1)E, (2)B, (1)C, (1)E, (1)D, (1)E
Row 202 (L): (4)E, (3)B, (1)E, (6)A
Row 203 (R): (7)A, (1)E, (3)B, (3)E
Row 204 (L): (4)E, (3)B, (1)E, (2)A, (1)B, (3)A
Row 205 (R): (4)A, (2)B, (1)A, (1)E, (4)B, (1)E, (1)D
Row 206 (L): (1)E, (1)C, (2)E, (1)D, (1)C, (1)B, (1)E, (2)A, (3)B, (1)A
Row 207 (R): (2)A, (3)B, (2)A, (1)E, (2)D, (2)B, (2)E
Row 208 (L): (3)D, (5)E, (2)A, (1)B, (1)C, (2)B
Row 209 (R): (1)D, (1)B, (2)D, (1)B, (2)A, (5)E, (1)A, (1)C
Row 210 (L): (1)B, (2)A, (1)D, (1)E, (1)C, (2)E, (2)A, (2)B, (1)E, (1)C
Row 211 (R): (1)E, (1)B, (1)E, (1)D, (4)A, (1)B, (1)A, (1)E, (1)D, (2)A
Row 212 (L): (2)B, (2)A, (1)D, (5)A, (2)B, (2)E
Row 213 (R): (1)B, (1)E, (1)D, (2)B, (5)A, (1)C, (3)A
Row 214 (L): (2)C, (8)A, (2)B, (1)D, (1)E
Row 215 (R): (2)E, (2)B, (9)A, (1)C
Row 216 (L): (1)C, (1)B, (12)A
Row 217 (R): (1)C, (1)E, (10)A, (1)B, (1)C
Row 218 (L): (1)C, (1)D, (1)C, (11)A

note
The pattern calls for the most common red/black/white color scheme, but I've also substituted turquoise for the red and love the way both turned out.

Maori Inspired

While traveling in New Zealand, I was captivated by the bold curved motifs created by the native Maori people. The motifs often decorate clothing and wall art, but are also frequently seen in tattoos. I've adapted one of those patterns for this bracelet.

SUPPLIES

- 11º cylinder beads
  - 5g color A (Miyuki DB-1490, opaque bisque white)
  - 4g color B (Miyuki DB-310, jet black matte)
  - 4–5g color C (Miyuki DB-723, opaque red)
- Beading needle, size 10, 11, or 12
- Fireline, crystal or smoke, 6-lb. test
- 3- or 4-loop tube clasp
- Scissors, thread snips, or thread burner

A   B   C

This pattern is a bit narrower than most of the others in the book; it is about 1¼ in. (3.2cm) wide and 7 in. (18cm) long, not including the clasp.

MAKE THE BRACELET

1. Follow the pattern or word chart below to complete the piece (see two-drop peyote stitch, p. 9), leaving an 8–10-in. (20–25cm) tail for adding the clasp. Add and end thread as needed.

2. Attach a 3- or 4-loop tube clasp to each end of the bracelet (see p. 7).

Row 1 and 2 (L): (1)A, (7)B, (1)A, (2)C, (9)A, (2)B, (2)A
Row 3 (R): (6)B, (3)A, (3)B
Row 4 (L): (2)A, (2)B, (2)C, (3)A, (3)B
Row 5 (R): (6)B, (6)A
Row 6 (L): (1)C, (3)A, (1)C, (1)A, (2)B, (2)A, (2)B
Row 7 (R): (3)B, (1)A, (2)B, (2)A, (2)C, (2)A
Row 8 (L): (4)C, (2)A, (3)B, (1)A, (2)B
Row 9 (R): (8)B, (1)A, (3)C
Row 10 (L): (4)C, (2)A, (6)B
Row 11 (R): (2)A, (6)B, (2)A, (2)C
Row 12 (L): (3)C, (1)A, (6)B, (2)A
Row 13 (R): (2)C, (2)A, (4)B, (2)A, (2)C
Row 14 (L): (2)C, (2)A, (4)B, (2)A, (2)C
Row 15 (R): (4)C, (2)A, (3)B, (1)A, (2)C
Row 16 (L): (2)C, (2)A, (2)B, (2)A, (4)C
Row 17 (R): (2)C, (2)A, (2)C, (2)A, (2)B, (1)A, (1)C
Row 18 (L): (2)C, (1)A, (1)B, (2)A, (2)C, (4)A

Row 19 (R): (4)C, (1)A, (3)C, (1)A, (1)B, (2)A
Row 20 (L): (2)C, (2)B, (4)C, (1)A, (2)C, (1)A
Row 21 (R): (1)C, (1)A, (7)C, (3)A
Row 22 (L): (1)C, (1)A, (1)B, (1)A, (8)C
Row 23 (R): (1)C, (1)A, (4)C, (2)A, (2)C, (1)B, (1)A
Row 24 (L): (1)C, (9)A, (1)C, (1)A
Row 25 (R): (1)C, (5)A, (2)B, (2)A, (2)B
Row 26 (L): (3)A, (7)B, (2)A
Row 27 (R): (1)A, (1)C, (6)B, (3)A, (1)B
Row 28 (L): (1)A, (9)B, (1)A, (1)C
Row 29 (R): (1)A, (1)C, (2)A, (3)B, (5)A
Row 30 (L): (4)B, (2)A, (3)B, (1)A, (2)C
Row 31 (R): (2)A, (2)C, (4)B, (1)A, (2)B, (1)A
Row 32 (L): (1)B, (1)A, (6)B, (1)A, (3)C
Row 33 (R): (1)B, (1)A, (2)C, (4)A, (3)B, (1)A
Row 34 (L): (2)A, (2)B, (4)A, (3)C, (1)A
Row 35 (R): (1)A, (1)B, (6)C, (4)A
Row 36 (L): (4)A, (6)C, (1)A, (1)B
Row 37 (R): (3)A, (9)C
Row 38 (L): (2)A, (3)C, (1)A, (4)C, (1)A, (1)B
Row 39 (R): (1)C, (3)A, (2)C, (2)A, (4)C
Row 40 (L): (1)B, (1)A, (7)C, (1)A, (1)B, (1)A
Row 41 (R): (2)C, (1)B, (1)A, (2)C, (1)A, (4)C, (1)A
Row 42 (L): (2)B, (6)C, (3)A, (1)C
Row 43 (R): (2)A, (2)B, (1)A, (1)C, (2)A, (2)C, (1)A, (1)B
Row 44 (L): (2)B, (4)A, (2)C, (1)A, (1)B, (1)A, (1)C
Row 45 (R): (2)C, (1)A, (1)B, (2)A, (2)C, (2)A, (2)B
Row 46 (L): (2)B, (2)A, (2)C, (2)A, (2)B, (2)A
Row 47 (R): (4)A, (2)B, (2)A, (2)C, (2)B
Row 48 (L): (4)B, (3)A, (3)B, (2)C
Row 49 (R): (3)C, (1)A, (2)B, (4)A, (2)B
Row 50 (L): (2)B, (4)A, (4)B, (2)C
Row 51 (R): (3)C, (1)A, (4)B, (4)A
Row 52 (L): (4)A, (5)B, (1)A, (2)C
Row 53 (R): (4)C, (7)B, (1)A
Row 54 (L): (2)A, (7)B, (1)A, (2)C
Row 55 (R): (4)C, (6)B, (2)A
Row 56 (L): (4)A, (5)B, (1)A, (2)C
Row 57 (R): (3)C, (1)A, (4)B, (2)A, (2)C
Row 58 (L): (4)C, (2)A, (4)B, (2)C
Row 59 (R): (3)C, (1)A, (2)B, (2)A, (4)C
Row 60 (L): (5)C, (3)A, (2)B, (2)C
Row 61 (R): (2)C, (4)A, (2)B, (2)A, (2)C
Row 62 (L): (2)C, (4)A, (2)B, (1)A, (1)B, (2)C
Row 63 (R): (1)A, (1)C, (1)A, (1)B, (1)A, (1)B, (2)A, (2)B, (1)A, (1)C
Row 64 (L): (2)C, (1)A, (3)B, (1)A, (1)B, (3)A, (1)C
Row 65 (R): (2)A, (1)B, (1)A, (2)B, (1)A, (3)B, (2)A
Row 66 (L): (2)C, (4)B, (1)A, (2)B, (3)A
Row 67 (R): (4)A, (2)B, (1)A, (4)B, (1)A
Row 68 (L): (1)C, (1)A, (3)B, (1)A, (4)B, (2)A
Row 69 (R): (1)B, (2)A, (3)B, (2)A, (3)B, (1)A
Row 70 (L): (1)C, (1)A, (8)B, (2)A
Row 71 (R): (8)B, (4)A
Row 72 (L): (1)C, (7)A, (2)B, (2)A
Row 73 (R): (1)B, (1)A, (2)B, (4)A, (3)C, (1)A
Row 74 (L): (1)C, (1)A, (6)C, (1)A, (3)B
Row 75 (R): (2)A, (2)B, (7)C, (1)A

Row 76 (L): (4)C, (2)A, (3)C, (1)A, (2)B

Row 77 (R): (1)A, (1)B, (2)A, (4)C, (1)A, (2)C, (1)A

Row 78 (L): (10)C, (1)A, (1)B

Row 79 (R): (2)B, (6)C, (4)A

Row 80 (L): (3)C, (1)A, (6)C, (2)A

Row 81 (R): (1)B, (3)A, (4)C, (1)A, (1)B, (1)A, (1)C

Row 82 (L): (2)C, (4)A, (2)C, (2)A, (2)B

Row 83 (R): (2)A, (2)B, (4)A, (2)B, (2)C

Row 84 (L): (1)A, (2)C, (1)A, (2)B, (2)A, (4)B

Row 85 (R): (2)A, (7)B, (1)A, (2)C

Row 86 (L): (2)A, (2)C, (4)B, (1)A, (3)B

Row 87 (R): (2)A, (6)B, (1)A, (2)C, (1)A

Row 88 (L): (2)A, (2)C, (2)A, (2)B, (2)A, (1)B, (1)A

Row 89 (R): (1)B, (1)A, (5)B, (1)A, (2)C, (2)A

Row 90 (L): (1)C, (2)A, (3)C, (3)B, (3)A

Row 91 (R): (2)B, (2)A, (2)B, (1)A, (3)C, (2)A

Row 92 (L): (2)C, (2)A, (2)C, (2)A, (4)B

Row 93 (R): (4)B, (2)A, (3)C, (1)A, (1)B, (1)A

Row 94 (L): (2)C, (1)B, (1)A, (4)C, (2)A, (2)B

Row 95 (R): (4)A, (4)C, (2)A, (1)B, (1)A

Row 96 (L): (1)C, (1)A, (2)B, (1)A, (5)C, (2)A

Row 97 (R): (8)C, (2)A, (2)B

Row 98 (L): (2)A, (2)B, (2)A, (6)C

Row 99 (R): (7)C, (2)A, (1)B, (2)A

Row 100 (L): (6)A, (3)C, (1)A, (2)C

Row 101 (R): (3)C, (1)A, (2)C, (2)A, (1)B, (3)A

Row 102 (L): (4)A, (1)B, (1)A, (2)C, (2)A, (2)C

Row 103 (R): (6)C, (4)A, (2)B

Row 104 (L): (4)B, (1)A, (1)B, (1)A, (1)C, (1)A, (3)C

Row 105 (R): (6)C, (1)A, (1)B, (1)A, (3)B

Row 106 (L): (4)B, (1)A, (1)B, (2)A, (1)C, (1)A, (2)C

Row 107 (R): (4)A, (1)C, (1)A, (2)B, (1)A, (3)B

Row 108 (L): (4)B, (1)A, (2)B, (1)A, (2)C, (2)A

Row 109 (R): (2)A, (2)C, (2)A, (2)B, (2)A, (2)B

Row 110 (L): (8)B, (1)A, (3)C

Row 111 (R): (1)A, (3)C, (1)A, (7)B

Row 112 (L): (8)B, (2)A, (2)C

Row 113 (R): (3)C, (1)A, (6)B, (2)A

Row 114 (L): (4)A, (5)B, (1)A, (2)C

Row 115 (R): (2)C, (2)A, (4)B, (2)A, (2)C

Row 116 (L): (4)C, (2)A, (4)B, (2)C

Row 117 (R): (2)C, (1)A, (3)B, (2)A, (4)C

Row 118 (L): (6)C, (2)A, (2)B, (1)A, (1)C

Row 119 (R): (2)C, (2)B, (2)A, (2)C, (2)A, (2)C

Row 120 (L): (2)C, (3)A, (3)C, (1)A, (1)B, (2)A

Row 121 (R): (1)C, (1)A, (2)B, (6)C, (2)A

Row 122 (L): (4)C, (1)A, (4)C, (1)A, (1)B, (1)A

Row 123 (R): (2)A, (1)B, (1)A, (4)C, (1)A, (2)C, (1)A

Row 124 (L): (10)C, (2)B

Row 125 (R): (1)A, (1)B, (2)A, (7)C, (1)A

Row 126 (L): (4)C, (4)A, (2)C, (1)A, (1)B

Row 127 (R): (2)B, (8)A, (1)C, (1)A

Row 128 (L): (2)C, (2)A, (4)B, (4)A

Row 129 (R): (1)B, (1)A, (8)B, (1)A, (1)C

Row 130 (L): (1)A, (1)C, (1)A, (8)B, (1)A

Row 131 (R): (2)A, (8)B, (2)C

Row 132 (L): (1)A, (2)C, (1)A, (8)B

Row 133 (R): (2)A, (6)B, (2)A, (2)C

Row 134 (L): (1)B, (1)A, (2)C, (2)A, (6)B

Row 135 (R): (2)A, (4)B, (2)A, (3)C, (1)A

Row 136 (L): (2)B, (4)C, (6)A

Row 137 (R): (6)A, (4)C, (2)A

Row 138 (L): (2)B, (10)C

Row 139 (R): (1)A, (9)C, (1)A, (1)B

Row 140 (L): (3)A, (9)C

Row 141 (R): (2)A, (2)C, (2)A, (4)C, (2)A

Row 142 (L): (2)C, (2)A, (3)C, (1)A, (4)C

Row 143 (R): (1)B, (1)A, (6)C, (3)A, (1)C

Row 144 (L): (2)C, (1)B, (1)A, (3)C, (1)A, (3)C, (1)A

Row 145 (R): (2)B, (6)C, (1)A, (1)C, (1)B, (1)A

Row 146 (L): (1)C, (1)A, (1)B, (3)A, (1)C, (1)A, (2)C, (2)A

Row 147 (R): (2)B, (4)A, (1)C, (1)A, (2)C, (2)B

Row 148 (L): (2)A, (1)B, (1)A, (3)C, (3)A, (2)B

Row 149 (R): (6)B, (1)A, (2)C, (1)A, (2)B

Row 150 (L): (1)A, (3)B, (2)C, (2)A, (4)B

Row 151 (R): (4)B, (2)A, (3)C, (1)A, (2)B

Row 152 (L): (4)B, (4)C, (2)A, (2)B

Row 153 (R): (4)A, (4)C, (2)A, (2)B

Row 154 (L): (4)B, (6)C, (2)A

Row 155 (R): (8)C, (1)A, (3)B

Row 156 (L): (4)B, (6)C, (1)A, (1)C

Row 157 (R): (2)C, (2)A, (4)C, (1)A, (3)B

Row 158 (L): (4)B, (4)C, (2)A, (2)C

Row 159 (R): (3)C, (3)A, (2)C, (2)A, (2)B

Row 160 (L): (1)A, (3)B, (3)C, (1)A, (1)B, (1)A, (2)C

Row 161 (R): (4)C, (1)B, (2)A, (2)C, (1)A, (2)B

Row 162 (L): (1)C, (1)A, (1)B, (1)A, (2)C, (4)A, (2)C

Row 163 (R): (2)C, (3)A, (1)B, (2)A, (1)C, (1)A, (1)B, (1)A

Row 164 (L): (4)A, (1)C, (1)A, (2)B, (1)A, (1)B, (1)A, (1)C

Row 165 (R): (2)C, (2)B, (2)A, (1)B, (1)A, (2)C, (2)B

Row 166 (L): (2)B, (4)A, (1)B, (1)A, (3)B, (1)A

Row 167 (R): (1)C, (1)A, (6)B, (1)A, (1)C, (1)A, (1)B

Row 168 (L): (2)B, (1)A, (1)C, (2)B, (2)A, (4)B

Row 169 (R): (1)A, (3)B, (1)A, (4)B, (3)A

Row 170 (L): (2)B, (1)C, (1)A, (3)B, (1)A, (4)B

Row 171 (R): (1)A, (3)B, (2)A, (4)B, (1)C, (1)A

Row 172 (L): (1)B, (3)A, (8)B

Row 173 (R): (4)A, (6)B, (1)A, (1)C

Row 174 (L): (1)A, (1)C, (1)A, (3)B, (6)A

Row 175 (R): (1)C, (1)A, (2)C, (4)A, (2)B, (2)A

Row 176 (L): (1)C, (1)A, (2)B, (3)A, (5)C

Row 177 (R): (8)C, (1)A, (2)B, (1)A

Row 178 (L): (1)C, (1)A, (2)B, (4)C, (2)A, (2)C

Row 179 (R): (4)C, (1)A, (4)C, (1)A, (2)B

Row 180 (L): (4)A, (5)C, (1)A, (2)C

Row 181 (R): (3)C, (1)A, (6)C, (1)A, (1)B

Row 182 (L): (1)A, (1)B, (1)A, (6)C, (1)A, (2)C

Row 183 (R): (2)C, (2)A, (6)C, (2)A

Row 184 (L): (1)A, (1)B, (4)A, (2)C, (3)A, (1)C

Row 185 (R): (1)A, (1)C, (1)A, (1)B, (8)A

Row 186 (L): (6)B, (2)A, (2)B, (2)C

Row 187 (R): (2)A, (1)C, (1)A, (7)B, (1)A

Row 188 (L): (1)B, (1)A, (7)B, (1)A, (1)C, (1)A

Row 189 (R): (1)B, (1)A, (2)C, (7)B, (1)A

Row 190 (L): (8)B, (4)A

Row 191 (R): (2)B, (2)C, (2)A, (4)B, (1)A, (1)B

Row 192 (L): (2)B, (2)A, (2)B, (2)A, (2)C, (1)A, (1)B

Row 193 (R): (2)B, (1)A, (3)C, (4)A, (2)B

Row 194 (L): (4)B, (2)A, (4)C, (1)A, (1)B

Row 195 (R): (2)B, (2)A, (4)C, (2)A, (2)B

Row 196 (L): (2)B, (2)A, (6)C, (2)B

Row 197 (R): (2)B, (2)A, (6)C, (2)A

Row 198 (L): (2)A, (7)C, (1)A, (2)B

Row 199 (R): (3)B, (1)A, (8)C

Row 200 (L): (8)C, (2)A, (2)B

Floral Ceramic

Ancient Persia (modern-day Iran) has a
long tradition of ceramic art, used not only
in the home, but to decorate mosques and
palaces. This pattern was based on a photo
I saw of a ceramic tile with bold flowers.

SUPPLIES

- 11º cylinder beads
  - 6g color A (Miyuki DB-1138, opaque cyan blue)
  - 3g color B (Miyuki DB-795, opaque cinnabar)
  - 5g color C (Miyuki DB-1490, opaque bisque white)
  - 1-2g color D (Miyuki DB-375, opaque turquoise blue satin)
- Beading needle, size 10, 11, or 12
- Fireline, crystal or smoke, 6-lb. test
- 4-loop tube clasp
- Scissors, thread snips, or thread burner

A   B   C   D

The pattern is 1½ in. (3.8cm) wide and nearly 7 in. (18cm) long, not including the clasp.

MAKE THE BRACELET

1. Follow the pattern or word chart below to complete the piece (see two-drop peyote stitches, p. 9), leaving an 8–10-in. (20–25cm) tail for adding the clasp. Add and end thread as needed.

2. Attach a 4-loop tube clasp to each end of the bracelet (see p. 7).

Rows 1 and 2 (L): (2)A, (1)B, (1)D, (4)B, (5)C, (1)B, (14)A
Row 3 (R): (8)A, (3)C, (2)B, (1)A
Row 4 (L): (2)A, (1)C, (1)B, (2)C, (1)D, (7)A
Row 5 (R): (8)A, (2)C, (3)B, (1)A
Row 6 (L): (1)B, (1)A, (2)C, (1)B, (1)D, (8)A
Row 7 (R): (3)B, (1)D, (6)A, (1)B, (1)C, (1)B, (1)A
Row 8 (L): (2)B, (2)C, (1)B, (5)A, (1)D, (1)C, (2)A
Row 9 (R): (4)A, (1)D, (5)A, (4)C
Row 10 (L): (4)C, (2)B, (4)A, (1)D, (1)B, (2)A
Row 11 (R): (4)A, (2)D, (4)A, (4)C
Row 12 (L): (4)C, (1)D, (1)B, (3)A, (1)B, (1)D, (1)B, (2)A
Row 13 (R): (4)A, (2)D, (4)A, (1)B, (2)C, (1)B

Row 14 (L): (1)B, (1)A, (3)C, (1)D, (2)A, (1)B, (1)C, (1)D, (1)B, (2)A

Row 15 (R): (4)A, (2)D, (4)A, (3)B, (1)A

Row 16 (L): (4)A, (1)B, (1)C, (2)A, (1)B, (2)D, (1)B, (2)A

Row 17 (R): (4)A, (2)D, (3)A, (2)B, (1)D, (2)A

Row 18 (L): (4)A, (2)C, (2)A, (3)D, (1)B, (2)A

Row 19 (R): (4)A, (2)D, (3)A, (1)B, (1)D, (1)B, (2)A

Row 20 (L): (1)B, (3)A, (2)C, (2)A, (1)C, (2)D, (1)B, (2)A

Row 21 (R): (4)A, (2)D, (1)B, (1)A, (1)B, (1)C, (1)B, (2)A, (1)B

Row 22 (L): (2)D, (2)A, (2)C, (2)A, (2)B, (1)C, (1)B, (2)A

Row 23 (R): (4)A, (1)D, (1)B, (1)C, (1)D, (1)D, (1)C, (1)B, (1)A, (1)B, (1)D

Row 24 (L): (2)D, (2)A, (4)B, (3)C, (3)A

Row 25 (R): (4)A, (1)C, (1)D, (6)C, (1)B, (1)D

Row 26 (L): (2)D, (1)A, (2)C, (2)B, (3)C, (2)B, (2)A

Row 27 (R): (3)A, (2)B, (4)C, (1)B, (2)C, (1)B, (1)D

Row 28 (L): (2)D, (1)B, (9)C, (2)A

Row 29 (R): (2)A, (1)B, (9)C, (1)B, (1)D

Row 30 (L): (2)D, (10)C, (1)B, (1)A

Row 31 (R): (2)A, (4)C, (1)B, (5)C, (1)B, (1)A

Row 32 (L): (2)A, (6)C, (2)B, (2)C, (1)B, (1)A

Row 33 (R): (2)A, (3)C, (1)B, (1)A, (1)B, (6)C

Row 34 (L): (1)B, (3)C, (1)B, (1)C, (1)B, (1)C, (2)A, (2)C, (2)A

Row 35 (R): (2)A, (1)D, (2)C, (1)B, (1)A, (3)C, (1)B, (3)C

Row 36 (L): (4)C, (1)A, (1)B, (2)C, (2)A, (2)C, (2)A

Row 37 (R): (3)A, (1)B, (1)C, (1)B, (1)A, (1)B, (1)C, (1)B, (1)A, (1)B, (2)C

Row 38 (L): (1)D, (3)C, (2)A, (1)D, (1)B, (2)A, (1)C, (1)B, (2)A

Row 39 (R): (2)A, (2)B, (2)C, (1)B, (2)D, (1)B, (1)A, (1)B, (2)C

Row 40 (L): (1)B, (3)C, (2)A, (3)B, (1)C, (1)A, (1)D, (1)C, (1)B

Row 41 (R): (1)B, (3)C, (2)B, (3)D, (2)B, (3)C

Row 42 (L): (1)A, (1)B, (3)C, (5)B, (4)C

Row 43 (R): (6)C, (8)B

Row 44 (L): (3)A, (3)B, (2)A, (1)B, (1)D, (4)C

Row 45 (R): (3)C, (4)B, (1)A, (1)D, (1)B, (2)C, (2)B

Row 46 (L): (1)A, (1)B, (3)C, (1)B, (2)A, (2)B, (1)A, (1)B, (2)C

Row 47 (R): (3)C, (1)B, (2)A, (1)B, (1)A, (2)B, (4)C

Row 48 (L): (4)C, (1)B, (1)A, (3)B, (2)A, (1)B, (2)C

Row 49 (R): (1)A, (1)B, (2)C, (2)B, (1)A, (3)B, (1)A, (1)B, (2)C

Row 50 (L): (4)C, (3)A, (2)B, (1)C, (1)A, (1)B, (2)C

Row 51 (R): (6)C, (4)B, (2)A, (2)C

Row 52 (L): (4)C, (2)A, (2)B, (1)D, (1)B, (4)C

Row 53 (R): (1)D, (4)C, (2)B, (1)A, (3)B, (3)C

Row 54 (L): (1)D, (3)C, (2)A, (1)C, (3)B, (4)C

Row 55 (R): (1)B, (3)C, (2)B, (2)A, (2)B, (4)C

Row 56 (L): (2)B, (2)C, (3)B, (1)A, (1)B, (1)D, (1)B, (3)C

Row 57 (R): (1)A, (3)C, (1)B, (1)C, (2)A, (2)B, (2)C, (1)B, (1)A

Row 58 (L): (2)A, (4)C, (1)B, (2)A, (1)D, (2)B, (2)C

Row 59 (R): (2)A, (1)B, (1)A, (2)C, (2)B, (1)C, (1)B, (2)C, (1)D, (1)A

Row 60 (L): (2)A, (5)C, (1)D, (3)C, (1)B, (2)A

Row 61 (R): (4)A, (5)C, (1)B, (2)C, (1)D, (1)A

Row 62 (L): (2)A, (3)C, (1)D, (5)C, (1)D, (2)A

Row 63 (R): (4)A, (5)C, (1)B, (2)C, (2)A

Row 64 (L): (2)A, (1)B, (2)C, (1)A, (5)C, (1)B, (2)A

Row 65 (R): (4)A, (5)C, (1)A, (2)D, (2)A

Row 66 (L): (3)A, (1)B, (2)A, (2)C, (3)B, (3)A

Row 67 (R): (4)A, (2)B, (2)C, (1)B, (5)A

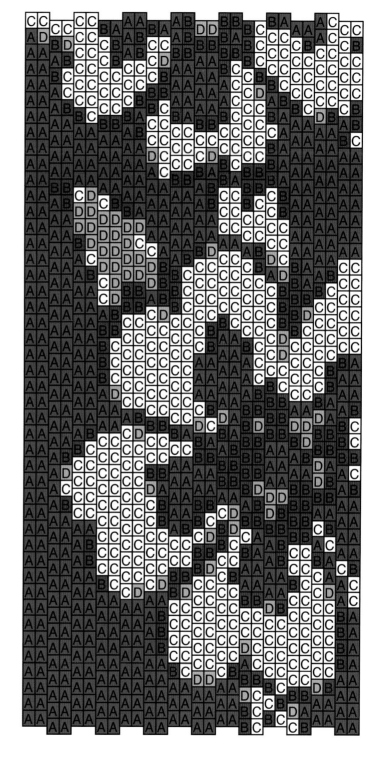

Row 68 (L): (6)A, (1)B, (1)C, (1)B, (5)A
Row 69 (R): (6)A, (2)B, (6)A
Row 70 (L): (6)A, (3)B, (5)A
Row 71 (R): (1)A, (1)B, (4)A, (1)C, (1)D, (1)B, (5)A
Row 72 (L): (2)B, (4)A, (2)C, (4)A, (1)D, (1)C
Row 73 (R): (2)A, (1)D, (1)B, (2)A, (1)C, (2)B, (3)A, (1)B, (1)D
Row 74 (L): (2)D, (1)B, (3)A, (1)C, (1)D, (4)A, (1)D, (1)B
Row 75 (R): (2)A, (1)D, (1)C, (2)A, (1)D, (2)B, (3)A, (2)D
Row 76 (L): (1)B, (2)D, (1)B, (2)A, (2)C, (3)A, (1)C, (1)D, (1)B
Row 77 (R): (2)A, (2)D, (2)A, (1)D, (1)C, (1)B, (2)A, (1)B, (2)D
Row 78 (L): (1)A, (3)D, (2)A, (2)C, (2)A, (2)C, (1)D, (1)B
Row 79 (R): (2)A, (2)D, (1)B, (1)A, (1)D, (1)C, (1)B, (2)A, (1)B, (2)D
Row 80 (L): (1)A, (3)D, (1)B, (1)A, (2)C, (2)A, (1)C, (2)D, (1)B
Row 81 (R): (2)A, (2)D, (3)B, (1)C, (3)B, (1)A, (2)D
Row 82 (L): (1)A, (2)D, (1)A, (2)C, (1)B, (1)C, (1)A, (1)D, (2)B, (1)D, (1)B
Row 83 (R): (2)A, (1)D, (1)B, (2)C, (1)B, (5)C, (2)D
Row 84 (L): (1)A, (3)B, (2)C, (1)B, (1)D, (3)C, (1)B, (1)D, (1)A
Row 85 (R): (2)A, (1)D, (1)B, (3)C, (1)B, (4)C, (1)B, (1)A
Row 86 (L): (2)A, (2)B, (3)C, (1)B, (4)C, (1)B, (1)A
Row 87 (R): (2)A, (1)C, (1)B, (3)C, (1)D, (4)C, (1)B, (1)C
Row 88 (L): (1)D, (6)C, (1)B, (4)C, (2)A
Row 89 (R): (4)A, (10)C
Row 90 (L): (7)C, (1)B, (3)C, (2)B, (1)A
Row 91 (R): (2)A, (12)C
Row 92 (L): (4)C, (2)B, (1)C, (1)B, (1)C, (1)B, (4)C
Row 93 (R): (1)A, (4)C, (1)B, (4)C, (1)A, (1)B, (2)C
Row 94 (L): (1)B, (3)C, (2)A, (1)C, (1)B, (2)A, (4)C
Row 95 (R): (1)B, (3)C, (1)B, (1)A, (3)C, (1)D, (2)A, (2)C
Row 96 (L): (1)B, (3)C, (2)A, (1)C, (1)B, (2)A, (1)D, (3)C
Row 97 (R): (1)A, (3)C, (2)A, (1)B, (1)D, (2)B, (1)A, (1)B, (2)C
Row 98 (L): (1)D, (1)B, (2)C, (2)A, (1)D, (1)B, (2)A, (4)C
Row 99 (R): (1)A, (1)B, (2)C, (1)B, (3)A, (1)B, (1)D, (3)C, (1)B
Row 100 (L): (1)C, (1)B, (2)C, (3)B, (1)A, (1)B, (1)A, (4)C
Row 101 (R): (2)A, (3)C, (2)D, (1)B, (2)D, (2)C, (2)B
Row 102 (L): (2)C, (7)B, (1)A, (2)C, (1)B, (1)A
Row 103 (R): (3)A, (1)B, (2)C, (2)B, (3)D, (1)B, (2)C
Row 104 (L): (4)C, (2)B, (1)A, (1)B, (2)A, (1)B, (1)A, (2)B
Row 105 (R): (1)B, (1)D, (2)C, (2)B, (1)A, (1)B, (1)A, (1)D, (1)B, (3)C
Row 106 (L): (2)C, (2)B, (2)D, (3)A, (1)B, (4)C
Row 107 (R): (4)C, (4)B, (1)A, (1)B, (3)A, (1)C
Row 108 (L): (2)C, (2)A, (1)D, (1)B, (2)A, (1)B, (2)A, (1)B, (2)C
Row 109 (R): (4)C, (2)A, (2)B, (1)A, (1)B, (3)A, (1)C
Row 110 (L): (2)C, (2)A, (5)B, (3)A, (2)C
Row 111 (R): (4)C, (3)A, (4)B, (2)A, (1)C
Row 112 (L): (2)C, (2)A, (1)C, (1)B, (2)D, (1)A, (1)B, (1)A, (1)B, (2)C
Row 113 (R): (1)A, (1)D, (2)C, (1)A, (1)B, (1)A, (2)B, (1)A, (2)C, (1)A, (1)C
Row 114 (L): (1)B, (1)C, (1)B, (2)C, (3)B, (2)C, (1)B, (1)C, (1)D, (1)B
Row 115 (R): (2)A, (2)C, (1)A, (5)B, (4)C
Row 116 (L): (5)C, (1)B, (2)A, (1)D, (1)C, (1)B, (1)C, (1)B, (1)A
Row 117 (R): (2)A, (4)C, (2)A, (1)B, (5)C
Row 118 (L): (4)C, (1)B, (1)C, (2)A, (1)B, (4)C, (1)B
Row 119 (R): (2)A, (4)C, (3)A, (1)C, (1)B, (3)C
Row 120 (L): (4)C, (1)D, (1)C, (2)A, (2)B, (3)C, (1)A
Row 121 (R): (2)A, (3)C, (1)B, (3)A, (1)C, (1)A, (1)B, (2)C
Row 122 (L): (1)B, (2)C, (1)B, (2)C, (2)A, (1)C, (1)B, (2)C, (1)B, (1)A

Row 123 (R): (2)A, (1)B, (1)C, (1)B, (1)A, (1)B, (1)A, (1)B, (1)C, (1)B, (1)A, (1)D, (1)B
Row 124 (L): (1)B, (3)A, (2)C, (2)B, (2)C, (2)B, (2)A
Row 125 (R): (5)A, (1)B, (5)C, (3)A
Row 126 (L): (1)C, (1)B, (2)A, (6)C, (4)A
Row 127 (R): (6)A, (4)C, (1)B, (3)A
Row 128 (L): (4)A, (2)C, (1)D, (2)C, (1)D, (4)A
Row 129 (R): (6)A, (2)C, (1)B, (1)C, (1)B, (3)A
Row 130 (L): (4)A, (2)B, (1)A, (1)B, (1)C, (5)A
Row 131 (R): (6)A, (3)B, (1)A, (1)B, (3)A
Row 132 (L): (4)A, (3)B, (5)A, (2)B
Row 133 (R): (2)A, (1)C, (1)D, (4)A, (3)C, (1)B, (2)A
Row 134 (L): (4)A, (1)C, (2)B, (3)A, (1)B, (1)C, (1)B, (1)A
Row 135 (R): (2)A, (2)D, (1)B, (3)A, (3)C, (1)B, (2)A
Row 136 (L): (4)A, (2)C, (4)A, (2)D, (2)A
Row 137 (R): (2)A, (4)D, (2)A, (4)C, (2)A
Row 138 (L): (4)A, (2)C, (4)A, (2)D, (2)A
Row 139 (R): (2)A, (1)B, (2)D, (1)C, (4)A, (2)C, (2)A
Row 140 (L): (4)A, (1)B, (1)A, (1)D, (1)B, (1)A, (1)C, (2)D, (2)A
Row 141 (R): (3)A, (1)C, (2)D, (1)A, (1)B, (2)C, (1)D, (1)C, (2)A
Row 142 (L): (2)C, (1)A, (2)B, (3)C, (1)B, (3)D, (2)A
Row 143 (R): (3)A, (1)B, (2)D, (1)B, (3)C, (1)A, (1)D, (1)A, (1)B
Row 144 (L): (2)C, (1)A, (1)B, (4)C, (1)B, (2)D, (1)C, (2)A
Row 145 (R): (4)A, (3)B, (4)C, (2)B, (1)C
Row 146 (L): (2)C, (2)B, (4)C, (1)B, (1)A, (1)D, (1)C, (2)A
Row 147 (R): (4)A, (3)B, (4)C, (1)B, (2)C
Row 148 (L): (2)C, (1)D, (1)B, (4)C, (1)D, (1)C, (1)B, (3)A
Row 149 (R): (4)A, (4)C, (1)B, (2)C, (1)B, (2)C
Row 150 (L): (3)C, (1)B, (2)C, (1)B, (3)C, (2)B, (2)A
Row 151 (R): (4)A, (4)C, (2)A, (1)C, (1)D, (2)C
Row 152 (L): (5)C, (2)B, (4)C, (1)B, (2)A
Row 153 (R): (4)A, (4)C, (2)A, (1)C, (1)D, (2)C
Row 154 (L): (1)A, (1)B, (3)C, (3)A, (3)C, (1)B, (2)A
Row 155 (R): (4)A, (4)C, (2)A, (3)C, (1)B
Row 156 (L): (2)A, (3)C, (3)A, (3)C, (1)B, (2)A
Row 157 (R): (4)A, (4)C, (2)A, (1)B, (2)C, (1)B
Row 158 (L): (2)A, (2)C, (1)B, (3)A, (2)C, (1)D, (3)A
Row 159 (R): (4)A, (4)C, (2)A, (3)B, (1)A
Row 160 (L): (1)B, (3)A, (3)B, (3)C, (4)A
Row 161 (R): (5)A, (1)B, (2)C, (1)D, (1)A, (2)B, (1)D, (1)A
Row 162 (L): (1)C, (1)B, (3)D, (1)B, (1)C, (1)D, (2)B, (4)A
Row 163 (R): (3)A, (1)B, (1)C, (1)D, (1)B, (1)A, (1)B, (1)A, (4)B
Row 164 (L): (1)C, (1)B, (1)D, (3)B, (1)A, (1)B, (4)C, (2)A
Row 165 (R): (2)A, (1)B, (5)C, (1)A, (1)B, (2)A, (2)B
Row 166 (L): (3)B, (1)A, (4)B, (4)C, (1)B, (1)A
Row 167 (R): (2)A, (4)C, (2)A, (2)B, (2)A, (1)D, (1)A
Row 168 (L): (1)C, (3)A, (2)B, (2)A, (2)B, (2)C, (1)D, (1)A
Row 169 (R): (2)A, (4)C, (2)A, (2)B, (2)A, (1)D, (1)B
Row 170 (L): (1)B, (1)A, (2)B, (1)D, (1)B, (3)A, (1)D, (3)C, (1)A
Row 171 (R): (2)A, (4)C, (4)A, (2)D, (2)B
Row 172 (L): (2)A, (3)B, (1)A, (3)B, (3)C, (1)B, (1)A
Row 173 (R): (2)A, (4)C, (2)A, (1)C, (2)D, (1)B, (2)A
Row 174 (L): (2)A, (4)B, (1)C, (2)B, (3)C, (2)A
Row 175 (R): (4)A, (2)C, (1)A, (2)B, (1)D, (2)B, (1)C, (1)B
Row 176 (L): (2)A, (2)B, (1)A, (1)C, (1)D, (5)C, (2)A
Row 177 (R): (3)A, (1)B, (4)C, (1)B, (1)C, (1)A, (1)B, (1)A, (1)C

Row 178 (L): (2)A, (2)C, (1)A, (3)B, (4)C, (2)A

Row 179 (R): (3)A, (1)B, (6)C, (1)A, (2)B, (1)A

Row 180 (L): (1)B, (3)C, (2)A, (1)D, (1)B, (4)C, (2)A

Row 181 (R): (4)A, (2)C, (2)B, (1)C, (1)B, (2)A, (1)C, (1)A

Row 182 (L): (1)C, (1)A, (1)C, (1)B, (2)A, (2)C, (1)D, (2)C, (1)B, (2)A

Row 183 (R): (4)A, (1)C, (1)D, (1)B, (1)D, (2)C, (2)A, (1)C, (1)D

Row 184 (L): (1)C, (1)A, (2)C, (2)B, (2)C, (6)A

Row 185 (R): (6)A, (4)C, (1)D, (1)B, (2)C

Row 186 (L): (1)A, (1)B, (6)C, (1)B, (5)A

Row 187 (R): (6)A, (8)C

Row 188 (L): (1)A, (1)B, (6)C, (1)B, (5)A

Row 189 (R): (6)A, (8)C

Row 190 (L): (1)A, (1)B, (3)C, (1)D, (2)C, (1)B, (5)A

Row 191 (R): (6)A, (8)C

Row 192 (L): (1)A, (1)B, (3)C, (1)A, (2)C, (6)A

Row 193 (R): (6)A, (1)B, (2)C, (1)B, (4)C

Row 194 (L): (2)A, (2)C, (2)B, (2)D, (6)A

Row 195 (R): (10)A, (1)B, (1)C, (1)D, (1)B

Row 196 (L): (2)A, (2)B, (1)C, (1)D, (8)A

Row 197 (R): (10)A, (1)C, (1)B, (2)A

Row 198 (L): (3)A, (1)D, (1)C, (1)B, (8)A

Row 199 (R): (10)A, (1)B, (1)C, (2)A

Row 200 (L): (2)A, (1)B, (2)C, (1)B, (8)A

Celtic Knot

Traditional Celtic motifs are often seen in Ireland, Scotland, and northern England. Celtic knots first appeared in the early 7th century and can be found in multiple variations, including the vertical one in this bracelet.

note
I find it interesting how different this pattern looks when reversing the same colors. It would also look great in green and gold.

SUPPLIES

- 11º cylinder beads
  - 10–11g color A (Miyuki DB-202, white pearl AB)
  - 3–4g color B (Miyuki DB-148, silver-lined green)
- Beading needle, size 10, 11, or 12
- Fireline, crystal, 6-lb. test
- 4-loop tube clasp
- Scissors, thread snips, or thread burner

A   B

The knot motif measures 3¾ in. (9.5cm) long. Adjusting the bracelet's length is easy; subtract 3¾ in. from your desired length, divide by 2, and that's how much solid color you'll need at each end.

MAKE THE BRACELET

1. Follow the pattern or word chart below to complete the piece (see two-drop peyote stitch, p. 9), leaving an 8–10-in. (20–25cm) tail for adding the clasp. Add and end thread as needed.
2. Attach a 4-loop tube clasp to each end of the bracelet (see p. 7).

Rows 1 and 2 (L): (28)A
Rows 3–38: (14)A
Row 39 (R): (2)A, (4)B, (4)A, (2)B, (2)A
Row 40 (L): (2)A, (4)B, (2)A, (6)B
Row 41 (R): (1)A, (1)B, (4)A, (1)B, (1)A, (2)B, (2)A, (2)B
Row 42 (L): (1)A, (1)B, (4)A, (2)B, (6)A
Row 43 (R): (1)A, (1)B, (5)A, (1)B, (6)A
Row 44 (L): (1)A, (1)B, (1)A, (2)B, (2)A, (1)B, (2)A, (2)B, (2)A
Row 45 (R): (1)A, (5)B, (3)A, (3)B, (2)A
Row 46 (L): (1)A, (2)B, (1)A, (3)B, (2)A, (1)B, (4)A
Row 47 (R): (1)A, (2)B, (5)A, (2)B, (4)A
Row 48 (L): (1)A, (2)B, (5)A, (2)B, (4)A
Row 49 (R): (1)A, (2)B, (2)A, (3)B, (1)A, (1)B, (4)A
Row 50 (L): (1)A, (3)B, (1)A, (1)B, (3)A, (1)B, (4)A
Row 51 (R): (1)A, (5)B, (1)A, (1)B, (6)A
Row 52 (L): (1)A, (1)B, (1)A, (2)B, (2)A, (1)B, (2)A, (1)B, (3)A

(Continues on p. 94)

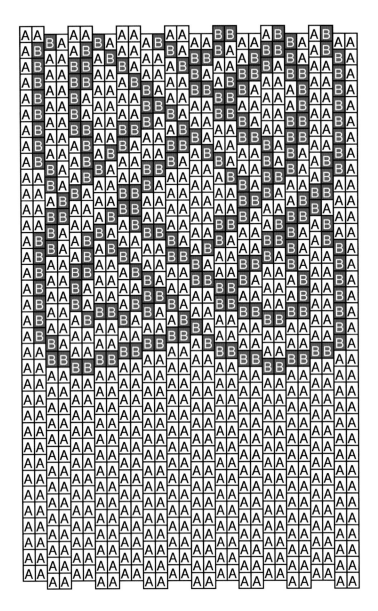

Row 53 (R): (1)A, (1)B, (1)A, (2)B, (1)A, (2)B, (2)A, (1)B, (2)A, (1)B

Row 54 (L): (1)A, (1)B, (1)A, (1)B, (2)A, (1)B, (1)A, (1)B, (1)A, (2)B, (1)A, (1)B

Row 55 (R): (3)A, (1)B, (4)A, (1)B, (2)A, (1)B, (1)A, (1)B

Row 56 (L): (8)A, (2)B, (1)A, (1)B, (1)A, (1)B

Row 57 (R): (2)A, (2)B, (1)A, (1)B, (3)A, (5)B

Row 58 (L): (4)A, (2)B, (6)A, (1)B, (1)A

Row 59 (R): (2)A, (1)B, (1)A, (2)B, (6)A, (1)B, (1)A

Row 60 (L): (2)A, (1)B, (1)A, (2)B, (4)A, (1)B, (1)A, (2)B

Row 61 (R): (5)A, (1)B, (3)A, (1)B, (2)A, (2)B

Row 62 (L): (3)A, (1)B, (5)A, (3)B, (1)A, (1)B

Row 63 (R): (1)A, (1)B, (1)A, (1)B, (4)A, (2)B, (1)A, (1)B, (1)A, (1)B

Row 64 (L): (1)A, (1)B, (1)A, (1)B, (2)A, (1)B, (1)A, (1)B, (2)A, (1)B, (1)A, (1)B

Row 65 (R): (1)A, (1)B, (1)A, (1)B, (2)A, (1)B, (3)A, (1)B, (3)A

Row 66 (L): (1)A, (1)B, (1)A, (2)B, (1)A, (2)B, (2)A, (1)B, (3)A

Row 67 (R): (1)A, (4)B, (2)A, (1)B, (6)A

Row 68 (L): (1)A, (5)B, (1)A, (1)B, (6)A

Row 69 (R): (1)A, (2)B, (2)A, (1)B, (3)A, (1)B, (4)A

Row 70 (L): (1)A, (2)B, (3)A, (1)B, (2)A, (1)B, (4)A

Row 71 (R): (1)A, (2)B, (5)A, (2)B, (4)A

Row 72 (L): (1)A, (2)B, (5)A, (2)B, (4)A

Row 73 (R): (1)A, (2)B, (2)A, (2)B, (2)A, (1)B, (4)A

Row 74 (L): (1)A, (3)B, (1)A, (1)B, (3)A, (1)B, (4)A

Row 75 (R): (1)A, (5)B, (1)A, (1)B, (6)A

Row 76 (L): (1)A, (4)B, (2)A, (1)B, (2)A, (1)B, (3)A

Row 77 (R): (1)A, (1)B, (1)A, (2)B, (1)A, (2)B, (2)A, (1)B, (3)A

Row 78 (L): (1)A, (1)B, (1)A, (1)B, (2)A, (1)B, (1)A, (1)B, (1)A, (2)B, (1)A, (1)B

Row 79 (R): (3)A, (1)B, (4)A, (1)B, (2)A, (1)B, (1)A, (1)B

Row 80 (L): (8)A, (2)B, (1)A, (1)B, (1)A, (1)B

Row 81 (R): (2)A, (2)B, (1)A, (1)B, (3)A, (5)B

Row 82 (L): (4)A, (2)B, (3)A, (1)B, (2)A, (1)B, (1)A

Row 83 (R): (2)A, (1)B, (1)A, (2)B, (4)A, (1)B, (1)A, (1)B, (1)A

Row 84 (L): (2)A, (1)B, (1)A, (2)B, (4)A, (1)B, (1)A, (1)B, (1)A

Row 85 (R): (4)A, (2)B, (3)A, (1)B, (2)A, (1)B, (1)A

Row 86 (L): (2)A, (2)B, (1)A, (1)B, (3)A, (5)B

Row 87 (R): (8)A, (2)B, (1)A, (1)B, (1)A, (1)B

Row 88 (L): (3)A, (1)B, (2)A, (1)B, (1)A, (1)B, (2)A, (1)B, (1)A, (1)B

Row 89 (R): (1)A, (1)B, (1)A, (1)B, (2)A, (1)B, (1)A, (1)B, (1)A, (2)B, (1)A, (1)B

Row 90 (L): (1)A, (1)B, (1)A, (2)B, (1)A, (2)B, (2)A, (1)B, (3)A

Row 91 (R): (1)A, (4)B, (2)A, (1)B, (6)A

Row 92 (L): (1)A, (5)B, (1)A, (1)B, (6)A

Row 93 (R): (1)A, (3)B, (1)A, (1)B, (3)A, (1)B, (4)A

Row 94 (L): (1)A, (2)B, (2)A, (2)B, (2)A, (1)B, (4)A

Row 95 (R): (1)A, (2)B, (5)A, (2)B, (4)A

Row 96 (L): (1)A, (2)B, (5)A, (2)B, (4)A

Row 97 (R): (1)A, (2)B, (2)A, (2)B, (2)A, (1)B, (4)A

Row 98 (L): (1)A, (3)B, (1)A, (1)B, (3)A, (1)B, (4)A

Row 99 (R): (1)A, (5)B, (1)A, (1)B, (6)A

Row 100 (L): (1)A, (4)B, (2)A, (1)B, (6)A

Row 101 (R): (1)A, (1)B, (1)A, (2)B, (1)A, (2)B, (2)A, (1)B, (3)A

Row 102 (L): (1)A, (1)B, (1)A, (1)B, (2)A, (1)B, (1)A, (1)B, (1)A, (2)B, (2)A

Row 103 (R): (1)A, (1)B, (1)A, (1)B, (2)A, (1)B, (1)A, (1)B, (2)A, (1)B, (1)A, (1)B

Row 104 (L): (8)A, (2)B, (1)A, (1)B, (1)A, (1)B

Row 105 (R): (2)A, (2)B, (1)A, (1)B, (3)A, (5)B

Row 106 (L): (4)A, (2)B, (3)A, (1)B, (2)A, (2)B

Row 107 (R): (2)A, (1)B, (1)A, (2)B, (4)A, (1)B, (1)A, (1)B, (1)A

Row 108 (L): (2)A, (1)B, (1)A, (2)B, (6)A, (1)B, (1)A

Row 109 (R): (4)A, (2)B, (3)A, (1)B, (2)A, (1)B, (1)A

Row 110 (L): (2)A, (2)B, (1)A, (1)B, (3)A, (5)B

Row 111 (R): (8)A, (2)B, (1)A, (1)B, (1)A, (1)B

Row 112 (L): (3)A, (1)B, (4)A, (1)B, (2)A, (1)B, (1)A, (1)B

Row 113 (R): (1)A, (1)B, (1)A, (1)B, (2)A, (1)B, (1)A, (1)B, (1)A, (2)B, (1)A, (1)B

Row 114 (L): (1)A, (1)B, (1)A, (2)B, (1)A, (2)B, (2)A, (1)B, (3)A

Row 115 (R): (1)A, (4)B, (2)A, (1)B, (2)A, (1)B, (3)A

Row 116 (L): (1)A, (5)B, (1)A, (1)B, (6)A

Row 117 (R): (1)A, (3)B, (1)A, (1)B, (3)A, (1)B, (4)A

Row 118 (L): (1)A, (2)B, (2)A, (3)B, (1)A, (1)B, (4)A

Row 119 (R): (1)A, (2)B, (5)A, (2)B, (4)A

Row 120 (L): (1)A, (2)B, (5)A, (2)B, (4)A

Row 121 (R): (1)A, (2)B, (3)A, (1)B, (1)A, (2)B, (4)A

Row 122 (L): (1)A, (3)B, (1)A, (1)B, (3)A, (1)B, (4)A

Row 123 (R): (1)A, (5)B, (1)A, (1)B, (6)A

Row 124 (L): (1)A, (5)B, (1)A, (1)B, (6)A

Row 125 (R): (1)A, (1)B, (1)A, (2)B, (1)A, (2)B, (2)A, (1)B, (3)A

Row 126 (L): (1)A, (1)B, (1)A, (1)B, (2)A, (1)B, (3)A, (1)B, (3)A

Row 127 (R): (1)A, (1)B, (1)A, (1)B, (2)A, (1)B, (1)A, (1)B, (1)A, (1)B, (2)A, (1)B

Row 128 (L): (1)A, (1)B, (1)A, (1)B, (4)A, (2)B, (1)A, (1)B, (1)A, (1)B

Row 129 (R): (3)A, (1)B, (5)A, (3)B, (1)A, (1)B

Row 130 (L): (5)A, (1)B, (3)A, (1)B, (3)A, (1)B

Row 131 (R): (2)A, (1)B, (1)A, (2)B, (4)A, (1)B, (1)A, (2)B

Row 132 (L): (2)A, (1)B, (1)A, (2)B, (6)A, (1)B, (1)A

Row 133 (R): (4)A, (2)B, (6)A, (1)B, (1)A

Row 134 (L): (2)A, (2)B, (1)A, (1)B, (4)A, (1)B, (1)A, (2)B

Row 135 (R): (5)A, (1)B, (2)A, (2)B, (1)A, (1)B, (1)A, (1)B

Row 136 (L): (3)A, (1)B, (4)A, (2)B, (1)A, (1)B, (1)A, (1)B

Row 137 (R): (1)A, (1)B, (1)A, (1)B, (2)A, (1)B, (1)A, (1)B, (1)A, (2)B, (1)A, (1)B

Row 138 (L): (1)A, (1)B, (1)A, (1)B, (2)A, (1)B, (3)A, (1)B, (2)A, (1)B

Row 139 (R): (1)A, (1)B, (1)A, (2)B, (1)A, (2)B, (2)A, (1)B, (3)A

Row 140 (L): (1)A, (1)B, (1)A, (3)B, (1)A, (1)B, (6)A

Row 141 (R): (1)A, (3)B, (1)A, (1)B, (8)A

Row 142 (L): (1)A, (2)B, (2)A, (3)B, (1)A, (1)B, (4)A

Row 143 (R): (1)A, (2)B, (5)A, (2)B, (4)A

Row 144 (L): (1)A, (2)B, (5)A, (2)B, (4)A

Row 145 (R): (1)A, (2)B, (2)A, (2)B, (1)A, (2)B, (4)A

Row 146 (L): (1)A, (5)B, (3)A, (3)B, (2)A

Row 147 (R): (1)A, (1)B, (1)A, (2)B, (2)A, (1)B, (2)A, (2)B, (2)A

Row 148 (L): (1)A, (1)B, (5)A, (1)B, (6)A

Row 149 (R): (1)A, (1)B, (4)A, (2)B, (6)A

Row 150 (L): (1)A, (1)B, (4)A, (1)B, (1)A, (2)B, (3)A, (1)B

Row 151 (R): (4)A, (2)B, (2)A, (2)B, (2)A, (2)B

Row 152 (L): (2)A, (4)B, (4)A, (4)B

Row 153 (R): (2)A, (2)B, (6)A, (2)B, (2)A

Rows 154–180: (14)A

note

If you reverse the colors (white knot on green background), use smoke Fireline.

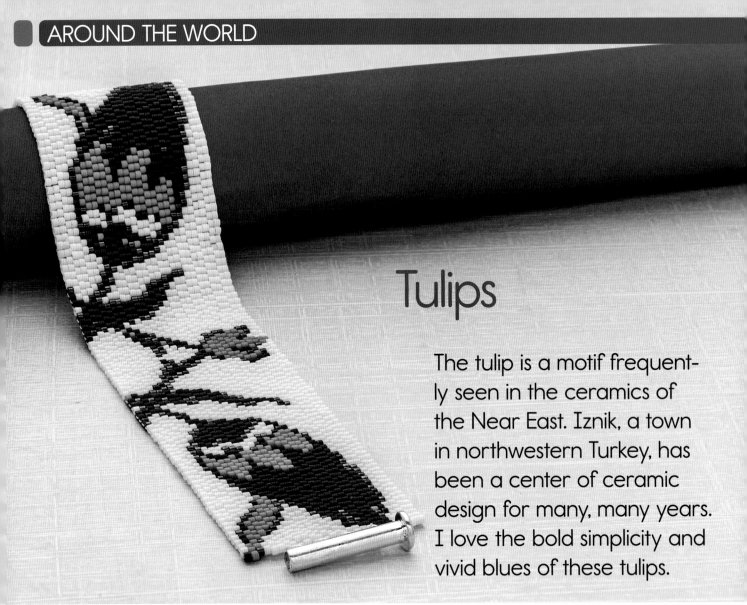

Tulips

The tulip is a motif frequently seen in the ceramics of the Near East. Iznik, a town in northwestern Turkey, has been a center of ceramic design for many, many years. I love the bold simplicity and vivid blues of these tulips.

SUPPLIES

- 11º cylinder beads
  - 9g color A (Miyuki DB-1490, opaque bisque white)
  - 2g color B (Miyuki DB-2, metallic dark blue AB)
  - 4g color C (Miyuki DB-756, matte opaque cobalt)
  - 2g color D (Miyuki DB-798, matte opaque capri blue)
- Beading needle, size 10, 11, or 12
- Fireline, crystal, 6-lb. test
- 4-loop clasp
- Scissors, thread snips, or thread burner

A   B   C   D

The pattern measures 1½ (3.8cm) wide and 7¼ in. (18.4cm) long, not including the clasp.

MAKE THE BRACELET

1. Follow the pattern or word chart below to complete the piece (see two-drop peyote stitch, p. 9), leaving an 8–10-in. (20–25cm) tail for adding the clasp. Add and end thread as needed.

2. Attach a 4-loop tube clasp to each end of the bracelet (see p. 7).

Rows 1 and 2 (L): (28)A
Row 3 (R): (2)B, (12)A
Row 4 (L): (2)A, (1)C, (1)B, (10)A
Row 5 (R): (1)A, (1)B, (9)A, (2)B, (1)A
Row 6 (L): (2)A, (2)B, (9)A, (1)C
Row 7 (R): (1)A, (1)B, (9)A, (2)B, (1)A

Row 8 (L): (2)A, (2)C, (8)A, (1)B, (1)D
Row 9 (R): (10)A, (1)B, (1)C, (2)A
Row 10 (L): (2)A, (1)B, (1)C, (8)A, (1)C, (1)D
Row 11 (R): (10)A, (1)B, (1)C, (2)A
Row 12 (L): (2)A, (1)B, (1)C, (2)B, (6)A, (2)D
Row 13 (R): (2)A, (1)C, (6)A, (1)B, (2)C, (1)B, (1)A
Row 14 (L): (2)A, (1)B, (1)C, (2)B, (6)A, (2)D
Row 15 (R): (2)A, (1)D, (1)B, (4)A, (2)B, (2)C, (2)B
Row 16 (L): (2)A, (2)B, (1)C, (1)B, (6)A, (1)D, (1)C
Row 17 (R): (2)A, (2)D, (4)A, (1)B, (3)C, (2)B
Row 18 (L): (2)A, (4)C, (1)B, (3)A, (1)B, (1)C, (1)D, (1)B
Row 19 (R): (2)A, (2)D, (4)A, (4)C, (2)B
Row 20 (L): (2)A, (4)C, (2)B, (2)A, (1)C, (1)D, (1)B, (1)A
Row 21 (R): (2)A, (1)C, (1)D, (1)C, (3)A, (4)C, (2)B
Row 22 (L): (2)A, (5)C, (1)B, (2)A, (2)D, (2)A
Row 23 (R): (3)A, (1)C, (1)D, (1)C, (1)A, (1)B, (4)C, (2)B

Row 24 (L): (2)A, (6)C, (2)A, (2)D, (2)A
Row 25 (R): (4)A, (1)D, (1)C, (1)B, (5)C, (2)B
Row 26 (L): (2)A, (6)C, (1)B, (1)A, (1)D, (1)B, (2)A
Row 27 (R): (4)A, (1)D, (7)C, (2)B
Row 28 (L): (2)A, (7)C, (1)B, (1)C, (3)A
Row 29 (R): (4)A, (1)D, (7)C, (2)B
Row 30 (L): (2)A, (8)C, (1)B, (3)A
Row 31 (R): (4)A, (1)D, (7)C, (2)B
Row 32 (L): (2)A, (8)C, (1)B, (3)A
Row 33 (R): (4)A, (1)B, (1)C, (1)B, (5)C, (2)B
Row 34 (L): (2)A, (6)C, (1)B, (1)C, (1)B, (3)A
Row 35 (R): (4)A, (2)C, (1)B, (5)C, (1)B, (1)A
Row 36 (L): (2)A, (7)C, (1)B, (1)C, (1)B, (2)A
Row 37 (R): (4)A, (1)C, (1)D, (6)C, (1)B, (1)A
Row 38 (L): (2)A, (6)C, (1)B, (1)D, (1)C, (1)B, (2)A
Row 39 (R): (4)A, (2)D, (6)C, (1)B, (1)A
Row 40 (L): (2)A, (4)C, (1)D, (3)C, (1)D, (1)C, (2)A
Row 41 (R): (3)A, (1)B, (2)D, (2)C, (2)D, (1)B, (1)C, (2)A
Row 42 (L): (2)A, (4)C, (2)D, (1)C, (3)D, (2)A
Row 43 (R): (2)A, (1)B, (3)D, (1)C, (3)D, (2)C, (2)A
Row 44 (L): (2)A, (4)C, (2)D, (1)C, (3)D, (2)A
Row 45 (R): (2)A, (1)B, (6)D, (3)C, (2)A
Row 46 (L): (2)A, (1)B, (3)C, (2)D, (1)C, (3)D, (2)A
Row 47 (R): (2)A, (1)C, (6)D, (3)C, (2)A
Row 48 (L): (2)A, (1)B, (1)C, (1)D, (1)C, (6)D, (2)A
Row 49 (R): (2)A, (1)C, (6)D, (1)C, (1)D, (1)C, (2)A
Row 50 (L): (2)A, (1)B, (1)C, (8)D, (2)A
Row 51 (R): (2)A, (1)C, (8)D, (1)C, (2)A
Row 52 (L): (3)A, (1)B, (4)D, (4)C, (2)A
Row 53 (R): (2)A, (1)C, (1)B, (1)C, (1)D, (1)B, (1)C, (3)D, (1)C, (2)A
Row 54 (L): (3)A, (1)B, (4)D, (1)A, (1)B, (4)A
Row 55 (R): (2)A, (1)B, (2)A, (1)B, (2)A, (3)D, (1)B, (2)A
Row 56 (L): (4)A, (2)D, (2)C, (6)A
Row 57 (R): (2)A, (2)B, (1)A, (1)B, (3)A, (1)C, (2)B, (2)A
Row 58 (L): (4)A, (2)D, (2)A, (4)C, (2)A
Row 59 (R): (2)A, (1)B, (3)C, (1)B, (3)A, (1)B, (3)A
Row 60 (L): (4)A, (1)B, (1)C, (2)A, (2)C, (1)D, (1)C, (2)A
Row 61 (R): (3)A, (5)C, (1)A, (1)B, (4)A
Row 62 (L): (5)A, (2)B, (1)C, (1)D, (1)C, (1)B, (1)C, (2)A
Row 63 (R): (3)A, (1)B, (2)C, (1)B, (1)D, (2)B, (4)A
Row 64 (L): (6)A, (6)C, (2)A
Row 65 (R): (4)A, (3)C, (2)B, (5)A
Row 66 (L): (6)A, (2)B, (3)C, (3)A
Row 67 (R): (4)A, (2)C, (2)B, (6)A
Row 68 (L): (8)A, (3)B, (3)A
Row 69 (R): (4)A, (1)B, (9)A
Row 70 (L): (10)A, (1)C, (1)B, (2)A
Row 71 (R): (14)A
Row 72 (L): (4)A, (2)B, (4)A, (1)B, (1)C, (2)A
Row 73 (R): (1)B, (2)A, (1)B, (4)A, (1)B, (1)C, (4)A
Row 74 (L): (6)A, (2)B, (3)A, (1)B, (2)A
Row 75 (R): (1)C, (1)A, (2)B, (3)A, (2)B, (5)A
Row 76 (L): (6)A, (1)B, (1)C, (4)A, (1)B, (1)A
Row 77 (R): (2)C, (1)B, (3)A, (1)B, (1)C, (6)A
Row 78 (L): (6)A, (1)B, (1)C, (4)B, (2)C
Row 79 (R): (1)A, (2)C, (1)B, (4)C, (6)A
Row 80 (L): (7)A, (1)B, (6)C

(Continues on p. 98)

(Continues on p. 99)

Row 81 (R): (1)B, (6)C, (1)B, (6)A
Row 82 (L): (8)A, (6)C
Row 83 (R): (6)C, (1)B, (7)A
Row 84 (L): (8)A, (2)B, (3)C, (1)B
Row 85 (R): (4)C, (1)B, (9)A
Row 86 (L): (11)A, (1)C, (1)B, (1)C
Row 87 (R): (1)C, (1)B, (1)A, (1)C, (10)A
Row 88 (L): (10)A, (1)C, (1)D, (2)A
Row 89 (R): (1)B, (3)A, (1)C, (9)A
Row 90 (L): (10)A, (1)D, (1)C, (2)A
Row 91 (R): (4)A, (2)C, (8)A
Row 92 (L): (9)A, (1)B, (1)C, (3)A
Row 93 (R): (4)A, (1)C, (1)B, (8)A
Row 94 (L): (8)A, (1)C, (1)B, (4)A
Row 95 (R): (4)A, (2)C, (1)B, (3)A, (4)B
Row 96 (L): (2)A, (2)D, (2)B, (2)A, (1)D, (1)C, (4)A
Row 97 (R): (5)A, (1)C, (1)B, (1)C, (2)A, (3)D, (1)B
Row 98 (L): (2)A, (3)D, (1)B, (1)A, (1)C, (1)A,
(1)B, (4)A
Row 99 (R): (5)A, (1)B, (1)A, (1)C, (1)A, (1)B,
(2)D, (1)B, (1)A
Row 100 (L): (2)A, (1)C, (3)D, (2)C, (1)A, (1)B, (4)A
Row 101 (R): (5)A, (1)B, (2)A, (1)C, (5)D
Row 102 (L): (6)D, (8)A
Row 103 (R): (8)A, (1)B, (5)D
Row 104 (L): (1)A, (5)D, (1)B, (7)A
Row 105 (R): (5)A, (1)C, (2)A, (2)C, (1)D, (1)C, (1)D, (1)B
Row 106 (L): (2)A, (2)C, (2)D, (2)C, (1)A, (1)B, (4)A
Row 107 (R): (5)A, (2)B, (1)C, (1)A, (1)B, (2)D, (1)B, (1)A
Row 108 (L): (2)A, (1)B, (2)D, (1)C, (1)A, (2)B, (1)C, (4)A
Row 109 (R): (4)A, (4)B, (2)A, (3)D, (1)B
Row 110 (L): (2)A, (2)D, (4)A, (2)C, (4)A
Row 111 (R): (4)A, (1)B, (1)C, (5)A, (1)B, (2)C
Row 112 (L): (2)A, (2)C, (4)A, (3)B, (3)A
Row 113 (R): (4)A, (2)B, (8)A
Row 114 (L): (10)A, (1)B, (3)A
Row 115 (R): (4)A, (1)B, (9)A
Row 116 (L): (10)A, (2)B, (2)A
Row 117 (R): (3)A, (1)B, (10)A
Row 118 (L): (10)A, (2)B, (2)A
Row 119 (R): (1)D, (1)C, (2)B, (10)A
Row 120 (L): (10)A, (1)B, (3)C
Row 121 (R): (1)C, (1)B, (4)C, (8)A
Row 122 (L): (8)A, (4)C, (1)B, (1)C
Row 123 (R): (3)C, (1)B, (3)C, (7)A
Row 124 (L): (8)A, (6)C
Row 125 (R): (1)A, (1)B, (2)C, (2)B, (2)C, (6)A
Row 126 (L): (7)A, (1)B, (4)C, (1)B, (1)C
Row 127 (R): (1)B, (1)C, (2)A, (2)B, (2)C, (6)A
Row 128 (L): (6)A, (1)B, (1)C, (4)A, (2)C
Row 129 (R): (1)C, (1)B, (1)C, (4)A, (1)C,
(1)B, (5)A
Row 130 (L): (6)A, (2)C, (4)A, (1)B, (1)A
Row 131 (R): (1)B, (1)A, (2)C, (4)A, (2)C, (4)A
Row 132 (L): (4)A, (2)C, (1)B, (4)A, (1)B, (2)A
Row 133 (R): (1)B, (2)A, (1)C, (4)A, (2)B,
(1)C, (1)B, (2)A

Row 134 (L): (11)A, (1)C, (2)A
Row 135 (R): (11)A, (1)B, (2)A
Row 136 (L): (3)A, (1)B, (6)A, (2)C, (2)A
Row 137 (R): (4)A, (1)C, (1)B, (8)A
Row 138 (L): (8)A, (3)C, (3)A
Row 139 (R): (4)A, (4)C, (6)A
Row 140 (L): (6)A, (1)B, (4)C, (1)B, (2)A
Row 141 (R): (3)A, (1)B, (4)C, (1)B, (5)A
Row 142 (L): (6)A, (1)B, (5)C, (2)A
Row 143 (R): (3)A, (1)B, (4)C, (1)A, (1)C, (4)A
Row 144 (L): (5)A, (1)C, (1)A, (1)B, (4)C, (2)A
Row 145 (R): (2)A, (1)B, (4)C, (1)B, (6)A
Row 146 (L): (4)A, (1)C, (1)B, (2)A, (4)C, (2)A
Row 147 (R): (2)A, (1)B, (1)C, (1)B, (1)C, (1)B, (2)A, (1)B, (4)A
Row 148 (L): (4)A, (2)D, (2)B, (2)C, (1)B, (1)C, (1)B, (1)A
Row 149 (R): (2)A, (1)B, (5)A, (1)C, (1)D, (1)C, (3)A
Row 150 (L): (4)A, (3)D, (1)C, (4)A, (1)B, (1)A
Row 151 (R): (2)A, (1)C, (1)A, (2)B, (1)A, (1)B, (3)D, (1)B, (2)A
Row 152 (L): (4)A, (3)D, (1)C, (1)A, (1)B, (2)A, (1)B, (1)A
Row 153 (R): (2)A, (1)D, (3)C, (1)B, (4)D, (1)C, (2)A
Row 154 (L): (4)A, (2)D, (1)C, (3)D, (3)C, (1)A
Row 155 (R): (2)A, (3)D, (1)C, (2)D, (1)C, (2)D, (1)C, (2)A
Row 156 (L): (3)A, (1)B, (8)D, (1)C, (1)A
Row 157 (R): (2)A, (6)D, (2)C, (1)D, (1)C, (2)A
Row 158 (L): (3)A, (1)C, (1)D, (1)C, (3)D, (1)C, (2)D, (1)B, (1)A
Row 159 (R): (2)A, (1)C, (5)D, (4)C, (2)A
Row 160 (L): (3)A, (3)C, (3)D, (1)C, (2)D, (2)A
Row 161 (R): (2)A, (1)C, (5)D, (4)C, (2)A
Row 162 (L): (2)A, (1)B, (3)C, (2)D, (2)C, (2)D, (2)A
Row 163 (R): (2)A, (1)B, (1)C, (1)D, (2)C, (1)D, (4)C, (2)A
Row 164 (L): (2)A, (1)B, (3)C, (2)D, (2)C, (1)D, (1)C, (2)A
Row 165 (R): (3)A, (1)C, (1)D, (7)C, (2)A
Row 166 (L): (2)A, (1)B, (9)C, (2)A
Row 167 (R): (3)A, (1)B, (8)C, (2)A
Row 168 (L): (2)A, (1)B, (9)C, (2)A
Row 169 (R): (4)A, (8)C, (1)B, (1)A
Row 170 (L): (2)A, (1)B, (8)C, (1)B, (2)A
Row 171 (R): (4)A, (8)C, (1)B, (1)A

Row 172 (L): (2)A, (9)C, (3)A
Row 173 (R): (4)A, (8)C, (1)B, (1)A
Row 174 (L): (2)A, (8)C, (1)D, (3)A
Row 175 (R): (4)A, (1)D, (7)C, (1)B, (1)A
Row 176 (L): (2)A, (8)C, (1)D, (1)B, (2)A
Row 177 (R): (4)A, (1)D, (1)B, (6)C, (1)B, (1)A
Row 178 (L): (2)A, (7)C, (1)B, (2)D, (2)A
Row 179 (R): (3)A, (1)B, (1)D, (1)B, (6)C, (1)B, (1)A
Row 180 (L): (2)A, (6)C, (1)B, (1)A, (2)D, (2)A
Row 181 (R): (2)A, (1)B, (2)D, (1)B, (6)C, (1)B, (1)A
Row 182 (L): (2)A, (6)C, (2)A, (2)D, (1)B, (1)A
Row 183 (R): (2)A, (2)D, (1)B, (2)A, (5)C, (1)B, (1)A
Row 184 (L): (2)A, (6)C, (2)A, (3)D, (1)B
Row 185 (R): (2)A, (2)D, (1)B, (2)A, (1)B, (4)C, (1)B, (1)A
Row 186 (L): (2)A, (6)C, (2)A, (1)B, (2)D, (1)C
Row 187 (R): (1)A, (1)B, (2)D, (4)A, (1)C, (1)B, (2)C, (2)A
Row 188 (L): (2)A, (1)C, (1)D, (3)C, (1)B, (3)A, (1)B, (2)D
Row 189 (R): (1)A, (1)B, (1)D, (1)B, (4)A, (1)C, (1)B, (2)C, (2)A
Row 190 (L): (2)A, (2)B, (3)C, (5)A, (2)D
Row 191 (R): (1)A, (1)C, (6)A, (1)C, (1)B, (2)C, (2)A
Row 192 (L): (3)A, (1)B, (1)C, (1)B, (6)A, (1)B, (1)D
Row 193 (R): (1)A, (1)D, (6)A, (1)C, (1)B, (2)C, (2)A
Row 194 (L): (3)A, (3)C, (7)A, (1)D
Row 195 (R): (1)A, (1)D, (8)A, (2)C, (2)A
Row 196 (L): (3)A, (1)C, (1)B, (8)A, (1)B
Row 197 (R): (1)B, (1)D, (8)A, (1)C, (1)B, (2)A
Row 198 (L): (2)A, (1)B, (1)C, (10)A
Row 199 (R): (2)B, (12)A
Row 200 (L): (2)A, (1)C, (1)B, (10)A
Row 201 (R): (14)A
Row 202 (L): (2)A, (1)B, (11)A
Row 203 (R): (12)A, (1)C, (1)A
Row 204 (L): (14)A
Row 205 (R): (14)A
Row 206 (L): (14)A
Row 207 (R): (14)A
Row 208 (L): (14)A

Birth of Venus

Because I really wanted to capture
the details of the beautiful face of
Venus, this bracelet zooms in on just
a portion of Botticelli's painting, as
if one is looking at her through a
partially open door.

note
The mix of galvanized
(metallic), matte, and shiny
beads results in a bracelet
with a sense of depth and
detail.

SUPPLIES

- 11º cylinder beads
  - 3g color A (Miyuki DB-1584, opaque matte currant)
  - 4g color B (Miyuki DB-2142, opaque cognac)
  - 3g color C (Miyuki DB-2109, opaque sienna)
  - 1g color D (Miyuki DB-340, copper-plated matte)
  - 3g color E (Miyuki DB-1165, galvanized matte muscat)
  - 3g color F (Miyuki DB-205, ceylon beige)
  - 1g color G (Miyuki DB-389, matte op light terracotta)
- Beading needle, size 10, 11, or 12
- Fireline, smoke, 6-lb. test
- 4-loop tube clasp
- Scissors, thread snips, or thread burner

A B C D E F G

This piece is 1½ in. (3.8cm) wide and 7¼ in. (18.4cm) long, not including clasp; shorten the length by omitting bottom rows until you reach your desired length. For the bracelet pictured here, I stitched 6½ in. (16.5cm) before adding the clasp, for a total bracelet length of 7 in. (18cm).

MAKE THE BRACELET

1. Follow the pattern or word chart below to complete the piece (see two-drop peyote stitch, p. 9), leaving an 8–10-in. (20–25cm) tail for adding the clasp. Add and end thread as needed.

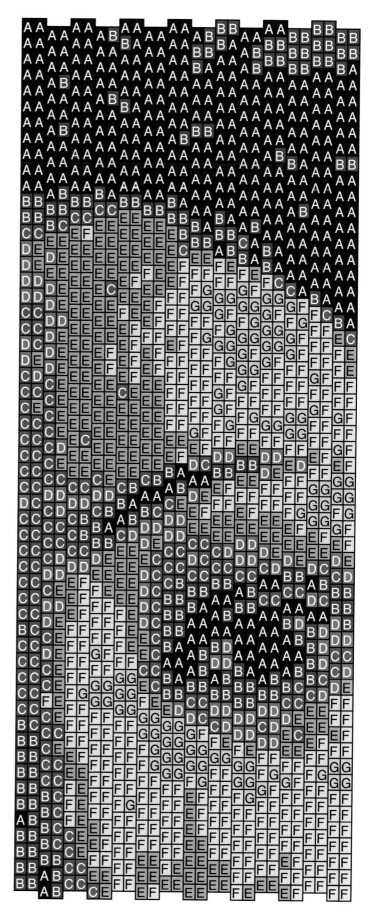

(Continues on p. 102)

2. Attach a 4-loop tube clasp to each end of the bracelet (see p. 7).

Row 1 and 2 (L): (6)B, (4)A, (3)B, (7)A, (1)B, (7)A
Row 3 (R): (4)A, (1)B, (3)A, (1)B, (1)A, (4)B
Row 4 (L): (5)B, (1)A, (2)B, (6)A
Row 5 (R): (10)A, (4)B
Row 6 (L): (1)A, (4)B, (2)A, (1)B, (6)A
Row 7 (R): (14)A
Row 8 (L): (12)A, (1)B, (1)A
Row 9 (R): (14)A
Row 10 (L): (10)A, (1)B, (3)A
Row 11 (R): (4)A, (1)B, (9)A
Row 12 (L): (14)A
Row 13 (R): (14)A
Row 14 (L): (6)A, (2)B, (4)A, (1)B, (1)A
Row 15 (R): (7)A, (1)B, (6)A
Row 16 (L): (14)A
Row 17 (R): (11)A, (1)B, (2)A
Row 18 (L): (2)B, (1)A, (1)B, (10)A
Row 19 (R): (14)A
Row 20 (L): (14)A
Row 21 (R): (14)A
Row 22 (L): (11)A, (2)B, (1)A
Row 23 (R): (7)B, (7)A
Row 24 (L): (2)A, (1)B, (5)A, (2)B, (2)C, (2)B
Row 25 (R): (2)B, (2)C, (2)E, (3)B, (5)A
Row 26 (L): (4)A, (1)B, (2)A, (1)B, (4)E, (1)C, (1)B
Row 27 (R): (2)C, (1)E, (1)F, (3)E, (3)B, (4)A
Row 28 (L): (5)A, (1)C, (2)B, (6)E
Row 29 (R): (1)D, (6)E, (1)C, (1)A, (2)B, (3)A
Row 30 (L): (5)A, (1)B, (7)E, (1)D
Row 31 (R): (1)D, (6)E, (2)F, (1)E, (1)B, (3)A
Row 32 (L): (4)A, (1)B, (3)F, (1)E, (1)F, (4)E
Row 33 (R): (2)D, (3)E, (1)F, (1)E, (4)F, (1)C, (2)A
Row 34 (L): (3)A, (1)C, (1)F, (2)G, (1)F, (2)E, (1)C, (2)E, (1)D
Row 35 (R): (2)D, (4)E, (2)F, (4)G, (1)B, (1)A
Row 36 (L): (2)A, (1)F, (5)G, (1)F, (4)E, (1)D
Row 37 (R): (2)C, (2)E, (1)F, (1)E, (2)F, (1)G, (1)F, (1)G, (2)F, (1)C
Row 38 (L): (1)A, (1)B, (1)G, (1)F, (1)G, (4)F, (3)E, (2)D
Row 39 (R): (2)C, (3)E, (4)F, (3)G, (2)F
Row 40 (L): (1)C, (1)E, (1)F, (4)G, (3)F, (3)E, (1)D
Row 41 (R): (1)D, (1)C, (3)E, (1)F, (1)E, (1)F, (4)G, (2)F
Row 42 (L): (1)E, (2)F, (1)G, (1)F, (1)G, (3)F, (1)E, (1)F, (2)E, (1)D
Row 43 (R): (1)D, (4)E, (4)F, (2)G, (3)F
Row 44 (L): (1)E, (3)F, (2)G, (3)F, (1)E, (1)F, (2)E, (1)D
Row 45 (R): (1)C, (1)D, (3)E, (7)F, (1)G, (1)F
Row 46 (L): (5)F, (1)G, (2)F, (5)E, (1)C
Row 47 (R): (2)C, (2)E, (1)C, (1)E, (2)F, (1)G, (5)F
Row 48 (L): (8)F, (5)E, (1)C
Row 49 (R): (1)C, (5)E, (2)F, (1)G, (3)F, (1)G, (1)F
Row 50 (L): (1)F, (4)G, (3)F, (5)E, (1)C
Row 51 (R): (2)C, (4)E, (3)F, (3)G, (2)F
Row 52 (L): (2)F, (2)G, (3)F, (1)G, (5)E, (1)C
Row 53 (R): (2)C, (1)E, (1)C, (4)E, (6)F
Row 54 (L): (1)F, (1)G, (2)F, (2)E, (1)F, (5)E, (1)D, (1)C

Row 55 (R): (2)C, (5)E, (1)F, (4)D, (1)E, (1)F
Row 56 (L): (1)F, (1)E, (1)D, (1)E, (2)B, (1)C, (1)D, (5)E, (1)C
Row 57 (R): (2)C, (4)E, (1)B, (1)A, (2)B, (1)D, (1)E, (2)F
Row 58 (L): (2)G, (2)F, (2)E, (2)A, (1)B, (1)C, (1)E, (3)C
Row 59 (R): (5)C, (1)B, (1)A, (1)B, (1)E, (3)F, (2)G
Row 60 (L): (2)G, (4)F, (1)E, (1)D, (2)A, (4)D
Row 61 (R): (1)D, (1)C, (2)D, (1)B, (1)A, (1)C, (1)E, (4)F, (2)G
Row 62 (L): (1)G, (1)F, (1)G, (2)F, (1)E, (1)F, (1)E, (1)C, (2)B, (1)C, (1)D, (1)C
Row 63 (R): (3)C, (1)B, (1)A, (1)B, (2)D, (4)E, (2)G
Row 64 (L): (1)F, (1)G, (1)F, (5)E, (2)D, (1)A, (1)B, (2)C
Row 65 (R): (3)C, (1)B, (1)C, (3)D, (5)E, (1)F
Row 66 (L): (1)F, (3)E, (2)D, (2)C, (1)E, (1)D, (2)B, (2)C
Row 67 (R): (4)C, (2)E, (3)C, (2)D, (3)E
Row 68 (L): (1)E, (1)D, (1)E, (3)D, (1)C, (1)D, (1)C, (2)E, (2)D, (1)C
Row 69 (R): (2)C, (2)D, (2)E, (5)C, (2)D, (1)C
Row 70 (L): (1)D, (1)C, (2)B, (5)C, (1)D, (2)E, (2)D
Row 71 (R): (2)C, (1)E, (1)F, (2)E, (1)C, (3)B, (3)A, (1)B
Row 72 (L): (2)B, (2)C, (1)B, (1)A, (2)B, (1)C, (1)D, (1)E, (1)F, (1)E, (1)C
Row 73 (R): (2)C, (1)E, (1)F, (2)E, (2)B, (2)A, (2)C, (1)D, (1)C
Row 74 (L): (2)B, (2)A, (2)B, (1)A, (1)B, (1)C, (1)D, (2)F, (2)D
Row 75 (R): (2)C, (1)E, (2)F, (1)E, (2)B, (1)A, (1)B, (4)A
Row 76 (L): (1)B, (2)D, (1)B, (4)A, (1)C, (1)D, (2)F, (1)E, (1)D
Row 77 (R): (1)B, (1)C, (3)F, (1)E, (2)B, (4)A, (1)B, (1)D
Row 78 (L): (2)D, (1)B, (5)A, (1)C, (1)E, (2)F, (1)E, (1)C
Row 79 (R): (2)C, (3)F, (1)E, (1)B, (1)A, (1)B, (1)D, (2)A, (1)B, (1)D
Row 80 (L): (2)C, (4)A, (1)B, (1)A, (1)C, (1)E, (1)F, (1)G, (1)E, (1)D
Row 81 (R): (2)C, (4)F, (2)A, (2)D, (2)A, (1)B, (1)D
Row 82 (L): (1)D, (1)C, (1)B, (2)A, (2)B, (1)A, (2)C, (2)F, (1)E, (1)C
Row 83 (R): (2)C, (2)F, (2)G, (1)B, (2)A, (1)B, (1)A, (2)B, (1)C
Row 84 (L): (1)E, (1)D, (1)C, (5)B, (1)C, (1)E, (2)G, (1)E, (1)C
Row 85 (R): (2)C, (1)F, (3)G, (6)B, (1)C, (1)D
Row 86 (L): (2)F, (2)C, (2)B, (2)C, (1)E, (1)F, (2)G, (1)E, (1)F
Row 87 (R): (2)C, (2)F, (2)G, (1)E, (5)D, (2)E
Row 88 (L): (2)F, (1)E, (3)D, (1)C, (1)D, (2)G, (2)F, (1)E, (1)C
Row 89 (R): (1)B, (1)C, (4)F, (2)G, (1)C, (1)D, (1)C, (1)D, (2)E
Row 90 (L): (1)F, (1)E, (1)C, (1)E, (2)D, (1)F, (3)G, (2)F, (2)C
Row 91 (R): (2)B, (4)F, (2)G, (1)F, (1)E, (2)D, (1)E, (1)F
Row 92 (L): (2)F, (3)E, (1)F, (3)G, (3)F, (1)E, (1)C
Row 93 (R): (2)B, (1)E, (3)F, (4)G, (4)F
Row 94 (L): (2)G, (2)F, (5)G, (3)F, (2)C
Row 95 (R): (2)B, (2)E, (2)F, (2)G, (3)F, (1)G, (1)F, (1)G
Row 96 (L): (2)G, (1)F, (4)G, (5)F, (2)C
Row 97 (R): (2)B, (1)F, (1)E, (6)F, (1)G, (3)F
Row 98 (L): (4)F, (1)G, (2)F, (1)E, (4)F, (1)C, (1)B
Row 99 (R): (2)B, (1)F, (1)E, (1)F, (1)G, (8)F
Row 100 (L): (7)F, (1)E, (4)F, (1)C, (1)B
Row 101 (R): (1)A, (1)B, (1)F, (1)E, (10)F
Row 102 (L): (7)F, (1)E, (3)F, (1)E, (1)C, (1)B
Row 103 (R): (2)B, (1)C, (1)E, (10)F
Row 104 (L): (6)F, (2)E, (3)F, (1)E, (1)C, (1)B
Row 105 (R): (2)B, (1)C, (1)E, (10)F

Row 106 (L): (3)F, (1)E, (2)F, (4)E, (2)F, (2)B
Row 107 (R): (2)B, (2)C, (3)F, (3)E, (4)F
Row 108 (L): (6)F, (6)E, (1)B, (1)A
Row 109 (R): (2)B, (2)C, (2)F, (6)E, (2)F
Row 110 (L): (3)F, (2)E, (1)F, (2)E, (1)F, (2)E, (1)C, (1)B, (1)A
Row 111 (R): (3)B, (1)C, (6)E, (4)F
Row 112 (L): (4)F, (1)E, (2)F, (2)E, (1)F, (1)E, (1)C, (1)B, (1)A
Row 113 (R): (1)B, (1)A, (1)B, (1)C, (1)E, (2)F, (4)E, (3)F
Row 114 (L): (2)F, (1)E, (1)F, (1)E, (1)D, (3)E, (1)F, (2)C, (1)B, (1)A
Row 115 (R): (1)B, (1)A, (2)B, (1)F, (1)E, (1)F, (5)E, (2)F
Row 116 (L): (2)F, (3)E, (2)C, (1)D, (1)C, (1)E, (2)C, (1)B, (1)A
Row 117 (R): (2)A, (2)B, (2)F, (3)C, (1)F, (1)E, (3)F
Row 118 (L): (4)F, (1)D, (1)C, (2)B, (1)C, (1)F, (1)C, (2)B, (1)A
Row 119 (R): (2)A, (2)B, (2)C, (1)B, (1)A, (1)B, (1)C, (3)F, (1)G
Row 120 (L): (1)F, (3)G, (1)E, (1)C, (2)A, (2)C, (3)B, (1)A
Row 121 (R): (2)A, (2)B, (2)C, (1)B, (1)D, (1)B, (1)C, (2)F, (2)G
Row 122 (L): (4)G, (2)F, (1)G, (1)F, (1)C, (1)F, (3)B, (1)A
Row 123 (R): (4)A, (2)B, (1)D, (1)F, (2)G, (1)F, (2)G, (1)F
Row 124 (L): (3)G, (2)F, (2)G, (1)F, (2)C, (1)B, (1)A, (1)B, (1)A
Row 125 (R): (5)A, (1)B, (1)C, (1)E, (5)F, (1)G
Row 126 (L): (1)F, (3)G, (1)F, (1)G, (2)F, (2)B, (4)A
Row 127 (R): (1)B, (5)A, (1)D, (1)E, (1)F, (2)G, (1)F, (2)G
Row 128 (L): (2)G, (1)F, (3)G, (2)F, (1)C, (1)B, (4)A
Row 129 (R): (2)B, (1)A, (3)B, (2)C, (3)F, (1)G, (2)F
Row 130 (L): (7)F, (1)E, (2)C, (4)B
Row 131 (R): (5)B, (3)C, (4)F, (2)E
Row 132 (L): (4)E, (3)F, (1)E, (1)D, (1)E, (4)B
Row 133 (R): (4)B, (3)C, (1)B, (4)F, (2)D
Row 134 (L): (1)D, (2)C, (2)F, (2)E, (1)C, (2)E, (2)C, (2)B
Row 135 (R): (4)B, (1)C, (1)B, (1)D, (1)B, (2)C, (2)E, (2)B
Row 136 (L): (1)C, (5)B, (3)C, (5)B
Row 137 (R): (2)B, (2)C, (4)B, (1)C, (2)B, (3)A
Row 138 (L): (2)C, (3)A, (1)B, (1)C, (1)F, (1)B, (1)A, (4)B
Row 139 (R): (5)B, (2)A, (1)B, (4)A, (2)E
Row 140 (L): (1)F, (1)E, (1)F, (1)C, (3)A, (1)B, (2)A, (4)B
Row 141 (R): (4)B, (4)A, (2)B, (2)C, (1)E, (1)F
Row 142 (L): (5)F, (1)E, (1)B, (4)A, (3)B
Row 143 (R): (2)B, (4)A, (2)B, (1)C, (5)F
Row 144 (L): (1)G, (3)F, (2)C, (4)B, (2)A, (2)B
Row 145 (R): (3)B, (3)A, (1)B, (1)C, (2)B, (1)C, (3)F
Row 146 (L): (2)G, (2)F, (1)C, (4)B, (2)A, (3)B
Row 147 (R): (4)B, (2)A, (2)B, (1)A, (1)B, (1)C, (1)E, (1)F, (1)G
Row 148 (L): (1)G, (1)F, (2)E, (2)B, (2)A, (6)B
Row 149 (R): (10)B, (2)C, (1)F, (1)G
Row 150 (L): (2)G, (1)F, (1)E, (1)C, (1)B, (1)A, (7)B
Row 151 (R): (10)B, (1)C, (1)E, (2)F
Row 152 (L): (2)G, (1)F, (1)E, (10)B
Row 153 (R): (10)B, (1)C, (1)E, (1)F, (1)G
Row 154 (L): (1)G, (1)F, (3)E, (1)D, (8)B
Row 155 (R): (8)B, (1)D, (1)E, (2)F, (2)G
Row 156 (L): (2)G, (4)F, (2)C, (6)B
Row 157 (R): (1)A, (6)B, (1)C, (1)F, (1)E, (2)F, (2)G
Row 158 (L): (3)G, (3)F, (1)E, (1)C, (6)B
Row 159 (R): (2)A, (5)B, (1)C, (2)E, (3)F, (1)G

Row 160 (L): (2)G, (2)F, (2)E, (2)C, (5)B, (1)A
Row 161 (R): (2)A, (5)B, (1)C, (3)E, (1)F, (2)G
Row 162 (L): (1)F, (1)G, (2)F, (2)E, (2)C, (4)B, (2)A
Row 163 (R): (3)A, (4)B, (1)C, (1)F, (2)C, (1)E, (1)F, (1)G
Row 164 (L): (2)F, (2)E, (1)B, (2)C, (5)B, (2)A
Row 165 (R): (4)A, (3)B, (4)C, (1)D, (1)E, (1)F
Row 166 (L): (2)F, (1)E, (1)D, (3)C, (4)B, (2)A, (1)B
Row 167 (R): (4)A, (3)B, (5)C, (1)E, (1)F
Row 168 (L): (2)F, (1)D, (4)C, (3)B, (4)A
Row 169 (R): (5)A, (3)B, (2)C, (2)B, (1)C, (1)E
Row 170 (L): (2)D, (1)C, (2)B, (1)C, (4)B, (2)A, (2)B
Row 171 (R): (5)B, (1)A, (2)B, (2)C, (2)B, (2)C
Row 172 (L): (3)C, (1)B, (2)C, (3)B, (2)A, (3)B
Row 173 (R): (3)B, (1)A, (9)B, (1)C
Row 174 (L): (2)E, (12)B
Row 175 (R): (7)B, (2)A, (3)B, (1)C, (1)E
Row 176 (L): (1)G, (1)F, (1)E, (1)D, (2)B, (1)A, (7)B
Row 177 (R): (7)B, (4)C, (1)E, (2)F
Row 178 (L): (2)G, (2)F, (1)E, (3)C, (6)B
Row 179 (R): (6)B, (4)C, (1)E, (3)F
Row 180 (L): (1)G, (3)F, (2)E, (3)C, (5)B
Row 181 (R): (6)B, (3)C, (2)E, (3)F
Row 182 (L): (2)F, (1)E, (1)F, (2)E, (2)D, (2)C, (4)B
Row 183 (R): (1)B, (1)A, (2)B, (1)C, (1)B, (3)C, (2)E, (3)F
Row 184 (L): (4)F, (3)E, (1)D, (2)C, (4)B
Row 185 (R): (5)B, (3)C, (3)E, (3)F
Row 186 (L): (2)F, (6)E, (2)C, (4)B
Row 187 (R): (4)B, (4)C, (5)E, (1)F
Row 188 (L): (1)G, (1)F, (4)E, (2)C, (1)D, (3)C, (2)B
Row 189 (R): (3)B, (3)C, (1)D, (5)E, (2)F
Row 190 (L): (2)G, (1)F, (3)E, (3)C, (1)D, (2)C, (1)B, (1)C
Row 191 (R): (2)B, (5)C, (1)D, (4)E, (2)F
Row 192 (L): (2)G, (1)E, (1)F, (3)E, (1)D, (5)C, (1)B
Row 193 (R): (4)B, (4)C, (4)E, (2)F
Row 194 (L): (1)G, (3)F, (3)E, (5)C, (2)B
Row 195 (R): (3)B, (4)C, (1)D, (4)E, (2)F
Row 196 (L): (4)F, (4)E, (4)C, (1)B, (1)C
Row 197 (R): (1)B, (1)C, (2)B, (1)C, (1)D, (2)C, (4)E, (2)F
Row 198 (L): (1)G, (3)F, (3)E, (5)C, (1)B, (1)C
Row 199 (R): (8)C, (1)D, (2)E, (3)F
Row 200 (L): (4)F, (2)E, (8)C
Row 201 (R): (1)C, (3)B, (4)C, (1)E, (1)C, (2)E, (2)F
Row 202 (L): (2)G, (3)E, (5)C, (2)B, (2)C
Row 203 (R): (4)C, (2)B, (4)C, (1)F, (1)E, (1)F, (1)G
Row 204 (L): (1)G, (3)F, (2)E, (2)C, (1)B, (5)C
Row 205 (R): (1)B, (8)C, (1)D, (2)E, (2)F
Row 206 (L): (3)F, (2)E, (1)D, (5)C, (1)E, (2)B
Row 207 (R): (4)B, (4)C, (1)E, (1)C, (2)E, (2)F
Row 208 (L): (1)G, (3)F, (1)E, (1)D, (1)B, (3)C, (3)B, (1)C
Row 209 (R): (3)B, (1)C, (2)B, (4)C, (2)E, (2)F
Row 210 (L): (1)G, (3)F, (1)E, (1)D, (3)C, (1)B, (3)C, (1)B
Row 211 (R): (2)B, (8)C, (2)E, (1)F, (1)G
Row 212 (L): (1)F, (1)G, (1)F, (1)E, (4)C, (1)B, (3)C, (2)B
Row 213 (R): (4)B, (2)C, (2)B, (2)C, (2)E, (2)F

Row 214 (L): (2)F, (2)E, (2)C, (1)B, (4)C, (3)B
Row 215 (R): (3)B, (4)C, (1)B, (2)C, (2)E, (2)F
Row 216 (L): (2)G, (2)E, (2)C, (2)B, (2)C, (1)B, (1)C, (2)B
Row 217 (R): (4)E, (1)B, (2)C, (2)B, (2)C, (2)E, (1)F
Row 218 (L): (1)G, (1)F, (3)E, (2)C, (2)B, (1)C, (4)E

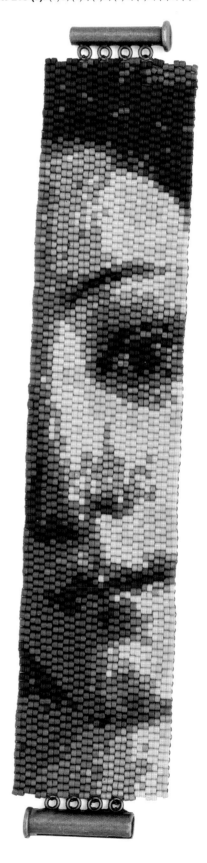

Sketch of a Woman

Leonardo da Vinci's famous sketch comes to life in this piece. As with the "Birth of Venus" pattern, this pattern captures a slice of the original sepia-tone artwork.

note
The six bead colors are a mixture of finishes, adding a sense of depth and detail to the finished bracelet, while remaining true to the original colors of the sketch.

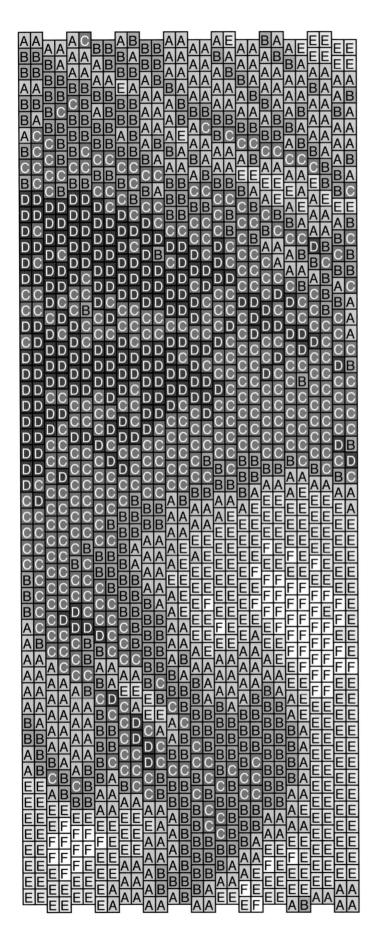

SUPPLIES

- 11° cylinder beads
  - 3g color A (Miyuki DB-389, matte opaque light terracotta)
  - 3g color B (Miyuki DB-1165, galvanized matte muscat)
  - 4g color C (Miyuki DB-340, copper-plated matte)
  - 3g color D (Miyuki DB-312, matte metallic copper)
  - 3g color E (Miyuki DB-1131, opaque pear)
  - 1g color F (Miyuki DB-157, opaque cream AB)
- Beading needle, size 10, 11, or 12
- Fireline, smoke, 6-lb. test
- 4-loop tube clasp
- Scissors, thread snips, or thread burner

A B C D E F

This pattern is 1½ in. (3.8cm) wide and 7¼ in. (18.4cm) long, not including the clasp. Shorten the length by omitting bottom rows until you reach your desired length. For the bracelet pictured here, I stitched 6½ in. (16.5cm) before adding the clasp, for a total bracelet length of 7 in. (18cm).

MAKE THE BRACELET

1. Follow the pattern or word chart below to complete the piece (see two-drop peyote stitch, p. 9), leaving an 8–10-in. (20–25cm) tail for adding the clasp. Add and end thread as needed.

2. Attach a 4-loop tube clasp to each end of the bracelet (see p. 7).

Rows 1 and 2 (L): (5)E, (2)A, (1)B, (2)A, (1)E, (5)A, (3)B, (1)A, (2)B, (1)C, (5)A

Row 3 (R): (2)B, (2)A, (1)B, (3)A, (1)B, (2)A, (1)B, (2)E

Row 4 (L): (2)E, (1)A, (1)B, (4)A, (3)B, (2)A, (1)B

Row 5 (R): (2)B, (2)A, (2)B, (3)A, (1)B, (4)A

Row 6 (L): (5)A, (1)B, (2)A, (1)B, (3)A, (2)B

Row 7 (R): (2)A, (2)B, (1)E, (1)A, (1)B, (5)A, (1)B, (1)A

Row 8 (L): (1)B, (3)A, (1)B, (5)A, (4)B

Row 9 (R): (2)B, (1)C, (3)B, (1)A, (1)B, (2)A, (1)B, (3)A

Row 10 (L): (1)A, (2)B, (3)A, (2)B, (2)A, (1)B, (1)A, (1)C, (1)B

Row 11 (R): (1)B, (1)A, (4)B, (1)A, (3)B, (1)A, (1)B, (2)A

Row 12 (L): (3)A, (3)B, (1)C, (3)A, (4)B

Row 13 (R): (1)A, (1)C, (2)B, (1)A, (1)B, (1)A, (1)E, (1)B, (1)C, (2)B, (2)A

Row 14 (L): (2)A, (1)B, (1)A, (2)C, (2)A, (1)B, (1)A, (3)B, (1)C

Row 15 (R): (1)B, (1)C, (1)B, (1)C, (3)B, (3)A, (2)C, (1)B, (1)A

Row 16 (L): (1)B, (1)A, (2)C, (1)B, (2)A, (1)B, (1)A, (1)B, (2)C, (1)B, (1)C

Row 17 (R): (6)C, (6)A, (1)C, (1)B

Row 18 (L): (1)A, (1)B, (2)A, (2)E, (1)B, (1)A, (2)C, (2)B, (2)C

Row 19 (R): (1)B, (1)C, (3)B, (1)C, (4)B, (3)E, (1)B

Row 20 (L): (1)C, (1)B, (1)A, (1)E, (1)A, (1)B, (2)C, (1)A, (1)B, (2)C, (1)B, (1)C

Row 21 (R): (4)D, (1)C, (3)B, (2)C, (1)A, (1)E, (1)A, (1)E

Row 22 (L): (3)E, (1)A, (1)B, (1)C, (2)B, (3)C, (3)D

Row 23 (R): (5)D, (1)C, (2)B, (1)C, (1)B, (1)C, (1)B, (2)A

Row 24 (L): (1)B, (2)A, (1)B, (5)C, (5)D

Row 25 (R): (1)D, (1)C, (4)D, (3)C, (2)B, (1)C, (2)A

Row 26 (L): (1)C, (1)B, (2)C, (1)B, (3)C, (6)D

Row 27 (R): (5)D, (1)C, (3)D, (1)C, (2)A, (1)D, (1)B

Row 28 (L): (1)B, (1)C, (1)B, (1)A, (3)C, (1)D, (1)B, (3)D, (1)C, (1)D

Row 29 (R): (1)D, (1)C, (4)D, (1)C, (2)D, (2)C, (1)A, (1)B, (1)C

Row 30 (L): (2)B, (2)A, (2)C, (8)D

Row 31 (R): (3)D, (1)C, (6)D, (2)C, (1)A, (1)B

Row 32 (L): (1)C, (1)A, (1)B, (3)C, (1)D, (1)C, (6)D

Row 33 (R): (4)C, (4)D, (3)C, (1)D, (1)C, (1)B

Row 34 (L): (1)A, (1)B, (1)C, (3)D, (1)C, (3)D, (1)C, (1)D, (1)C, (1)D

Row 35 (R): (3)C, (1)B, (2)C, (2)D, (2)C, (1)D, (2)C, (1)B

Row 36 (L): (1)A, (3)C, (1)D, (2)C, (1)D, (2)C, (1)D, (1)C, (1)D, (1)C

Row 37 (R): (3)D, (6)C, (3)D, (2)C

Row 38 (L): (1)A, (1)C, (3)D, (8)C, (1)D

Row 39 (R): (1)C, (2)D, (1)C, (1)D, (1)C, (3)D, (3)C, (1)D, (1)C

Row 40 (L): (2)C, (1)D, (3)C, (8)D

Row 41 (R): (7)D, (4)C, (1)D, (2)C

Row 42 (L): (1)B, (1)D, (5)C, (7)D

Row 43 (R): (8)D, (2)C, (1)D, (3)C

Row 44 (L): (2)C, (1)B, (3)C, (8)D

Row 45 (R): (5)D, (1)C, (3)D, (5)C

Row 46 (L): (6)C, (5)D, (3)C
Row 47 (R): (2)D, (4)C, (1)D, (7)C
Row 48 (L): (6)C, (1)D, (1)C, (2)D, (2)C, (2)D
Row 49 (R): (2)D, (2)C, (1)D, (9)C
Row 50 (L): (9)C, (2)D, (2)C, (1)D
Row 51 (R): (6)D, (8)C
Row 52 (L): (1)B, (1)D, (9)C, (1)D, (2)C
Row 53 (R): (2)D, (12)C
Row 54 (L): (1)D, (2)C, (4)B, (3)C, (1)D, (3)C
Row 55 (R): (2)D, (2)C, (1)D, (3)C, (1)B, (1)C, (3)B, (1)C
Row 56 (L): (1)C, (1)B, (2)A, (2)B, (6)C, (1)D, (1)C
Row 57 (R): (1)D, (7)C, (2)B, (4)A
Row 58 (L): (2)A, (1)E, (2)A, (3)B, (6)C
Row 59 (R): (1)C, (1)D, (3)C, (1)B, (1)A, (1)B, (2)A, (4)E
Row 60 (L): (1)A, (4)E, (3)A, (2)B, (4)C
Row 61 (R): (4)C, (2)B, (3)A, (5)E
Row 62 (L): (6)E, (2)A, (3)B, (3)C
Row 63 (R): (4)C, (2)B, (2)A, (6)E
Row 64 (L): (8)E, (2)A, (4)C
Row 65 (R): (3)C, (2)B, (2)A, (3)E, (1)F, (3)E
Row 66 (L): (3)E, (1)F, (3)E, (3)A, (2)B, (2)C
Row 67 (R): (2)C, (1)B, (1)C, (1)B, (2)A, (5)E, (1)F, (1)E
Row 68 (L): (4)E, (1)F, (3)E, (2)A, (2)B, (2)C
Row 69 (R): (1)B, (3)C, (2)B, (4)E, (2)F, (2)E
Row 70 (L): (2)E, (2)F, (4)E, (2)A, (1)B, (3)C
Row 71 (R): (1)B, (3)C, (2)B, (1)A, (3)E, (4)F
Row 72 (L): (1)E, (4)F, (1)E, (1)F, (1)E, (1)A, (1)B, (4)C
Row 73 (R): (1)B, (1)C, (1)D, (1)C, (2)B, (1)A, (3)E, (3)F, (1)E
Row 74 (L): (1)E, (3)F, (4)E, (2)B, (2)C, (1)D, (1)C
Row 75 (R): (1)A, (1)C, (2)D, (1)C, (1)B, (2)A, (1)F, (2)E, (3)F
Row 76 (L): (2)E, (2)F, (1)A, (3)E, (2)B, (1)C, (1)D, (2)C
Row 77 (R): (1)A, (1)B, (1)C, (1)B, (1)C, (1)B, (2)A, (4)E, (2)F
Row 78 (L): (1)E, (3)F, (2)A, (1)E, (1)A, (2)B, (1)C, (1)B, (2)C
Row 79 (R): (2)A, (1)C, (1)B, (2)C, (1)A, (1)B, (3)A, (1)E, (2)F
Row 80 (L): (3)F, (1)E, (4)A, (2)B, (2)A, (1)C, (1)A
Row 81 (R): (2)A, (2)C, (2)A, (1)B, (5)A, (2)F
Row 82 (L): (4)E, (3)A, (1)B, (1)C, (1)B, (1)A, (1)B, (2)A
Row 83 (R): (3)A, (1)B, (2)E, (2)B, (2)A, (1)B, (1)A, (2)F
Row 84 (L): (3)E, (1)A, (1)B, (2)A, (2)B, (1)E, (1)D, (1)C, (2)A
Row 85 (R): (4)A, (1)C, (1)A, (1)C, (2)B, (1)A, (2)B, (2)E
Row 86 (L): (3)E, (1)A, (4)B, (2)E, (1)C, (1)B, (2)A
Row 87 (R): (1)B, (3)A, (1)C, (1)D, (1)A, (1)C, (4)B, (2)E
Row 88 (L): (2)E, (1)A, (5)B, (1)A, (1)C, (2)B, (2)A
Row 89 (R): (2)B, (2)A, (1)C, (1)D, (1)A, (5)B, (2)E
Row 90 (L): (2)E, (1)A, (4)B, (2)C, (1)D, (2)B, (2)A
Row 91 (R): (1)A, (1)B, (2)A, (2)C, (6)B, (2)E
Row 92 (L): (2)E, (1)A, (1)B, (1)C, (1)B, (3)C, (1)D, (1)C, (1)B, (1)A, (1)B
Row 93 (R): (1)A, (1)B, (1)A, (1)B, (4)C, (1)B, (1)C, (2)B, (2)E
Row 94 (L): (2)E, (1)A, (1)B, (3)C, (2)B, (1)C, (1)A, (2)B, (1)C
Row 95 (R): (2)E, (1)C, (2)B, (1)C, (2)B, (1)C, (3)B, (2)E
Row 96 (L): (2)E, (2)A, (2)C, (1)B, (1)C, (1)B, (1)C, (2)A, (1)B, (1)A
Row 97 (R): (2)E, (2)B, (2)A, (6)B, (2)E
Row 98 (L): (3)E, (1)A, (2)B, (1)C, (1)B, (4)A, (2)E
Row 99 (R): (6)E, (1)A, (1)B, (1)C, (1)B, (2)A, (2)E
Row 100 (L): (2)E, (2)A, (2)B, (1)C, (1)B, (1)A, (3)E, (1)F, (1)E
Row 101 (R): (2)E, (2)F, (2)E, (1)A, (1)B, (1)C, (1)B, (2)A, (2)E
Row 102 (L): (4)E, (1)A, (3)B, (2)A, (1)E, (3)F

Row 103 (R): (2)E, (2)F, (2)E, (1)A, (3)B, (4)E
Row 104 (L): (3)E, (1)F, (2)A, (2)B, (2)A, (2)E, (2)F
Row 105 (R): (2)E, (1)F, (1)E, (3)A, (2)B, (1)A, (1)F, (3)E
Row 106 (L): (5)E, (1)A, (3)B, (1)A, (2)E, (1)F, (1)E
Row 107 (R): (4)E, (2)A, (2)B, (2)A, (4)E
Row 108 (L): (2)A, (3)E, (1)F, (1)A, (2)B, (2)A, (3)E
Row 109 (R): (4)E, (3)A, (1)B, (4)E, (2)A
Row 110 (L): (2)A, (1)B, (1)A, (1)F, (1)E, (5)A, (3)E
Row 111 (R): (8)A, (3)E, (1)A, (2)B
Row 112 (L): (2)B, (2)C, (1)F, (2)E, (5)A, (1)E, (1)A
Row 113 (R): (8)A, (2)E, (1)A, (1)D, (1)C, (1)B
Row 114 (L): (1)B, (3)C, (3)E, (7)A
Row 115 (R): (3)A, (1)B, (4)A, (2)E, (2)A, (2)C
Row 116 (L): (5)C, (1)A, (2)E, (4)A, (2)B
Row 117 (R): (2)B, (5)A, (1)E, (2)F, (1)B, (1)A, (2)C
Row 118 (L): (1)D, (2)C, (1)A, (1)D, (1)C, (1)F, (1)E, (5)A, (1)B
Row 119 (R): (2)C, (5)A, (1)E, (1)F, (1)E, (1)D, (1)B, (2)C
Row 120 (L): (2)D, (1)C, (1)A, (1)D, (1)C, (2)E, (5)A, (1)B
Row 121 (R): (1)C, (1)D, (2)A, (1)B, (1)A, (3)E, (1)B, (1)D, (1)C, (2)D
Row 122 (L): (3)D, (1)C, (1)D, (1)C, (2)E, (4)A, (1)C, (1)D
Row 123 (R): (2)D, (1)C, (1)B, (2)A, (2)E, (1)A, (1)B, (4)D
Row 124 (L): (5)D, (1)C, (3)E, (1)A, (2)B, (2)D
Row 125 (R): (3)D, (1)C, (2)A, (2)E, (2)C, (4)D
Row 126 (L): (6)D, (1)B, (2)E, (1)A, (2)C, (2)D
Row 127 (R): (1)C, (3)D, (1)B, (1)A, (2)E, (6)D
Row 128 (L): (6)D, (1)C, (1)A, (2)E, (4)D
Row 129 (R): (1)C, (3)D, (1)B, (1)A, (2)E, (6)D
Row 130 (L): (7)D, (1)B, (2)E, (4)D
Row 131 (R): (1)C, (4)D, (1)B, (2)E, (6)D
Row 132 (L): (7)D, (1)C, (1)E, (1)A, (4)D
Row 133 (R): (4)D, (1)C, (1)B, (1)A, (1)B, (6)D
Row 134 (L): (3)D, (1)C, (4)D, (2)B, (4)D
Row 135 (R): (6)D, (1)C, (7)D
Row 136 (L): (3)D, (1)C, (10)D
Row 137 (R): (2)C, (3)D, (1)C, (6)D, (2)C
Row 138 (L): (1)C, (1)D, (1)C, (6)D, (1)C, (2)D, (2)C
Row 139 (R): (3)C, (1)D, (2)C, (6)D, (2)C
Row 140 (L): (3)C, (7)D, (1)C, (1)D, (2)C
Row 141 (R): (13)D, (1)C
Row 142 (L): (1)B, (2)C, (11)D
Row 143 (R): (13)D, (1)C
Row 144 (L): (1)A, (1)B, (2)C, (10)D
Row 145 (R): (11)D, (2)C, (1)B
Row 146 (L): (2)B, (3)C, (9)D
Row 147 (R): (8)D, (1)C, (1)D, (2)C, (2)A
Row 148 (L): (2)A, (1)B, (2)C, (1)D, (1)C, (7)D
Row 149 (R): (9)D, (3)C, (2)A
Row 150 (L): (2)A, (2)B, (1)D, (2)C, (7)D
Row 151 (R): (7)D, (5)C, (1)A, (1)B
Row 152 (L): (1)E, (1)A, (1)B, (3)C, (1)D, (1)C, (6)D
Row 153 (R): (6)D, (6)C, (2)A
Row 154 (L): (2)A, (1)B, (7)C, (4)D
Row 155 (R): (5)D, (6)C, (1)B, (1)C, (1)A
Row 156 (L): (1)E, (1)A, (2)B, (6)C, (4)D
Row 157 (R): (5)D, (3)C, (1)D, (3)C, (1)A, (1)C
Row 158 (L): (2)E, (1)A, (1)B, (2)C, (1)B, (3)C, (4)D
Row 159 (R): (5)D, (7)C, (1)A, (1)E

Row 160 (L): (1)A, (1)C, (1)A, (1)B, (3)C, (1)B, (3)C, (1)D, (1)C, (1)D
Row 161 (R): (1)C, (4)D, (2)C, (1)B, (4)C, (2)A
Row 162 (L): (1)B, (1)A, (1)B, (7)C, (4)D
Row 163 (R): (2)D, (1)C, (1)D, (3)C, (1)B, (4)C, (2)A
Row 164 (L): (1)B, (1)A, (2)B, (1)C, (1)B, (1)C, (1)B, (2)C, (1)D, (1)C, (1)D, (1)C
Row 165 (R): (7)C, (1)B, (4)C, (2)A
Row 166 (L): (2)A, (2)B, (7)C, (1)D, (1)C, (1)D
Row 167 (R): (6)C, (2)B, (3)C, (1)B, (2)A
Row 168 (L): (1)E, (2)A, (1)B, (4)C, (1)B, (3)C, (1)D, (1)C
Row 169 (R): (4)C, (2)D, (6)C, (1)A, (1)B
Row 170 (L): (1)E, (2)A, (1)B, (1)C, (1)B, (8)C
Row 171 (R): (2)C, (1)B, (1)C, (1)D, (5)C, (3)B, (1)A
Row 172 (L): (2)E, (1)A, (3)B, (1)C, (1)D, (4)C, (1)B, (1)C
Row 173 (R): (1)C, (3)B, (2)C, (1)B, (3)C, (2)B, (2)E
Row 174 (L): (3)E, (2)A, (1)B, (6)C, (1)B, (1)C
Row 175 (R): (5)B, (1)C, (1)B, (1)C, (2)B, (2)A, (2)E
Row 176 (L): (4)E, (1)A, (1)B, (1)C, (1)D, (2)C, (4)B
Row 177 (R): (1)C, (7)B, (1)C, (1)B, (1)E, (1)A, (2)E
Row 178 (L): (5)E, (1)A, (1)C, (1)B, (1)C, (4)B, (1)A
Row 179 (R): (1)C, (1)B, (1)A, (1)B, (1)A, (5)B, (1)E, (1)A, (2)E
Row 180 (L): (3)E, (2)A, (5)B, (1)A, (3)B
Row 181 (R): (2)B, (3)A, (5)B, (4)E
Row 182 (L): (3)E, (2)A, (3)B, (1)A, (5)B
Row 183 (R): (6)B, (1)C, (2)A, (1)B, (4)E
Row 184 (L): (2)E, (1)A, (1)E, (1)A, (4)B, (2)A, (1)B, (1)A, (1)B
Row 185 (R): (1)B, (1)A, (1)B, (3)A, (2)B, (3)A, (3)E
Row 186 (L): (2)E, (2)A, (1)E, (1)A, (2)B, (6)A
Row 187 (R): (1)B, (6)A, (2)B, (2)A, (3)E
Row 188 (L): (3)E, (1)A, (2)E, (2)B, (2)A, (2)B, (2)A
Row 189 (R): (1)E, (3)A, (1)B, (1)A, (4)B, (3)A, (1)E
Row 190 (L): (2)E, (1)B, (3)A, (1)B, (2)E, (1)A, (1)B, (1)A, (1)E, (1)A
Row 191 (R): (2)A, (1)E, (1)A, (1)B, (1)A, (2)E, (2)C, (2)A, (2)E
Row 192 (L): (2)E, (4)A, (1)E, (1)B, (1)E, (2)A, (1)B, (1)E, (1)A
Row 193 (R): (5)A, (1)B, (1)A, (5)E, (1)A, (1)E
Row 194 (L): (1)E, (2)A, (6)E, (3)A, (2)E
Row 195 (R): (2)E, (3)A, (1)B, (1)A, (2)E, (5)A
Row 196 (L): (1)A, (1)E, (2)A, (2)E, (2)A, (1)E, (3)A, (2)E
Row 197 (R): (1)A, (2)E, (1)A, (1)E, (1)A, (1)E, (1)A, (2)E, (2)A, (2)E
Row 198 (L): (2)B, (3)E, (1)A, (6)E, (2)A
Row 199 (R): (2)E, (1)A, (6)E, (1)A, (4)E
Row 200 (L): (2)E, (1)A, (7)E, (4)A
Row 201 (R): (3)A, (1)E, (1)A, (3)E, (1)A, (3)E, (1)A, (1)E
Row 202 (L): (12)E, (1)A, (1)B
Row 203 (R): (1)A, (1)B, (11)E, (1)A
Row 204 (L): (14)E
Row 205 (R): (1)B, (1)E, (4)A, (8)E
Row 206 (L): (2)A, (1)B, (7)E, (1)A, (1)B, (1)A, (1)E
Row 207 (R): (2)E, (2)A, (7)E, (1)A, (2)E
Row 208 (L): (3)E, (1)B, (6)E, (2)B, (1)A, (1)E
Row 209 (R): (2)E, (2)A, (7)E, (3)B
Row 210 (L): (1)B, (1)E, (2)B, (9)E, (1)A

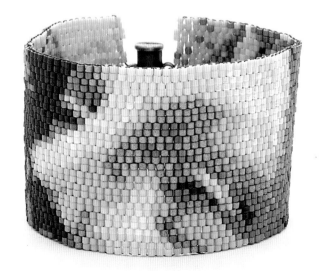

GALLERY

Ukrainian Embroidery ▼
This pattern, based on traditional Ukrainian embroidery, was originally designed in red, black, and white—but I wanted to change it up a bit and used turquoise instead of red.

Bruce Springsteen, ▲
based on a photo by Herb Ritts. How to combine two of my loves? Use one (two-drop peyote stitch) to create a portrait of another (Bruce Springsteen).

Tougher Than the Rest ▲
We all have days when we lack confidence or feel overwhelmed. It's on those days when I can use a reminder that I am strong, so Bruce Springsteen's song "Tougher Than the Rest" becomes my mantra—now I can wear it on my wrist.

Portuguese Azulejo ▶
When I visited Lisbon a couple of years ago, I fell in love with the azulejo tiles that adorn many homes and buildings in the city. Though shades of blue and white are traditional, there are many examples of different colors as well. This one reminds me of an antique map's compass rose, so it's also symbolic of my love of travel.

Icarus by Henri Matisse ▶
This bold graphic image makes a statement and pays homage to Matisse, who originally published this cutout in 1947. It's his interpretation of the Greek legend of Icarus, a young man obsessed with the idea of flying who got too close to the sun.

Acknowledgments

To Cathy, who had endless patience and a sense of humor when I was first learning peyote stitch; you have no idea what you've unleashed.

To Charlotte, for suggesting I create designs based on Renaissance art and the ceramics of the Near East.

To the entire editorial team at Kalmbach Books, especially Erica Barse; you have made the publishing process easy and fun for a first-time author.

All designs in this book were created with BeadTool4 software.

About the Author

Author photo by Matilde Holloway

Holly's designs are influenced by the places she's lived—New York City, San Francisco, Kauai, and currently Occitanie (France)—as well as the many places she's traveled across the U.S. and the world. Born and raised in New York City, Holly moved to San Francisco for work and love, and she lived there for nearly 30 years. A job transfer took her to the island of Kauai for 18 months during that time; who would turn down an opportunity to live in paradise? Now residing in the historic center of a small town in the south of France, near to both the Mediterranean and the mountains, Holly is surrounded and inspired by history, vineyards, and beauty.

Being a professional career coach and trainer is a fulfilling profession, but creating unique two-drop peyote stitch designs is a passion and obsession. The possibilities of what can be created with a needle, thread, and a pile of beads are endless. Holly's work has appeared in BeadStyle magazine, and you can find more of patterns at etsy.com/shop/hillcreststudio.

Must-Have Books for
BEAD STITCHERS

Project-packed books from Kalmbach Media feature step-by-step instructions from the bead stitching experts.

**Beader's Guide:
Peyote Stitch**
This in-depth look at one of the most popular stitches covers all the possibilities of peyote stitch.
#67916 • $19.99

**Beader's Guide:
Right-Angle Weave**
Perfect this popular stitch, right-angle weave, with creative, expert-tested jewelry projects!
#67921 • $19.99

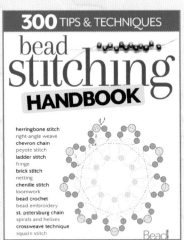

**Bead Stitching
Handbook**
Discover information, instructions, and hundreds of tips for the 15 major bead stitches.
#67910 • $19.99

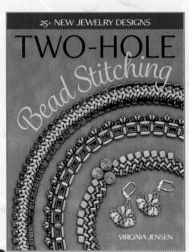

**Two-Hole
Bead Stitching**
Enjoy 25+ all-new projects that showcase popular two-hole shaped beads.
#67913 • $22.99